The Mac Internet Tour Guide™

Cruising the Internet the Easy Way

Second Edition

Michael Fraase

Revised for the Second Edition
by
Ted Alspach & Jan Weingarten

VENTANA
PRESS

D1404924

The Mac Internet Tour Guide™: Cruising the Internet the Easy Way
Copyright © 1995 by Michael Fraase and Ventana Communications Group, Inc.

Library of Congress Cataloging-in-Publication Data

Fraase, Michael.
     The Mac Internet tour guide : cruising the Internet
     the easy way / Michael Fraase. -- 2nd ed.
        p.   cm.
     Includes bibliographical references and index.
     ISBN 1-56604-173-2
     1. Internet (Computer network) 2. Macintosh (Computer)
     TK5105.875.I57A44 1995
   004.6'7--dc20   94-44116
                                               CIP

Book design: Karen Wysocki
Cover design and icons: John Nedwidek, Sitzer:Spuria
Design staff: Dawne Sherman, Marcia Webb
Index service: Richard T. Evans, Infodex
Technical review: Matthew Saderholm, Kelly Garner
Editorial staff: Angela Anderson, Walter R. Bruce III, Eric Edstam, Tracye Giles, Nathaniel
   Mund, Ruffin Prevost, Pam Richardson
Production staff: Patrick Berry, John Cotterman, Dan Koeller

Second Edition 9 8 7 6 5 4 3 2 1
Printed in the United States of America

Ventana Press, Inc.
P.O. Box 2468
Chapel Hill, NC 27515
919/942-0220
FAX 919/942-1140

Trademarks

Trademarked names appear throughout this book. Rather than list the names and entities that own the trademarks or insert a trademark symbol with each mention of the trademarked name, the publisher states that it is using the names only for editorial purposes and to the benefit of the trademark owner with no intention of infringing upon that trademark.

About the Authors

Michael Fraase is the proprietor of Arts & Farces, a multifaceted communications and professional services business specializing in hypermedia production, technical writing, desktop/electronic publishing, general Macintosh consulting and software interface design.

Fraase is the author of numerous books, including the 3-volume *Macintosh Hypermedia* series (ScottForesman, 1990–1991), *Farallon's MediaTracks* (Business One Irwin, 1991), *Groupware for the Macintosh* (Business One Irwin, 1991), *Structured Publishing From the Desktop: Frame Technology's FrameMaker* (Business One Irwin, 1992) and the 15-volume *Rapid Reference Series* (Business One Irwin, 1992–1993).

Ted Alspach is a contributing editor to *Mac Home Journal* and author of the *Macworld Illustrator 5.0/5.5 Bible*, *The Complete Idiot's Guide to QuarkXPress*, *The Complete Idiot's Guide to Photoshop* and the *Internet E-Mail Quick Tour* (Ventana Press). As the owner of Bezier, a leading computer training company in Scottsdale, Arizona, Ted has been training users in desktop publishing, graphics, the Internet and commercial online services for Macintosh- and Windows-based computers since 1988, and has been fiddling with his modem even longer. Ted is also the creator of Lefty Casual and Ransom Note, two very popular shareware fonts.

Jan Weingarten is a software trainer, consultant and writer in Seattle, Washington. Her most recent book is *Teach Yourself WordPerfect 6.0 for Windows*. In addition, she has authored or co-authored books on Windows, Word, Lotus 1-2-3, Excel and CorelDRAW.

Acknowledgments

This is my twenty-second computer book, and the first one in a long
time that has been a load of fun. Writers don't make much money, so
most of us insist that what we do be fun. At least I do. Thanks to Dennis
Fazio and Dave Bergum at Minnesota Regional Network for support
and advice on all things Internet. My most heartfelt gratitude is offered
to my wife, Karen Caldwell Fraase, who continues to make my life fun.

While the task of writing is a solitary one, the act of creating a book
isn't. Thanks to everyone at Ventana Press for proving what I suspected: small publishers can make a Big Difference.

Thanks to Joe and Elizabeth Woodman for seeing the potential in this
project. Thanks especially to Elizabeth for recognizing that Mac users
needed this book and Joe for a rich sense of humor. I will forever carry
the image of a "spaghetti book" in my mind's eye.

Thanks to Pam Richardson for routing and scheduling everything.
Thanks to Diane Lennox for publicity and promotion. Thanks to Fran
Phillips and Larry Levitsky for sales. Thanks to Karen Wysocki for the
interior page design and managing a feverish production schedule.
Most of all, thanks for reminding me, with your design, that I'm a
writer and not a designer.

Thanks to John Nedwidek of Sitzer:Spuria for the cover design and
icons. Everyone who's seen the cover has had the same reaction:
"Wow! That's really neat. I like it...." then a sideways glance and "Do
you like it?" Anyone who can evoke that kind of reaction is doing
something right.

And finally there's Ruffin Prevost, my editor. Writers' nightmares
are populated with bad editors. Ruffin is the exception that proves
the rule; he's a real writer's editor, and approached this project as a
true collaboration. He made this a better book with a reasoned, even
hand. The world would be a better place if there were more editors
like Ruffin.

—*Michael Fraase*

Thanks to everyone at Ventana for their efforts. I would especially
like to thank John Cotterman and Patrick Berry in the Production
Department; Eric Edstam, Angela Anderson and Pam Richardson in
the Editorial Department; and Dykki Settle and Walt Bruce for their
help in the development and progression of the Second Edition.

—*Ted Alspach*

The publisher would also like to acknowledge a number of individuals and organizations who made invaluable contributions to this book.

For advice, support, technical expertise and general friendly assistance, thanks goes to a number of people at MCNC's Center for Communications in Research Triangle Park, North Carolina. Thanks especially to Naomi L. T. Courter and Alan Clegg at the CONCERT Network and Jane Smith and Kevin Gamiel at the Clearinghouse for Networked Information Discovery and Retrieval.

Thanks also goes to Paul Jones and the staff at the University of North Carolina's Office of Information Technology in Chapel Hill for their cooperation and support.

For their help in testing, reviewing and otherwise trying to crash various Internet client applications and software resources and verifying tons of tips, tricks and inside information, thanks goes to Mac Internet cybergeeks Rob Terrell and Shea Tisdale. Thanks to Matthew Saderholm and Kelly Garner for their thorough technical review of the Second Edition.

A special thanks also goes to Aladdin Systems (makers of the StuffIt Expander utility), Steve Dorner and the University of Illinois Computing Services Office (author of the Eudora e-mail program), and Jim Matthews of Dartmouth College (author of the Fetch FTP software) for graciously allowing their excellent Mac applications to be included on the companion disks. Thanks also to InterCon Systems for assistance and advice regarding their TCP/Connect II integrated Macintosh Internet software.

For advice on telecommunications and modems, technical information and hardware support, special thanks goes to Hayes Microcomputer and Global Village Communications.

About the Images in This Book

The graphic images shown on the opening page of each chapter of *The Mac Internet Tour Guide* are from the OTIS (The Operative Term is Stimulate) Project. OTIS is an electronic art gallery containing hundreds of images and animations. According to OTIS Project founder Ed Stastny, OTIS exists "to distribute original creative images over the world's computer networks for public perusal, scrutiny and retransmission, and to facilitate communication, inspiration, critique and to set the foundations for digital immortality."

According to Stastny, "The basic idea behind 'digital immortality' is that computer networks are here to stay, and anything interesting you deposit on them will be around nearly forever. The images of today will be the artifacts of an information-laded future. Perhaps the images will be converted into newer formats when the current formats become obsolete—perhaps only surviving on forgotten backup reels. But they'll be there, and someone will dig them up—data-archeologists sifting through the cobwebs of an old storage room."

The OTIS Project is currently accessible by anonymous FTP at three sites:

- no-name-broadband.med.umich.edu in the /projects/otis/ directory
- sunsite.unc.edu in the /pub/multimedia/pictures/OTIS/ directory
- aql.gatech.edu in the /pub/OTIS/ directory

For more information about the OTIS Project, contact

OTIS Project
Ed Stastny
PO Box 241113   ed@cwis.unomaha.edu
Omaha, NE 68124   ed@sunsite.unc.edu

A special thanks goes out to those OTIS artists who generously allowed us to reproduce their images. Thanks to Ed Stastny (Information Web, Chapter 1; VR2, Chapter 5; ©1993 Ed Stastny, used with permission); Tom Nawara (Stigmata, Chapter 2; Eye See U, Chapter 9; ©1993 Tom Nawara, used with permission); Michael Maier (Future Culture, Chapter 3; ©1993 Michael Maier, used with permission); David Anjo (No Roof, Chapter 4; ©1993 David Anjo, used with permission); Barrett Ryker (Fractal Moon, Chapter 6; Castle Spirit, Chapter 7; ©1993 Barrett Ryker, used with permission); Eric Weber (Clock, Chapter 8; Quarry, Chapter 10; ©1994 Eric Weber, used with permission.)

Contents

Introduction xvii

Chapter 1 What Is the Internet? 1

It's Easier Than You Think 2

Roadside Attraction Ahead 2

Cruising the Easy Way 3

A Sense of Place 4

Internet Benefits for the Average User 5

A General Overview of the Internet 6

Internet Governance

A Brief History of the Internet 8

The Future of the Internet 10

Commercialization • Privatization • Bandwidth

Chapter 2 Getting Connected 13

Where to Sign Up 14

University Users • Government Users • Business
Users • Individual Users

Types of Connections 18
Dedicated Connection • SLIP & PPP Connection
• Other Types of Connections
Resource Requirements 22
Macintosh • Network Interface Card or Modem
• MacSLIP or MacPPP • MacTCP • Client Application
Software
Making the Leap 26

Chapter 3 Network Infrastructure 29
An Information Democracy 30
The Internet Rosetta Stone 30
Transmission Control Protocol (TCP)
• Internet Protocol (IP)
Where.Is.That.Thing@on.the.Net? 33
Have Your .Org Call My .Gov About That .Com
When in Rome... Don't Tie Up the Phone Lines 37
Acceptable Use Policies • Security Issues
First Names Are Lousy Passwords 40
Usage Courtesy

Chapter 4 Electronic Mail 43
What Is E-Mail & How Does it Work? 44
E-Mail Etiquette & Courtesy 46
E-Mail Privacy
How to Send E-Mail Anywhere 51
Internet to UUCP & Back • Internet to CompuServe
& Back • Internet to MCI Mail & Back • Internet to
America Online & Back • Internet to AT&T Mail &
Back • Internet to AppleLink & Back • Cross-Network
E-Mail Addressing Quick Reference

Quick Guide to Using Eudora 58

Configuring Eudora • Using Eudora

Quick Guide to Using TCP/Connect II 75

Configuring the TCP/Connect II Mail Module • Using
the TCP/Connect II Mail Module • Working With
E-Mail Filters

Finding Addresses 91

Using Finger • Using MIT's USENET User List • Using
Whois • Using the PSI White Pages • E-Mail Address
Starter Kit

Electronic Mailing Lists 96

Subscribing to Mailing Lists • Canceling Subscriptions
to Mailing Lists

E-Mail & Attached Files 99

Sending Files in E-Mail Messages • Receiving Files in
E-Mail Messages • Files in E-Mail Caveats

Chapter 5 Network News & Newsgroups **107**

What Is Network News & What Are Newsgroups? 108

An Overview of Newsgroups 111

Interesting Newsgroups • Macintosh Newsgroups

A Primer on Newsgroup Etiquette 114

Flames, Flame-Bait & Flaming

Selecting a News Reader 120

Configuring Nuntius • Configuring the TCP/Connect II
News Module

How to Read, Post & Reply to Articles 129

Using Nuntius • Using the TCP/Connect II News Module

Chapter 6 Transferring Files **143**
What Is FTP? 144
Why Would You Want to Transfer Files? 144
A Primer on Software Resources 145
   Public Domain • Freeware • Shareware
A Primer on File Types 148
A Disinfectant for Viruses 150
   Using Disinfectant
Using Fetch to Transfer Files 152
   Configuring Fetch • Downloading Files With Fetch
   • Uploading Files With Fetch
Using TCP/Connect II to Transfer Files 165
   Configuring the TCP/Connect II FTP Module
   • Downloading Files With TCP/Connect II • Uploading
   Files With TCP/Connect II

Chapter 7 Using Gopher **179**
What Is Gopher? 179
What Can I Use Gopher For? 180
Why Should I Use Gopher Instead of FTP? 181
Using TurboGopher 181
   Configuring TurboGopher • Browsing Information
   With TurboGopher • Downloading Files With
   TurboGopher • Using TurboGopher Bookmarks
Gopher Servers 198
TurboGopher Tips 199

Chapter 8 The World Wide Web **201**
What Is the World Wide Web? 201
What Is Mosaic? 203

Browsing the Web With Mosaic 203
Navigating in the Document Window • All About
Links • A Quick Tour Through the Web • Retrieving
Files • Going Directly to Another Page • Setting Up
a New Home Page • Graphics & Modem Connections

Accessing FTP Sites With Mosaic 220

Accessing Gopher Sites With Mosaic 221

Building Your Own Web Pages 222

Chapter 9 Other Internet Resources 225

What Is Telnet? 226
Using NCSA Telnet • Using the TCP/Connect II
Telnet Module

Knowbots 234

Netfind 235

Finger 236

WAIS 239

Archie 242
Using the Macintosh Archie Client • Using
TurboGopher for Archie Searches

RFCs 248

FAQs 250

Internet Organizations 250
Electronic Frontier Foundation • Internet Society

Chapter 10 Hot Spots on the Net 255

Art 256

Books, Literature & 'Zines 260

Business 263

Computing 266

Culture & Diversity 268

Education 270

Environment 272

Finance 275

Food & Drink 277

Fun & Games 280

Health, Medicine & Recovery 282

History 287

Humor 288

Internet Stuff 291

Jobs 300

Languages 301

Law 303

Miscellany 305

Multimedia 306

Music 307

New Age 313

News 313

Occult 314

Philosophy 315

Politics, Government & Social Issues 316

Reference 322

Religion & Spirituality 323

Romance 326

Science 326

Science Fiction 335

Security 336

Showbiz 337

Software 338

Sports 338

Star Trek 343

Strange USENET Newsgroups 344

Technology 345

Theater & Film 345
Travel 348
Weather 351
Gateways to More Internet Resources 351

Appendix A **The Companion Disks & Ventana Online** 361
The Companion Disk Software 361
Ventana Mosaic • Eudora • Fetch • Nuntius • StuffIt
Expander • TurboGopher • InterSLIP & MacTCP
Ventana Online & the Visitor's Center 363

Glossary 365

Bibliography 381

Index 383

Introduction

These are the days of lasers in the jungle
Lasers in the jungle somewhere
Staccato signals of constant information...
—Paul Simon

Part of the experience of using a Macintosh is a sense that there's a collection of actual places behind the screen—places you can't see, but know are in there. Or, rather, out there. This feeling really hit home for me when I saw a photo a friend used to replace his usual Macintosh desktop pattern. It showed his face and hands scrunched up against a window pane, creating the illusion of someone *out there* trying to get *in here*. If you've ever used your Macintosh to connect to another computer—either by network or modem—you know this experience, and you know it's real. Tapping into the Internet not only confirms but also *validates* this feeling.

These days, it's hip to call this collection of not-quite-real places *cyberspace*. William Gibson created the term in his novel *Neuromancer* to represent a universe sustained by a vast network of computers and telecommunications lines.

"People jacked in so they could hustle. Put the trodes on and they were out there, all the data in the world stacked up like one big neon city, so you could cruise around and have a kind of grip on it, visually anyway, because if you didn't, it was too complicated, trying to find your way to a particular piece of data you needed."

But cyberspace isn't some wild future dream; it's here now. John Perry Barlow—sometime Wyoming cattle rancher and sometime lyricist for the Grateful Dead—describes cyberspace as where you are when you're on the telephone. Think about that for a minute, and then realize that cyberspace is also where your bank accounts, credit history and tax records are. And in the near future, cyberspace is also likely to be where you earn a good portion of your income.

This book is about the Internet—a vast computer network of many component networks. Think of it as a web. Think of it as the first *really real* cyberspace.

For too many years, the Internet was the playground of propeller-heads and spooks, inaccessible to mere mortals. But lately, the Internet has changed, becoming a critical tool for millions of computer users. Powerful but simple software tools have made the network accessible to practically anyone—especially anyone with a Macintosh. And that's what this book is all about: making the Internet as friendly and familiar as everything else you do with your Mac.

Explosive Growth

The past few years have seen the Internet expand at an astonishing rate. Individuals and businesses are rushing to the Internet in droves for a good reason: it's an invaluable resource for anyone who works with information. Its power and potential are practically limitless. Just a few of the most popular features of the Internet include

- **Electronic mail.** Send electronic mail (e-mail) to virtually any networked computer user. Internet e-mail reaches its destination—practically anywhere on the planet—in a matter of a few minutes.

- **Network news.** Participate in a wide variety of electronic discussion groups on just about any topic you can think of. There are literally thousands of in-depth discussions on topics ranging from the essential to the arcane. Molecular biology, politics, comic books, the stock market, computers and practically anything else you can think of are all covered in the Internet's network news.

- **File transfer.** Transfer any kind of file between your computer and any other computer on the Internet. The Internet boasts the largest collection of Macintosh software and shareware in the world, and its libraries are growing every day.

- **Information browsing.** You can browse through a never-ending collection of information resources available throughout the Internet. Weather reports, electronic information databases and electronic journals (and much more) are available—free to anyone with access to the Internet.

Who Can Use *The Mac Internet Tour Guide*?

If you use a Macintosh and already have Internet access, or if you're interested in obtaining Internet access in the future, this book is for you. If you subscribe to one of the commercial information services (such as Prodigy or GEnie or America Online), you can use this book for exchanging electronic mail with Internet users, subscribing to mailing lists and retrieving files available on the Internet via electronic mail. If you subscribe to AOL, Delphi or CompuServe, you have an impressive array of Internet options available to you.

This *Tour Guide* is written for Internet newcomers. No knowledge of the Internet is assumed (although experienced Internet users are sure to find plenty of interest here as well). I do assume, however, that you're comfortable finding your way around a Macintosh. You should be able to copy files from a floppy to your hard drive, launch application programs, work with control panels, and connect peripherals to your Macintosh. If you haven't yet mastered these simple skills, don't despair. A couple of hours with your Macintosh manuals (or a beginning Macintosh tutorial) will bring you up to speed.

Although the *Tour Guide* will help you navigate the Internet and lead you through its vast resources, regardless of what hardware or software you have, you'll need a few things to get the most out of this book:

- A Macintosh with at least 4mb of RAM.

- An Internet account (or an account with one of the commercial information services, depending on your Internet requirements), and an appropriate network connection or full SLIP/PPP access. To make the most of the tools and techniques discussed in this book, you should have SLIP or PPP access or a direct connection to the Internet. (See the offer in the back of this book for information on establishing your own SLIP/PPP connection.) If you have an Internet shell account, you will find many of the tips and resources useful, but you won't be able to make full use of the companion software.

- MacTCP, properly configured and installed. MacTCP is provided on the companion disks that come with this book. See your service provider or network system administrator for specific configuration information for your network connection.

- The companion disks that come with this book.

If some of this sounds like Greek to you, don't despair. Information on joining the Internet can be found throughout these pages, particularly in Chapter 2.

The Mac Internet Tour Guide will not only show you the most fascinating and helpful places on the Internet, it will also give you the tools and techniques you need to navigate the vast landscape of information out there. The software on the enclosed companion disks will bring new power and simplicity to everything you do on the Internet. Best of all, every detail of configuring and using the companion software is discussed in detail throughout the book—using real-world examples to show you how to get the most out of your time on the Net. Here's a brief look at what you'll find in the *Tour Guide:*

What's Inside?

Chapter 1, "What Is the Internet? (And Why Should I Use It?)," covers network benefits for the average user and provides a general overview of the Internet for beginners. It also includes information about the history, growth and future of the Internet.

Chapter 2, "Getting Connected (The Big Plug-In)," provides information for all different types of users about how to physically connect to the Internet. If you work for a medium or large organization, you may want to talk with your system administrator; you may already have an Internet account and not even know it. If you're with a smaller firm, or simply an individual looking to "plug in," this chapter also covers the basics of all the various kinds of Internet connections.

Chapter 3, "Network Infrastructure (Electronic Alphabet Soup)," offers background on how the Internet is organized, what you need to know about networking protocols, and the parts of an Internet address. We'll also go over some basic information about being a good Internet citizen. This chapter is a must-read before venturing out into the Net—it will make future chapters easier to understand.

Chapter 4, "Electronic Mail (The Pony Express Goes Digital)," covers everything you need to know about sending, receiving and replying to electronic mail (e-mail). You'll learn how to send e-mail from the Internet to virtually any other networked computer. You'll also learn how to use Eudora (an invaluable e-mail program included on *The Mac Internet Tour Guide Companion Disks*) and TCP/Connect II, a favorite commercial mail program used by thousands of Macintosh Internet enthusiasts. Finally, you'll also learn how to find addresses, participate in mailing lists and send and receive attached files with your e-mail messages.

Chapter 5, "Network News & Newsgroups (Broadsheets of the Broadband)," offers information on reading, posting and replying to the tens of thousands of news articles available via the Internet. This chapter shows you how to quickly and effectively browse, track and search newsgroups and articles using Nuntius (included on the companion disks) and TCP/Connect II. A brief discussion of posting etiquette and a general overview of available newsgroups are also provided.

Chapter 6, "Transferring Files (The Mother Download)," provides complete instructions for using the File Transfer Protocol (FTP) for downloading and uploading files on any of the thousands of publicly accessible file archives on the Net. Again, two excellent software products are covered: Fetch (included on the companion disks) and TCP/Connect II. We'll also cover the basics of computer viruses and how to use the popular Disinfectant antivirus shareware program.

Chapter 7, "Using Gopher (Burrowing for Information)," covers the details of using the powerful and user-friendly TurboGopher software (included on the companion disks) to browse information resources and download files on any Gopher server on the Internet. Information on creating and sharing TurboGopher bookmarks (electronic crumb trails through vast amounts of information) is also included.

Chapter 8, "The World Wide Web (Browsing With Mosaic)," provides detailed instructions for using Ventana Mosaic (included on the companion disks), a powerful graphical "front end," or interface, used for browsing the World Wide Web (WWW), an online hypertext system spanning most of the Internet.

Chapter 9, "Other Internet Resources (Geez, What Is All This Stuff?)," offers information on various Internet resources, both human and electronic. The Electronic Frontier Foundation (EFF) and the Internet Society, for instance, are bountiful organizations that provide a wealth of information for Internet users of any level of expertise. This chapter also includes information about relatively "minor" or esoteric Internet services that sometimes get overlooked, including time- and money-saving gems like Netfind, Finger, Archie, RFCs and FAQs.

Chapter 10, "Hot Spots on the Net (Notable Sites & Servers)," provides an extensive listing of fascinating Internet sites you can access using the software included with this book.

Appendix A gives information about the programs included on the companion disks, and about Ventana Online, including the Visitor's Center and *The Mac Internet Tour Guide Online Companion*.

A complete glossary, bibliography and index are also included in the last sections of the book.

But perhaps the best thing about *The Mac Internet Tour Guide* is that you can't get lost or left behind—just follow along at your own pace. Everything is covered in simple, step-by-step detail. Even if you've never used the Internet before, you'll find the software and instructions in this *Tour Guide* as easy to use as all your other favorite Macintosh applications.

And to keep the trip interesting, our tour will take frequent sidetrips to visit some of the most fascinating people, places and resources throughout the Internet. Keep an eye out for these "roadside attraction" sidebars—they'll feature people profiles, file reviews, resource listings, and fun and intriguing examples of the kinds of information you'll find (by chance or design) as you cruise the Internet.

So forget what you've heard about how complicated and frustrating the Internet can be. With the right software and a few pointers from a pro, it's a lot easier than you think—in fact, it's actually fun. Hop aboard, our tour is about to begin!

CHAPTER 1

WHAT IS THE INTERNET?
And Why Should I Use It?

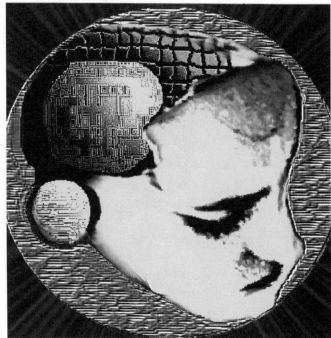

Imagine downloading Dante's *Inferno* from a computer in Massachusetts or California, just as quickly as if you were copying the file from a floppy disk. Imagine corresponding with anyone on almost a billion different computers, anywhere in the world, as easily as typing a letter with a word processor. Imagine reading the latest news practically as soon as it's written, or cruising through a web of connected computer networks and information resources so vast that no one knows for sure how big it is or how many people it reaches.

Need to know what the weather is like for your trip to New England this weekend? No problem—weather reports and even weather maps are only a few mouse clicks away. Want to find out who wrote a particular book or article? You don't even have to leave your chair to browse the holdings of the Library of Congress. This isn't a scenario from some commercial for a futuristic telephone company or a guess at what television will be like in the year 2050. This is a snapshot of the Internet as it exists right now.

It's Easier Than You Think

Forget everything you've heard about how complicated it is to use the Internet. Tools with a familiar Macintosh interface are available for just about every Internet service. You don't need to know any arcane UNIX commands or have an office next door to a mainframe computer. The myth is still there, but it's all smoke and no fire. Oh, sure, you can still plod around the Net the hard way, pecking out abbreviated gibberish on your keyboard like so much secret code. But there's a much easier way to cruise the Internet—one that will make your time online more fun and more productive—and that's what this book is all about.

I grew up in cities when I was a kid, and my cousins all grew up on farms in the country. Whenever I went to visit, they would tease me because I didn't know much about driving a tractor, saddling a horse or tossing a cowpie. I couldn't tease them about not knowing how to play stickball or dodge traffic, because I was on their turf—my city experiences weren't relevant. It's sort of like that on the Internet, but now the turf is common to everyone. If the UNIX fans and command-line aficionados want to pump water by hand, that's fine. Smile at them politely while you turn on your Macintosh faucet.

The main reason my country cousins teased me was because I wasn't familiar with their turf. I didn't have a tour guide or a map of the territory. The same is true for new Internet users. It's a daunting task to navigate new terrain without a guide to point out the landmarks.

This book is a tour guide to the Internet, designed to provide you with the tools and information you need to effectively navigate its vast information resources. You'll also find step-by-step tutorials for using a wide array of Macintosh software tools that help you communicate with people and travel to both the "cities" and the "rural areas" that make up this vast information resource. In fact, many of these tools are included on *The Mac Internet Tour Guide Companion Disks*.

Roadside Attraction Ahead

One of the greatest features of the Internet is that it provides all sorts of interesting areas to explore as well as virtually unlimited opportunities for rest, relaxation and diversion. Even the most serious researchers will wander occasionally into some offbeat area of the network, perhaps a newsgroup about a favorite band or a Web site dedicated to basketball (more about what the World Wide Web is in Chapter 8). I have tried to structure this book in a similar way, placing occasional roadside attractions along the highway. These attractions include discussions of various resources as well as some background insights into the culture, history and folklore of the Internet. Of course you are free to ignore these extra nuggets of information, and we hope we've made it easy to distinguish them by setting them apart from the regular text. Here's what a typical roadside attraction looks like:

You can't judge a book by what's between its covers.

It used to be that a book was a discrete object, something you could only change or supplement when you reprinted it. Nowadays more and more publishers are creating books that spill beyond their covers, that are amplified and even kept up to date by information provided on the Internet.

Most of the files mentioned in this book, as well as megabytes of related information, are maintained at Ventana Online's FTP and World Wide Web sites. What you hold in your hands is really only the core of *The Mac Internet Tour Guide*. The full package includes all the carefully organized data and programs available to you on the Ventana Online Internet server. The server's anonymous FTP address is ftp.vmedia.com, and the address for the World Wide Web site is http://www.vmedia.com/. A little later we'll show you how easy it is to access these sites and extend this tour guide in all kinds of exciting ways.

And now, since we stopped for a moment anyway, this is a perfect time to check the map and our tour itinerary for a quick overview of where we're headed and what we'll see.

Cruising the Easy Way

Neal Cassady was one of the most tenacious drivers of his generation. He'd think nothing of hopping in a Buick and driving Jack Kerouac coast to coast—stopping only for gas—with only a hip flask and a pack of smokes. Cassady was a pretty lousy guide, though, especially when he was trundling along in the big Merry Prankster bus on one of Ken Kesey's intrepid trips.

This book is a tour guide of the Internet, but my pace is a little less frantic than Cassady's (then again, I'm still alive). Since getting there is half the fun, we'll be making frequent stops to wander the nooks and crannies of cyberspace. And the great thing about this bus trip is that, although I'm driving, you can take things at your own pace. If you're anxious to get moving, you can bail out and catch up with the group at the next stop. If you're a slow starter, you can slow things down to a more leisurely pace. So, before we leave the station, let's take a couple minutes to check the map and itinerary for a quick overview of where we're headed and what we'll see.

A Sense of Place

People often describe the Internet as a worldwide network of computer networks. That's as good a description as anything I can come up with, but the experience of using the Internet—*being in the Net*—is something completely different. For instance, when I log into the simple local area network in my office, I'm pretty certain of what I'll find there; it doesn't really feel like a place. It's instead sort of like insipid American hotel chains. There's hardly ever anything different—never a surprise—the same bedspreads, brown Formica, loud air conditioner and view of the interstate.

But when I log into the Internet, it feels like a real place, just as real as the bar on the corner or the deli down the street. There's always something new to explore, and usually an interesting message or two in my e-mail box. And you can no more explore the entire Internet than you could visit every country on the globe. Things change too quickly and dramatically for you to ever become bored.

In this chapter, we'll take a look at what the Internet is, what kinds of information it contains, and how you can use that information to your advantage. We'll also explore a little of the history of the Internet, and speculate about what the future might hold for network users. But best of all, we'll take a look at the places, people and things you'll discover on your tour through the Net.

If you're already familiar with the Internet and how it works, or if you're just anxious to get connected and start exploring, you may want to skip ahead to Chapter 2, "Getting Connected."

Internet Benefits for the Average User

The Internet is much more than a network of networks. It's also much more than a huge repository of information. The Internet is a virtual community, existing only ephemerally in physical reality. While all this philosophical mumbo-jumbo is a great mental exercise—something interesting to think about while you're waiting in the dentist's office or the airport—it probably doesn't have much impact on your daily life.

But the Internet provides several very real benefits that can have an enormous impact on your daily life:

- **Electronic mail.** You can use the Internet to send electronic mail (e-mail) to virtually any networked computer user on the planet. Traditional post office mail ("snail mail" or the "paper net" to e-mail users) may take several days to reach its destination. Internet e-mail can be delivered anywhere on the planet in a matter of minutes, or at the most, a few hours. I used e-mail to correspond with my editor (who is also on the Internet), sending chapters back and forth during the entire writing cycle of this book. When the manuscript was finished, I used e-mail to correspond with the publisher's marketing and publicity staff—and they weren't even on the Internet.

- **Network news.** You can participate in a wide variety of electronic discussion groups on just about any topic imaginable, from investment strategies to molecular biology, from comic books to politics. If you can think of a topic that isn't already represented by a *newsgroup*, you can start your own. As of mid-October 1994, there were more than 9,000 active newsgroups accessible through the Internet. That number continues to exponentially grow, and there are hundreds of additional commercial newsgroups that are available for a fee. When the Clinton administration announced its support for the Clipper encryption chip, lively and informative discussions on all sides of the issue were taking place in various newsgroups within minutes of the announcement.

- **File transfer.** You can use the Internet's standard protocols to transfer computer files between your Macintosh and just about any other computer on the Internet. It doesn't matter where the other computer is located, how it's attached to the network or even if it uses the same operating system as yours. You can just as easily download a file from a UNIX-based mainframe in Tokyo as you can copy it from another Mac in the next room. The same day that Apple released QuickTime 2.0, I was able to download it from Stanford University's Macintosh archive. Just for fun, I called several local dealers to see if they had it in stock. Not one did.

■ **Information browsing.** You can use specialized software tools to browse through an almost limitless collection of information resources. Everything from weather reports and electronic journals to university and government databases is available. After I began work on this book, for example, the Clinton administration began to make position papers and speeches available on the Internet.

And that's just the beginning of what the Internet has to offer. As you explore, you'll discover people, places and other resources that will become invaluable to you. Because of its size, depth and diversity, the Internet can truly be all things to all people. But if you're new to the Net, you may be still wondering exactly what it *is*. The answer is at the same time simple and complicated. And the Internet changes so quickly, it's become something of a moving target—like a lemon seed on your kitchen counter: just when you think you have it in your grasp, it slips away.

A General Overview of the Internet

If you're a technophobe and don't much care about how things work, feel free to skip this section. It contains information about the plumbing of the Internet, and you can always read it later.

The Internet is a collection of various computer networks, linked together and communicating via a common protocol known as TCP/IP (Transmission Control Protocol/Internet Protocol). Because every computer on the Internet agrees to communicate using this protocol, it doesn't matter what kinds of computers you travel to, or even what operating system they are running.

In order for your Macintosh to communicate with other computers using TCP/IP, you must have the MacTCP software installed and properly configured. This process is discussed in more detail in the next chapter.

Although most of the computers that are connected to the Internet run some form of UNIX (the software that controls the computers), as a Macintosh user, you don't need to know one whit about UNIX. Though it probably wouldn't kill you to know a little UNIX, it's important to understand that, for the purposes of basic Internet activity, you don't need to know anything about UNIX—especially if you follow the advice and step-by-step instructions in this book.

The Internet is often defined as that group of computer networks that cooperatively form a seamless network using TCP/IP. But what about those computer systems that don't use TCP/IP but appear to be part of the Internet? For example, I can send electronic mail and even file enclosures from my Internet account to any user on MCI Mail. Yet MCI Mail's computers technically aren't on the Internet. MCI Mail maintains a *gateway* that's used to transfer electronic mail between their computers and the Internet. So, if you have an MCI Mail account, you can be reached from the Internet even though you don't have a computer on the Internet.

Internet Governance

Consensual anarchy best describes the governance of the Internet. While the individual networks that make up the Internet are likely to have executive officers, there's no such person running the entire Internet. The closest thing to an absolute governing authority is the Internet Society. The Internet Society is a group of volunteers whose charter is to promote the exchange of information using Internet technology. The Internet Society appoints a subgroup, the Internet Architecture Board, that authorizes standards and allocates and keeps track of Internet resources (like unique computer addresses). Another volunteer group, the Internet Engineering Task Force, handles acute operational and technical problems.

If you've ever driven in Paris, you'll understand this notion of consensual anarchy. The French have traffic lights, but they don't pay much attention to them. The traffic sort of develops a rhythm of its own without regard to the traffic lights. Drivers take account of the weather, the time of day, the number of vehicles, but not the traffic lights. If you come to a dead stop at a red light in Paris, people will honk their horns and shout silly-sounding French epithets at you. It's hard for an American mind to grasp a situation where there's a sense of everyone doing the right thing without external rules or order. But that's the way it is with the Internet. There are only two "rules" for life on the Internet, and they're unwritten:

- ▪ Don't waste bandwidth.

- ▪ Don't do anything that threatens the network.

You can do just about anything you like on the Internet, so long as you keep these two guidelines in mind. Would that the rest of life were as easy.

Each member network maintains its own Network Operations Center. These centers communicate with each other and arrive at a consensus on how to facilitate communications and resolve problems.

Since the Internet doesn't really exist in physical reality, there's nowhere to send a check for access. Each of the component networks that make up the Internet pays for its own operations. I send payment for my organization's connection to a regional network, which in turn pays a national provider for its connection. In theory, everyone on the Internet pays for his or her share, and in practice, this actually works amazingly well.

A Brief History of the Internet

The Internet began in the early 1970s as a Defense Department network called ARPAnet. The ARPAnet was originally implemented to support military research about how to build networks that could withstand partial outages and still function properly.

This network design approach assumed that the network itself was unreliable—a very realistic approach in hindsight, bomb attacks not-withstanding. Because the original ARPAnet model called for all communication to occur between two computers directly, any segment of the network could suffer an outage and the communication would still take place using any available alternative route across the network. The *computers* on the network—rather than the *network* itself—were responsible for correctly addressing and verifying communications. In network lingo, this is called *peer-to-peer* networking.

All that was needed for two computers to communicate on the ARPAnet was a message enclosed in a standard envelope—called an Internet Protocol (IP) packet—with a correct "address" for the destination computer.

In the early 1980s, Ethernet-based local area networks were developed. Most of the workstations that made up a local area network (LAN) in the early 1980s ran the UNIX operating system. The UNIX operating system came with IP networking capabilities built in. Organizations using these workstations wanted to connect their LANs to the ARPAnet, rather than connecting to one large timesharing computer at each site. Since all of the networks were speaking IP, the benefits of enabling users on one network to communicate with those on any other network became obvious.

In the late 1980s, the National Science Foundation (NSF) created five regional supercomputer centers, making the resources of the world's fastest computers available for academic research. Because the supercomputer centers were so expensive, only five could be created, and their resources were to be shared. A communications problem became immediately apparent: researchers and administrators at the different supercomputer sites needed to connect their centers together and also had to provide access for their clients. The ARPAnet seemed to be the solution to the communications problem but was abandoned, mostly because of bureaucratic problems.

The NSF built its own network—NSFNET—based on the ARPAnet's IP technology, with connections running at 56,000 bits per second (56 kbps) over specially conditioned telephone lines. This kind of connection was capable of sending about two pages per second across the network—slow by today's standards. Because these special telephone lines were expensive (the telephone companies charge for these lines by the mile) the NSF decided to create regional networks allowing sites to connect to their nearest neighbor, in daisy-chain fashion. Each daisy chain was connected to one of the regional supercomputer centers, and the centers themselves were linked together. This strategy allowed any computer to communicate with any other computer by passing messages up and down the daisy chain.

This strategy was successful—too successful, actually, and the network quickly became overloaded when the researchers discovered that the network was also useful for sharing resources not directly related to the supercomputer centers. In 1987, Merit Network received a contract to maintain and upgrade the network. Merit, in conjunction with IBM and MCI, ran Michigan's educational network. The original NSF network was replaced with telephone lines that were 20 times faster, and quicker computers were also installed. The network was subsequently opened to most academic researchers, government employees and contractors. Access was extended to international research organizations in countries that were allies of the United States.

In the early 1990s the network was opened up to a few large commercial sites, and international Internet access has also started expanding rapidly.

Today, the Internet is a collection of high-speed networks composed of the national backbone network provided by the National Science Foundation and a hierarchy of more than 5,000 attached regional, state, federal, campus and corporate networks. Links to networks in Canada, Europe, Japan, Australia, Central America and South America are in place. There are more than 2 million computers and workstations of various sizes connected to the Internet, with millions of users.

The Future of the Internet

The Internet is growing at a rate of about 10 percent per month as more colleges, universities and businesses come online. As of January 1994 there were 2,217,000 Internet hosts, and a new Internet address is registered every 30 minutes. The future of the Internet lies in three key areas: *commercialization*, *privatization* and *bandwidth*.

Commercialization

Lots of large multi-national corporations have been on the Internet for years, although their access has been limited to research and engineering departments.

Corporations have recently discovered how expensive running multiple networks can be and have begun to look for ways to consolidate their separate networks. Many have discovered that the Internet is at least part of the answer to their problems. In 1992, many of the restrictions on commercial use of the network began to change. In fact, there are already more commercial sites on the Internet than educational and research sites combined.

Privatization

Internet proponents have always wanted the various telephone companies—or other commercial organizations—to provide Internet connections. They claim you should be able to order an Internet connection just like you order Call Waiting or a second line for your telephone service. The telephone companies haven't jumped on this idea right away, but the recent corporate interest in the Internet has not gone unheeded, and this attitude is (slowly) changing.

But before the Internet can be fully privatized, users must find a method for funding the connections that are already in place. As soon as enough small businesses and individuals—the driving force of our economy—decide that connection to the Internet is an important asset, privatization of the Internet will occur very quickly.

One of the short-term changes likely to be brought about by commercialization and privatization is that transactions will become commonplace on the Internet. You will soon be able to order and pay for software and information via e-mail. More importantly, people will actually begin to make their livings in cyberspace.

Bandwidth

Bandwidth is the range of transmission frequencies a network can use. What this means is that as bandwidth increases (which it will dramatically in the next few years), you can transfer *more* information *faster*.

Increasing available bandwidth will not necessarily change the way many people currently use the Internet, but it will improve certain aspects of the way we use the Internet:

- Electronic mail will be richer in media type and benefit from faster delivery.

- File transfers will take much less time—a mere fraction of their current rate.

- Electronic publications—telepublications—will be richer in media type and benefit from faster delivery.

- Telecommuting (working from home via phone, fax and modem) will be more enjoyable and effective.

- Remote collaboration will become easier, more rewarding and more effective.

In short, the way we use and work with information will change drastically. More than ever before, information will take on new value and urgency, while at the same time becoming more accessible and available.

Moving On

This chapter has introduced you to the basic aspects of the Internet as well as its history and future. By now, you're probably ready to get connected and see for yourself what the Internet is all about. Don't worry, we'll get there. But first, you should know how to establish an Internet account and learn a little bit about the mechanics of the network. The next chapter explains how to establish your actual account on the Internet.

The road ahead is long and winding, and it's not without its pitfalls. But if you stick with the group and follow instructions, you're guaranteed to enjoy every second of the journey. Let's get started!

CHAPTER 2

GETTING CONNECTED
The Big Plug-In

Before actually starting our tour of the Internet, we'll spend this chapter covering the details of how to get connected. If you already have an Internet connection, you can probably skip all this and go straight to Chapter 3, "Network Infrastructure," where you'll learn about how the places and pathways of the Internet are constructed and connected. Getting connected to the Internet traditionally has been either exceptionally easy or almost impossible. If you're with a university, government agency or corporation that already has computers connected to the Internet—or "on the Net," as veteran netters say—your task is remarkably easy: sweet-talk the folks in your computer support department to create an account for you. It will take them less than 15 minutes, but they'll probably tell you it will take anywhere from a few hours to a few weeks. Don't argue; bite your tongue, smile pleasantly, thank them for their time and efforts, and count your blessings—you are one of the lucky few. If you're not a part of an organization that's already on the Net, don't worry; it's not nearly as hard to get connected as it was just a few years ago.

Where to Sign Up

Because the Internet is not a single computer system—it's not even centrally managed—there is literally no "where" to sign up. For years, it was nearly impossible to get connected to the Internet. Most people talked to a friend of a friend, or found someone inside an organization who could provide them with a news and mail *feed*, sending packets of electronic mail and a limited number of newsgroups.

MacPGP v2.2 encryption software.

Encryption is an important way to assure privacy and authentication of e-mail messages. MacPGP v2.2 uses the non-NSA approved IDEA cipher patented in Switzerland. You can download the current version of MacPGP by FTP at ftp.csua.berkeley.edu in the /pub/cypherpunks/pgp/ directory.

In those days when "real people" could only wheedle their way onto the Internet, there was always a feeling of dealing with an "information black market." People passed around secret tips and covert instructions for bluffing your way into getting an account on the sly. Invariably, these instructions were to approach a sympathetic librarian in the musty basement of the local university computer center and imply that you were either a student or on the faculty. (The feeling was always one of begging for an audience with a scribe in the Holy Roman catacomb.) If luck was with you, your account would be activated later that day, and you were off to explore the nether regions of the Net, hoping nothing would go wrong and you wouldn't be found out.

These days, it's much easier. The following four sections provide general instructions about whom to befriend and what arcane terms to utter so you'll sound like a seasoned expert. You'll be able to obtain your very own Internet connection, regardless of what type of user you are—academic, government, business or individual.

University Users

If you're a university user—faculty, staff or student—you're in luck. Chances are, your college or university is already directly connected to the Internet. Contact anyone in the computing center and ask them for—or perhaps tell them you *must have*—access to the network. After you've been shuttled to the right person, he or she will probably ask you a series of questions like the ones shown in Table 2-1. Note that these questions are general in nature and the responses are merely examples, so your mileage will surely vary depending on your situation. But since half the game of getting the kind of Internet connection you want is just knowing what to ask for, the table shows you how to ask for the most and best of everything. If you sound like you know what you're talking about, most people will assume that you do. Don't worry about what it means; that's all explained later.

Table 2-1: University users Internet information.

They'll Ask	Your Response
Do you want a full or partial connection?	I need a connection to both my department's local area network, the campus wide area network and the Internet.
What kind of computer do you have?	I have a Macintosh IIci with 8mb of RAM running System 7.0.1, with a LocalTalk connection to my office's LaserWriter.
Do you want a dedicated, SLIP/PPP, UUCP or dial-in connection?	Preferably both a dedicated and a SLIP/PPP connection. I have a second Macintosh in my home office, and I'd like to have a PPP or SLIP connection to the network.
Do you want LocalTalk or Ethernet for your dedicated connection?	I'd prefer an Ethernet connection, but I also need to connect to my office's LaserWriter.
What speed modem do you need for your home office connection?	I need a V.32bis/V.42/V.42bis modem and the appropriate software to make the network connection.
Do you want a PPP or a SLIP connection?	I'd prefer a PPP connection.
What do you want for your username?	I'd like my username to be jsmith, which is my first initial and last name with no punctuation.

After all that, the odds are in your favor that you'll get at least some of what you asked for; and at this point you'll probably be scheduled to have your office computer network connection upgraded. Your account should be activated in a day or two. You will probably be given a packet of software, an instruction manual and the name, telephone number and e-mail address of your network administrator (often known as a "net god"). Most important, you'll probably get the telephone number of the campus help desk for any problems you have while using your connection. That's it—you're now an Internet citizen.

Government Users

If you work for a government agency, it's likely your agency is already connected to the Internet. Begin by asking your supervisor (or the appropriate computer techie) if your office has an Internet connection. He or she may not know but will probably be able to point you toward someone who can help. The person responsible for maintaining Internet accounts within your agency may or may not be affiliated with your local office.

In any case, finding the right person to help set up your connection is probably the hardest part. The questions—and your responses—will likely be similar to the ones shown in Table 2-1. It's not likely that you'll be able to request a dial-in connection—government agencies are fairly stingy with that type of connection, which is usually reserved for work-at-home types or people who travel extensively. But who knows; maybe you'll get lucky.

You'll probably have duplicate requisition forms to fill out, you may have to demonstrate that you have a direct need for an Internet account (a little creativity goes a long way here), and it will probably take you several attempts to fill out all the forms properly.

When your forms are correct and complete and your access has been authorized, someone will wire your computer for the network connection. This person will install a network card if necessary and provide you with software and an instruction manual.

Here's an important tip: try to get the installer to test the connection for you. The installation person will also give you the name, telephone number and e-mail address of your local network administrator. You probably won't be provided with a help desk telephone number (but you can always call the nearest university help desk and try to sound professorial). You'll also be instructed where to report network problems. Once that's done, you're all set.

Business Users

Many large businesses—especially those involved with the computer industry—are old-timers when it comes to the Internet. Here you may find one person (or even a whole department) in charge of maintaining Internet connections. These are the people you want to seek out: ask your supervisor or refer to your corporate employee manual or inter-office directory. If you've been using a local area network within your department, ask the person who comes to fix your computer when it breaks or when the network goes down. (Odds are, they'll be so happy to hear from someone who isn't reporting a problem, they'll be happy to hook you up to the Net.)

The procedure for acquiring an Internet connection within most businesses usually falls somewhere between the looseness of a university connection and the structure of a government connection. You may be able to get a dial-in connection, depending on your organization and its corporate culture. But as a starting point, you should be able to use the responses from Table 2-1.

If the company you work for isn't on the Internet, you may have to look into opening an individual account on your own and seek reimbursement from the company (for more information on this approach, see the "Individual Users" section later in this chapter). Alternatively, you may be able to generate enough interest within your workgroup or department to have management look into connecting existing local and wide area networks to the Internet.

Flame wars, affirmative action and babies (oh my!).

People love to carry out heated debates via the electronic messages they can post throughout the Internet. Here's a great "net.story" from Mikki Barry:

"In 1991, a huge flame war [a heated debate carried out via electronic messages] erupted over affirmative action in the soc.women newsgroup. The flames were exchanged for many months, tensions getting higher and higher. Not being one to let anyone else have the 'last word,' I helped fuel this war with my obviously eloquent articles, made increasingly virile through the evil hormones prevalent through late pregnancy. However, nobody on the Net knew I was pregnant, since I was at work until the day I went into labor.

"Just as the flame war reached its peak, however, I had the strange feeling that I wasn't going to be able to participate for awhile. So I posted a message saying, in effect, 'Sorry, I can't respond to this thread anymore. I have to go have a baby now.' Morgan Elizabeth Baumann was born later that night."

The procedure for establishing an Internet account varies widely from business to business. Some firms create an account for all new employees, while others offer accounts only to "critical" employees. In most medium and large businesses, there will be a help desk (or at least an MIS specialist) available if you have any questions or problems with your Internet account.

Individual Users

Unlike universities and large companies, individuals and small business users rarely need a full-time connection and are well served with only a dial-in connection. With a *dial-in* connection, you use your Macintosh and a modem to dial another computer or server where your Internet account is stationed. This is less convenient (but usually cheaper) than a standard connection, where your Macintosh is always connected directly to the Internet. For more information on the advantages and disadvantages of a dial-in connection, see "Types of Connections" later in this chapter.

Individuals and small businesses typically have the hardest time establishing an Internet account. Until recently, the Internet has been geared for users within large organizations communicating only with users inside other large organizations. Thankfully, this is changing rapidly, and now it's fairly common to find individuals and small businesses with full Internet access.

The main difference in individuals and small businesses using the Internet is that *you (or your business) must foot the complete bill for your account.* Needless to say, this affects the kind of connection and level of service you select. But Internet access is not nearly as expensive as it used to be—usually well within the means of most small businesses.

Take a quick look at the "Types of Connections" and "Resource Requirements" sections before you jump in and order the most expensive Internet connection offered by your service provider. You run the risk of buying a fully loaded Cadillac with power windows, sunroof and Corinthian leather interior when a more sensible Saturn or even a VW Microbus will do.

Types of Connections

This book assumes that your Internet connection is a "full" connection—one that includes electronic mail, telnet, FTP (File Transfer Protocol), network news and all the other network niceties. "Partial" connections with only some of the features of a full connection are also available from some institutions and service providers, but they are not powerful enough to be of much use to the dedicated Internet cybernaut. With that understanding, there are only two types of individual or small business connections you need concern yourself with: a dedicated connection and a SLIP (Serial Line Internet Protocol) or PPP (Point-to-Point Protocol) connection.

Dedicated Connection

If you have a dedicated Internet connection, your Macintosh—or the local area network to which your Mac is connected—is directly connected to the Internet. These connections are most common for users within universities, government agencies and large corporations; they're usually too expensive for individuals and small businesses.

Dedicated connections offer three distinct advantages over SLIP or PPP connections:

- You can set up an FTP server, allowing anyone else on the Internet to access your files when it is most convenient for them (be careful, this can also be seen as a disadvantage in some organizations).

- You don't have to connect to the network each time you want to use it—you're always connected. Wherever you go, there you are.

- Your file transfers (and any other work you do on the Internet) will be accomplished much faster.

When you contract for a dedicated Internet connection, your service provider will lease a dedicated telephone line at the speed you specify and will install a *router* at your site. The faster the telephone line you specify, the more you'll pay.

The only disadvantage to a dedicated connection is that it's expensive; but like most everything else, you get what you pay for. If you need convenient, constant access or lightning-fast file transfer and data throughput, you won't be happy with anything less than a dedicated connection. But that performance comes at a great cost. As of fall 1994, a dedicated Internet connection would cost most small businesses between $15,000 and $20,000 for the first year and about $5,000 to $10,000 each subsequent year. Organizations with more than 50 employees pay fees tied to their usage rates, but the average per-employee cost is as much or more than for small businesses.

SLIP & PPP Connection

Luckily, access to the Internet needn't cost several thousands of dollars. Using a modem, you can get most of the benefits of a dedicated connection at only a fraction of the cost. SLIP and PPP allow you to establish an Internet connection over standard telephone lines via high-speed modems. If you have a SLIP or PPP Internet connection, your Macintosh is also directly connected to the Internet—*but only while the SLIP or PPP link is active.*

Although SLIP is currently the more common protocol, PPP will probably surpass SLIP in the near future. PPP offers more features and better throughput during interactive sessions where small bits of information are passed in both directions. Additionally, PPP is a recognized Internet standard for transferring IP information over serial lines (SLIP isn't). If you're given a choice, you're better off to go with a PPP connection—it's the up-and-coming standard.

InterCon Systems Corporation has released SLIP software for the Macintosh—InterSLIP—as freeware. It's available by anonymous FTP at ftp.intercon.com in the /InterCon/sales/Mac/Demo_Software/ directory. InterSLIP is also included on the companion disks at the back of this book, and the latest version is always available from Ventana Online (see Appendix A for more about Ventana Online).

MandelTV.

MandelTV is one of the slickest Mandelbrot set (fractal) generators available for the Macintosh. It's implemented as a desk accessory and requires color QuickDraw and a math coprocessor. You can download it by FTP from mac.archive.umich.edu in the /mac/system.extensions/da/ directory.

MacPPP 2.0.1 is available as freeware by anonymous FTP at merit.edu in the /pub/ppp/mac/ directory. (For information on using FTP, see "Using Fetch to Transfer Files" or "Using TCP/Connect II to Transfer Files" in Chapter 6, "Transferring Files.")

SLIP or PPP connections lack many of the features of a dedicated connection:

■ Because you're using a modem rather than a direct network connection, getting files from here to there (and back again) will take significantly longer over a SLIP or PPP connection than with a dedicated connection.

■ You cannot offer a reliable, constant FTP archive, so other users can't directly access your files at any time.

■ Your connection to the Internet is active only while the modem connection is active; when you hang up the modem, you are no longer on the Internet.

■ The connection isn't fast enough to support more than two or three users.

■ You have to pay for at least one high-speed modem.

The biggest advantage to a SLIP or PPP connection is that you pay much lower connection costs. And unlike a less powerful dial-in connection, you are actually on the Internet while the connection is active. With the exception of offering a full-time FTP archive (something most individuals and small businesses would have limited use for anyway), you can do anything on the Internet with a SLIP or PPP connection that you can do with a dedicated connection at a literal fraction of the cost.

SLIP or PPP access is usually the best alternative for individuals and is the method I use to connect myself and my very small business to the Internet. See the special offer in the back of this book for information on establishing your own SLIP/PPP Internet connection.

Other Types of Connections

You can dial in to gain access to the Internet if you have an account on a computer that has a dedicated connection to the Internet (a university mainframe, for instance). Dial-in access to another computer is not as useful, powerful or easy to use as a SLIP or PPP connection, but it's much easier (and usually cheaper—sometimes free) to set up. Unfortunately for Macintosh users, dial-in access methods most often require you to use the archaic UNIX commands to traverse the Internet. And your dial-in connection may limit which Internet services you can use.

UUCP (UNIX to UNIX Copy Protocol) can also be considered an alternative type of connection. Every UNIX system supports UUCP as a method of moving information across standard telephone lines. You can usually find a service provider or an existing UUCP site that will allow you to use UUCP to transfer Internet mail and network news to your Macintosh—via a modem—but you won't really be "connected" to the Internet itself.

While this *Tour Guide* is geared for users with dedicated or SLIP/PPP connections, if you only have limited dial-in access, you'll still find much of the information on electronic mail, network news and other Internet resources highly useful.

Resource Requirements

Hang on, you're almost there! Now that you know about the different types of available connections, and assuming you have an appropriate network connection and your account has been activated, let's explore exactly what hardware and software resources are required to connect to the Internet.

Macintosh

You'll need a Macintosh of course. Almost any Macintosh will do, although you'll be hard-pressed if your Mac doesn't have a hard drive and at least 4mb of RAM. (As in all things Macintosh, you can never have too much hard drive space or memory.) You should be running System 7 or System 7.5.

Library of Congress Information System (LOCIS).

It's a great spectator sport—watching Congress in action. And you can do it if you have an IBM 3270-compatible terminal emulator. Luckily, the popular Mac Internet software, TCP/Connect II, can emulate just such a terminal. TELNET to locis.loc.gov and browse through the legislation that Congress introduces.

Sometimes it's rather alarming:

OFFICIAL TITLE(S):

AS INTRODUCED: (DATA FURNISHED BY THE HOUSE)

A concurrent resolution stating that Congress supports the suspension, with respect to the leadership of Iraq, of the prohibition of Executive Order 12333 on assassinations until Iraq has complied fully with all United Nations Security Council resolutions concerning the withdrawal of Iraqi military forces from Kuwait.

COMMITTEE(S) OF REFERRAL: House Foreign Affairs

SUBCOMMITTEE(S) OF REFERRAL:

Hsc International Security and Scientific Affairs

Hsc Europe and the Middle East

COSPONSORS

Rep. Holloway

Rep. Solomon

Rep. Paxon

Rep. Inhofe

Rep. Santorum

Rep. Barton

Rep. Rohrabacher

Rep. Spence

Rep. Ravenel

Network Interface Card or Modem

You'll also need a way of connecting to the Internet: either a high-speed modem or a network interface card. If you're with a large organization, someone will probably install and configure your network card hardware for you. If you're on your own, simply refer to the instructions that came with the card.

If you plan to access the Internet by SLIP or PPP, use at least a V.32 (9600 bps) modem, although I'd highly recommend a V.32bis/V.42bis (14,400 bps) modem, assuming your service provider supports the higher speed (and most do).

Buying a modem is simple in theory but difficult in practice: purchase the modem supporting the fastest *standard* modulation protocol and the best error correction and data compression you can afford.

MacSLIP or MacPPP

If you're connecting to the Internet with either SLIP or PPP, you'll need the appropriate LAP (Link Access Protocol) driver for MacTCP. (MacTCP, included on the companion disks, is special software that allows you to access the Internet. In most cases, your service provider or network administrator will configure MacTCP for you.) If you have a dedicated Internet connection, you do not need either of these drivers; you can skip the rest of this section and continue with "MacTCP" (the following section).

InterSLIP is available by anonymous FTP at ftp.intercon.com in the /InterCon/sales/Mac/Demo_Software/ directory, and the current version is included on the companion disks at the back of this book (the latest version is also always available from Ventana Online). MacPPP is available by anonymous FTP at merit.edu in the /pub/ppp/mac/ directory. (For information on using FTP, see "Downloading Files With Fetch" or "Downloading Files With TCP/Connect II" in Chapter 6.)

The SLIP software I use and recommend is Hyde Park Software's MacSLIP. It's usually available from your service provider or network administrator. If you are an individual user, you can order MacSLIP directly from the manufacturer for about $50.

> Hyde Park Software
> PO Box 7133
> Austin, TX 78713
> 512/454-1170
> info@hydepark.com

MacTCP

You'll also need to properly configure MacTCP, the software that lets your Macintosh communicate with other computers on the Internet. If you're dying to know the technicalities of it all, MacTCP enables your Macintosh to use Transmission Control Protocol/Internet Protocol (TCP/IP) to communicate with non-AppleTalk devices on the Internet.

Important Note: MacTCP is included on the companion disks that came with this book. It is required to establish an Internet connection and use Macintosh-specific TCP/IP software programs. Regardless of whether you have a direct connection to the Net via Ethernet or a SLIP or PPP connection via ordinary telephone lines, you must properly configure MacTCP. Even though the basic procedures for configuring MacTCP are generally the same, the exact details (which are crucial) are always different for everyone. For that reason, it's best to work directly with your network administrator or service provider to get MacTCP up and running. It is absolutely crucial that you not misconfigure MacTCP or use bogus IP addresses.

Alice in Wonderland.

The complete text of *Alice in Wonderland* has been made available by Project Gutenberg. Project Gutenberg was formed to encourage the creation and distribution of electronic text.

You can download the complete text of this and other works by FTP at mrcnext.cso.uiuc.edu in the /pub/etext/etext91/ directory.

Client Application Software

Unless you're part of a large organization, getting a network connection and an account on the Internet is only half the battle. You'll also need some client application software (or software that lets you navigate and take advantage of the Internet). This can be something of a chicken-and-the-egg situation, since no such software is built into the Macintosh operating system or provided with your Mac when you buy it. If you need a special program to transfer other software programs to your Macintosh (*and you do*), how do you download a program that you need the program to download?

The Mac Internet Tour Guide Companion Disks are the best place to start. You can use the programs provided on the disks to transfer, convert and decompress virtually any other program or utility you will need for using your Internet connection effectively. Best of all, the later chapters in this book address where to find and how to use the hottest software available on the Internet.

Making the Leap

OK, you've got your account established, you've got your network connection or modem configured, you've got the software that came with this book loaded, and you've got MacTCP configured. Congratulations! You're finally ready to make the leap and make your first Internet connection.

If you enjoy a dedicated Internet connection, simply launch the client software program you want to use.

If you use a PPP or SLIP Internet connection, you will have to establish a modem connection to the network before you can launch any of the client software programs you may want to use. For information on how to establish a modem connection with your PPP or SLIP driver, refer to the documentation that came with the software or talk to your service provider or network administrator, who should give you a customized settings document to use with your PPP or SLIP driver to establish your Internet connection.

Moving On

Now you know how to get an Internet account—who to talk to and what to ask for—and a little bit about what you need to actually establish the connection.

As the bus pulls out of the station, go ahead and take a nap or stretch your legs as we get up to speed; that was a long time to spend in the terminal waiting for our old bus to be gassed up and made roadworthy. But the weather ahead looks favorable—feels like we even have a bit of a tail wind.

If you're anxious to get on the road and take a quick sidetrip on your own, feel free to skip ahead to Chapter 4, "Electronic Mail," where you'll learn how to send e-mail, search for addresses and even subscribe to mailing lists. Or, you can jump to Chapter 6 and download some software. But if you want to stay with the main group, we're heading for Chapter 3, where we'll learn what we need to know about the terrain and the natives we're likely to encounter.

CHAPTER 3

NETWORK INFRASTRUCTURE
Electronic Alphabet Soup

As the bus wends its way along the back-roads route (I hate the interstates—they all look the same—so this tour will follow the roads less traveled), now might be a good time to talk about the customs of the people you'll be meeting and the places you'll be visiting as we continue to explore the Internet.

I know you're eager to begin prowling the Internet, but reading this brief chapter before resuming our tour will pay off down the road. This chapter covers what absolute beginners need to know about how the Internet works. One of the most crucial aspects of navigating and using the Internet is understanding the complex and sometimes confusing addressing schemes used throughout the Net. It's important to know how Internet addresses work, not only for sending e-mail, but for locating and using the vast resources available throughout the Net. This chapter explores all you need to know about network addresses to find your way to any resource on the Internet.

We'll also cover what it means to be a good Internet citizen.

An Information Democracy

The Internet's strongest single organizing principle is the democratization of information. As open and untamed as the wild west, the Internet has no formal organization.

What organization there is can be thought of as a sort of "consensual information anarchy," a network of networks connected by everything from standard telephone lines to high-speed, dedicated, leased lines to fiber-optic links. Think of each component network as a fiefdom with its own organizational structure.

When someone talks about being "on" the Internet, his or her computer is connected to one of the interconnected networks that make up the Internet. Computers on the Internet talk to each other by passing notes to each other—just like we all did when we were in grade school. Only the computers on the Internet are a lot more particular about the whole process, as I'll explain shortly.

The Internet has only two practical organizing principles:

- It serves to democratize information. Your network communications are handled in exactly the same manner, whether you are the chief executive of a Fortune 100 corporation or a junior high student.

- Every computer on the Internet agrees to follow the same protocol—to speak a common language: TCP/IP, which is short for Transmission Control Protocol/Internet Protocol.

The Internet Rosetta Stone

To understand how your communications on the Internet are handled, you have to know a little bit about TCP/IP, the network's common language. Rather than bore you with unnecessary details, I'll only discuss the main points of TCP/IP. You need to know a good bit about TCP/IP to *administer* an Internet connection, but not to *use* one.

As I mentioned earlier, computers on the Internet talk to each other by passing notes, just like we did in grade school. Unfortunately, the Internet's component networks—and the computers that use the Net to communicate—aren't as intelligent as grade-schoolers. Grade-school kids can decipher just about any kind of note, folded any which way.

Computers on the Internet are like a picky penmanship teacher; they require the message to be in a very specific language, and the note has to be folded just so. If the Internet note doesn't comply with the TCP/IP standard, it gets tossed faster than a school love poem intercepted by a lunchroom monitor.

So, if you want to communicate on the Internet, the software you use has to pass properly worded, carefully formatted notes. You can't just shout across the lunchroom, *"Hey! Augie! Pass me those peas!"* You have to use the proper decorum. You have to quietly pass your message in a note to your neighbor closest to Augie.

Transmission Control Protocol (TCP)

The Transmission Control Protocol (TCP)—the first piece of the protocol puzzle—controls the information you want to send across the Internet and separates it into smaller pieces that are easily managed. This allows you to send virtually any type of information, from text and graphics to sounds and video, or even actual shareware and software programs. And that information can range in size from a brief e-mail message to the complete works of William Shakespeare.

As TCP separates your information into manageable chunks, it numbers each piece, so the receiving end can put the pieces back together again in the proper order. As soon as each piece of information is received at the destination, TCP verifies it. If some pieces of your information are missing or garbled, TCP requests the originator to resend the missing or garbled pieces. When TCP has assembled all the information in the correct order, it sends it to the software program using its services. But remember, all this is going on at several thousands of bits per second, even if you're working over a modem, so the whole process is transparent to you.

Going back to Augie in the lunchroom, Augie would number each pea before putting them in a bowl and then pass you the bowl. You'd then take the bowl and eat each pea in numerical sequence. If you found a squished or missing pea, you'd pass a note back to Augie asking for a specific replacement pea. Hey now, I've seen stranger things in a lunchroom.

Internet Protocol (IP)

When you mail a paper message to a friend via the U.S. Postal Service, you seal your message in an envelope containing both a destination and return address. When you drop your message in the mailbox, a mail carrier transports the message to a local post office where your message is combined with others bound for the same general destination. The messages are then loaded on trucks and planes and shipped off to their destinations. Once there, the sorting process is reversed, and your message is delivered.

Messages sent on the Internet (and everything you do on the Internet is basically a message) work in roughly the same way, thanks to the Internet Protocol (IP). The networks that make up the Internet are connected by special-purpose computers, called *routers*. These routers are the network equivalent of post offices; they determine how to route the information traffic on the Internet. Each router need only know what different connections are available and which is the best next destination to get a message closer to its final destination. The routers are physically linked by Ethernet networks and telephone lines—the network equivalents of the Postal Service's trucks and planes.

The Internet Protocol manages each message's addressing, working just like an addressed envelope for your paper mail.

Once again, returning to the lunchroom metaphor—and I promise this is the last time—think of the Internet Protocol as the lunchroom monitor. The monitor makes sure the bowl of peas Augie passes down the line gets routed most efficiently among all the schoolmates between the two of you, including the class bully, until it finally reaches you.

Travel advisories.

The State Department of the United States provides foreign travel advisories by FTP from ftp.std.com in the /obi/US.StateDept/Travel directory. I've always wanted to go to Belize; let's check out the travel advisory:

Belize—Consular Information Sheet—December 15, 1992

Embassy Location: The U.S. Embassy in Belize is located at the intersection of Gabourel Lane and Hutson Street in Belize City; telephone (501-2) 77161.

Country Description: Belize is a developing country. Its tourism facilities vary in quality.

Entry Requirements: A passport, a return/onward ticket, and sufficient funds are required for travel to Belize. US citizens who stay less than three months do not need visas. However, for visits exceeding one month, travelers must obtain permits from the immigration authorities in Belize. For further information, the traveler can contact the Embassy of Belize at 2535 Massachusetts Avenue N.W., Washington, D.C. 20008, (202) 332-9636. Or contact the Belize Mission to the U.N. in New York.

Medical Facilities: Medical care is limited. Doctors and hospitals often expect immediate cash payment for health services.

Crime Information: Petty crime, including pickpocketing and muggings, occurs. Visitors who walk alone on city streets, especially at night, or travel alone to a remote tourist site are particularly at risk.

Drug Penalties: Penalties for possession and trafficking in drugs are strict, and convicted offenders can expect jail sentences and fines.

Where.Is.That.Thing@on.the.Net?

While messages sent across the Internet may travel in a fashion similar to regular letters, the Internet addressing system looks nothing like a street address. Many beginners are intimidated by the complex and seemingly arcane—or apparently random—way Internet sites are named, or addressed. But a closer look at the process reveals a method to the madness, and learning that method will help you avoid plenty of confusion, panic and frustration.

Each computer on the Internet has two unique addresses:

■ *IP address,* like 134.84.101.48 (always four numbers—each less than 256—separated by periods).

■ *Domain name,* like deeper.farces.com (always at least two words—or numbers—separated by periods).

All you really have to know is the domain name (the nonnumeric one) of any computer on the Internet you want to communicate with. The Internet addressing schemes were designed so that people only had to use the domain name address, while the computers would use the IP address.

Each person on the Internet has his or her own unique address: username@domain.top domain. My Internet address, for example, is mfraase@farces.com. My machine name address is deeper.farces.com ("deeper" is the name of my Macintosh). An example of this domain name address and its structure is shown in Figure 3-1.

Figure 3-1: Example domain-name address and structure.

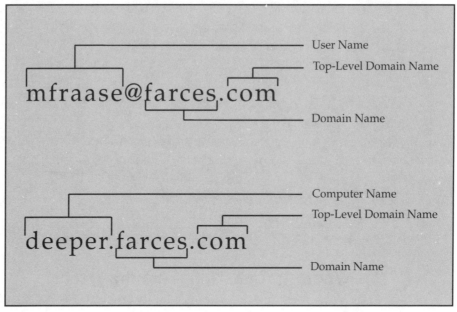

'Zine scene.

Lots of electronic 'zines are available at the Electronic Frontier Foundation's Gopher server and FTP archive. *Athene*, *CORE*, *Quanta*, *Unplastic News* and *ScreamBaby* are all available. Point your TurboGopher to gopher.eff.org port 70. Alternatively, you can FTP to ftp.eff.org and browse through the /pub/publications/ directory.

Domain-name addresses have special pronunciation rules:

- mfraase@farces.com is pronounced "em-frazy at farces dot com."

- deeper.farces.com is pronounced "deeper dot farces dot com."

Usernames aren't always a first initial followed by the last name, as mine is. Sometimes they're a first and last name separated by an underscore, like Ida_Jones@idacorp.com. Others may be almost indecipherable, like mx121bc@cowcollege.edu. If you get a chance to choose your own username, remember that people who send you e-mail will have to remember it. So pick something that's meaningful to other people as well as yourself.

Similarly, domain names aren't always a recognizable company or organization name. Domain names can be virtually anything, so long as they're unique, and they don't always refer to a specific business or other organization.

Generally, you can refer to computers on the Internet with either their IP address or their domain-name address (although it's usually much easier to remember a domain-name address), and you always refer to people with their domain-name address.

Have Your .Org Call My .Gov About That .Com

The last portion of a domain-name address is called the top-level domain. It provides a clue about the computer or the person you're addressing. Top-level domain names are standardized throughout the Internet, as shown in Table 3-1.

Table 3-1: US top-level domain names.

Domain	Represents
com	Businesses and commercial organizations
edu	Educational institutions
gov	Government institutions
mil	Military organizations
net	Network resources
org	Other (usually nonprofit) organizations

All Internet sites outside the United States are identified by a unique two-character top-level domain name, as shown by the examples in Table 3-2.

Table 3-2: International top-level domain names.

Domain	Represents
au	Australia
at	Austria
bz	Belize
ca	Canada
dk	Denmark
fi	Finland
fr	France
de	Germany
it	Italy
jp	Japan
no	Norway

The top-level domain name for the United States is "us," although it's not used very often. Some Internet users identify themselves by their geographic location in their domain names. For example, the domain name username@well.sf.ca.us indicates a user on the Whole Earth 'Lectronic Link (WELL) located in San Francisco, California, United States.

Finger.

Finger is a Macintosh implementation of the UNIX finger command. The archived file contains two programs: a Finger client and a Finger daemon. When Internet users finger you or your machine, they'll see a report you can customize. The program is available by FTP from mac.archive.umich.edu in the /mac/util/comm/ directory.

Here are a few tips to help you deal with the alphabet soup of Internet domain-name addresses:

- The example addresses used in this chapter are very simple. My editor's Internet address, for example, is ruffin@gibbs.oit.unc.edu. Ruffin's account is on a computer named Gibbs (gibbs) in the Office of Information and Technology (oit) at the University of North Carolina (unc), an educational facility (edu).

- The computer networks on the Internet aren't picky about case-sensitivity. For instance, mFraase@Farces.COM, Mfraase@farces.Com, and MFRAASE@FARCES.COM will all reach me just as efficiently.

- Make sure to write down important e-mail addresses. I can't tell you the number of times I thought I could remember an e-mail address only to have forgotten it by the time I needed it. Keep a hard-copy record of your e-mail address book. You never know when it might be accidentally deleted from the computer that maintains your account.

Eudora.

Eudora is one of the best Internet e-mail programs available for the Macintosh. Freeware and commercial versions are available. You can always download the latest release of the freeware version and its associated documentation by FTP from mac.archive.umich.edu in the mac/util/comm/ directory. The current version is included on the companion disks at the back of this book, and the latest version is also always available from Ventana Online. Information about the commercial version of the software is available by e-mail from eudora-info@qualcomm.com.

When in Rome... Don't Tie Up the Phone Lines

If your friend Augie invites you to dinner, you have to know more than just how to get to his house. You also need to know which water glass is yours (is it the one on the left or the one on the right?) and which fork to use for the salad. Before you set out on your Internet explorations, take a moment to review a few tips that may keep you from alienating anyone or making a fool out of yourself right away. We all make fools of ourselves on the Net at one time or another; here's hoping you can delay your fool debut for a while.

Acceptable Use Policies

Although the acceptable use policies of the various networks that make up the Internet are rapidly changing, we'll all probably have to deal with them at least until the mid-1990s. Instead of reprinting all of the different acceptable use policies, I'll just go over the main points.

To some extent, your category of Internet connection determines how you can use the Internet. If you're classified as an educational, research or noncommercial user, your Internet activities must be restricted to the purpose of research, education, charitable activities, government affairs, individual professional development or public service. If you're classified as a commercial user, your Internet activities are unrestricted (except, of course, for activities that are specified as unacceptable). Research and educational network traffic is routed over connections subsidized by taxpayers; commercial network traffic is routed over private connections. You don't have to worry about how your traffic is routed; that's the responsibility of your service provider.

Most service providers specify these uses as unacceptable:

- Distribution of unsolicited advertising.
- Transmission of anything that causes disruption of service to others.
- Propagation of computer worms or viruses.
- Use of the network to make unauthorized entry to any resource.

In addition, most service providers require you to abide by some general commonsense usage guidelines:

- Respect the privacy of other users.
- Usage must be consistent with common ethical practice and community standards.
- Respect copyrights and licenses of programs, information and documents.

Nuntius.

Nuntius is a Macintosh network news reader that employs the familiar Mac interface. It uses the NNTP protocol and allows you to follow message threads within the various newsgroups. The program is available by FTP from mac.archive.umich.edu in the /mac/util/comm/usenet/ directory. The current version is included on the companion disks at the back of this book, and the latest version is also always available from Ventana Online.

Finally, some service providers may require you to comply with the NSFNET Backbone Services Acceptable Use Policy. Ask your service provider or network administrator if your Internet activity is affected by this policy.

And if your idea of a good time is to wade through pages of legalese, you can always retrieve the complete documents from various archives on the Internet. For more information on how and where to get these documents, refer to "Downloading Files With Fetch" in Chapter 6 and "Downloading Files With TurboGopher" in Chapter 7.

Security Issues

With the rapid growth of the Internet, computer security becomes a more serious issue each year, especially when you're sharing resources across the Net. While your Internet connection is active, your computer—and perhaps more important, any other resources attached to your computer via a local-area network—are all on the Internet. It is your responsibility to protect your own system.

You also have a responsibility to be a good Internet citizen. You have been granted access to a worldwide resource and should respect the privacy and property of others.

If we, as Internet inhabitants, don't manage our own security wisely, it's likely that some less-than-benevolent government agency will take it upon itself to manage things for us.

Fetch.

Fetch is currently the best Macintosh FTP client software program. Fetch is distributed as freeware for non-profit and educational users and as shareware for commercial users. The current version is included on the companion disks at the back of this book, and the latest version is always available from Ventana Online. You can also download the latest release of the software and its associated documentation by FTP from dartmouth.edu in the /pub/mac/ directory. Site license information for commercial users is available by e-mail from fetch@dartmouth.edu.

First Names Are Lousy Passwords

Your login password is your security key, and is the most likely way someone will gain unauthorized access to your Internet account. Guard your password with care. Don't write it down, don't allow others to use it, and change it often.

A good password

- is made up of at least six characters that do not form a word.
- includes both uppercase and lowercase letters and numerals.
- is easily remembered, but is something no one can guess.

If you think your Internet account is being hacked—or if you suspect that your computer has been broken into—talk to your network administrator or service provider immediately.

TurboGopher.
Gopher lets you burrow through information resources using a series of easy to navigate menus that appear as standard Macintosh file folders and icons. You can use TurboGopher on the Macintosh to navigate huge dataspaces just by double-clicking the mouse button. TurboGopher is always available by FTP (or Gopher) from boombox.micro.umn.edu in the /pub/gopher/Macintosh-TurboGopher/ directory, and is also available from Ventana Online. The current version is included on the companion disks at the back of this book.

Usage Courtesy

Everything you do on the Internet has potential ramifications beyond the Net. The unwritten rule underlying all Internet activity is simple: *The Internet is a good thing and it must be protected.* While unwritten, this rule is enforced with impartial severity. If you screw up badly enough, you can expect to lose your access privileges. While there are no etiquette handbooks or Internet finishing schools, the same common sense and social grace you use in the real world will generally be enough to get you through most potentially sticky Internet situations.

While some of the tips and advice in this section may mean little to you now, they'll become second nature once you get your Internet legs:

- *Anonymous FTP isn't.* Always use your e-mail address as your login password when accessing remote FTP servers as an anonymous user. (See Chapter 6 for more on accessing FTP sites.) You can always make up a phony e-mail address when you visit far-flung spots on the Net, but don't bother. Cookie-crumb trails will lead back to your site, if not directly to you.

- *Leave your ethnocentricity at the door.* Many juicy Internet resources reside in foreign countries. Be careful with the cultural references you use.

- *Don't tie up popular sites at busy times.* Be aware that shared resources on the Internet may actually be in use by real people trying to do real work. Try to access the busiest resources during off-peak hours whenever possible (unless, of course, you're a real person doing real work). Be sensitive to time zones; think about what time it is where you're *going* rather than where you *are*. Try to find alternative routes to the busiest and most popular resources. Many popular archives have less crowded "mirror" sites elsewhere on the Net. Learn where they are and use them when possible.

- *Try to find the closest source for what you need.* Don't FTP or Gopher to Finland for a file you know is available a mere one or two hops away from your local site.

- *Don't use remote resources when you can use local ones.* Don't use archive space clear across the world for your personal files, just because you can't afford a bigger hard drive.

- *Log off properly.* Make sure you leave all resources in the same condition and state in which you found them. If you log off improperly, you may leave certain tasks or processes running in the background of the host machine, causing problems for other users or worse, network administrators.

Keep in mind that nothing on the Internet is really free. Somebody is paying for it. And if everyone takes a "free ride" on the most popular and expensive Net resources, it won't be long before those same resources are protected, restricted or closed to public access.

You'll find more Internet etiquette advice in the chapters that deal with specific network services.

Moving On

Now you know how the Internet works and how computers and people are identified. You've also looked at how to best get along with your fellow Internet inhabitants. The next chapter guides you through the wonders of using electronic mail on the Internet. You'll learn how to use the best Mac Internet e-mail software and how to communicate via e-mail with people who aren't even on the Internet.

CHAPTER 4

ELECTRONIC MAIL
The Pony Express Goes Digital

Our tour bus has been making pretty good time sticking to the back roads. But we've been rolling along for some time now, and some of you may want to send a message to your friends and family back home, just to let them know you're having a great time. So let's take a look at how to use electronic mail to communicate privately with individuals and small groups on the Internet.

With the exception of gestures, e-mail is arguably the most efficient means of communications yet devised by humans. Because it uses recycled phosphors on your Macintosh screen, e-mail is ecological—nary a tree and very little energy is used to create, deliver and read e-mail messages. You can choose to read your e-mail whenever is most convenient for you, not when it's convenient for someone else. You can scan an electronic in-box full of e-mail faster than you can open a single paper mail envelope. You can easily forward, store or reply to e-mail messages with the touch of a button. Sending messages to dozens of people is a snap with the multiple-addressing capabilities of e-mail. And there's a host of other features that make e-mail one of the most powerful and convenient ways to communicate.

But lots of people never get the most from their e-mail systems because they have to wrestle with arcane and obscure commands and abbreviations just to send a simple message. Forget about all that command-line nonsense. You're a Macintosh user, and there are excellent tools available that provide an elegant Mac interface for the Internet's electronic mail services. After all, electronic mail is only effective if you actually use it, and who wants to put up with a UNIX-based, command-driven e-mail program, when simple, Mac-specific options are available?

E-mail is an incredibly powerful form of communication, and there are plenty of Internet users who do little on the Net besides send mail. Consequently, we'll be spending more time discussing e-mail than any other topic in the course of our tour. So before we get started, let's pull off to the side of the road and take a look at the map of what we'll be covering in this chapter:

- What is E-Mail & How Does it Work?
- E-Mail Etiquette & Courtesy
- How to Send E-Mail Anywhere
- Quick Guide to Using Eudora
- Quick Guide to Using TCP/Connect II
- Finding Addresses
- Electronic Mailing Lists
- E-Mail & Attached Files

We've got a long road ahead, so hang on tight and let's get started!

What Is E-Mail & How Does it Work?

Most people who have never used e-mail have trouble understanding why it's touted over regular mail, fax or even phone conversations. It takes anywhere from a few seconds to a few minutes to deliver an e-mail message (complete with attached files) anywhere in the world. A postal delivery usually takes several days to reach its destination, and the telephone system is immediate, but both parties have to be on the phone at the same time. Fax was the rage in the '80s because it was fairly easy to use and didn't require a computer. But this chapter shows why so many people prefer e-mail to phone, fax or paper mail.

You can use e-mail to

- *Send text-based messages to any other Internet user.* You can also send messages to users on commercial electronic mail and information services. Soon you'll be able to send messages that contain fully formatted text, pictures, sound and even video—*between different types of computers and operating systems.*

- *Attach computer files to text messages.* You can send binary files— complete software programs or fully formatted files—to any other Internet user and users on most of the commercial electronic mail and information services. (Why send a static, dead document via fax when you can work with a live one via e-mail?)

- *Send messages and files to multiple recipients.* Where telephones tend to be useful for one-to-one communications, e-mail is useful for both one-to-one and one-to-many communications.

- *Reply to or forward messages you receive.* You can quickly and easily dash off a reply to a message, or forward it to other users around the world.

- *Subscribe to electronic mailing lists.* You can add your name to any of the thousands of mailing lists whose topics range from Macintosh hardware and software to political debates and discussions.

- *Communicate with mail list servers.* By sending e-mail queries to special addresses, you can query list servers that automatically respond to special commands by returning to you specific information, documents or other files.

Electronic mail is different from other Internet services in one important way—the sending and the receiving computers need not be able to connect directly with each other. You create e-mail messages on your computer and send them to a *mail server.* The mail server determines the best route to reach the recipient and passes the e-mail to the next closest mail server. The e-mail is passed through any number of mail servers and is eventually delivered to the final recipient's mail server. This is called a *store-and-forward* service, and it happens much faster than it took you to read about the process.

Smithsonian Institution photograph archive.
The Smithsonian Institution has begun to archive electronic versions of its photographs and art collections. The archive is accessible by FTP at photo1.si.edu in the directory /pub/images/. Unfortunately, this machine has a poor network connection. Daily updates are mirrored at the University of North Carolina and are accessible by FTP at sunsite.unc.edu in the /pub/multimedia/pictures/smithsonian/ directory.

Like the phone system and the postal service, e-mail isn't infallible. Occasionally, an e-mail message doesn't reach its intended destination. Any e-mail that does not reach its recipient is returned to the sender as undeliverable mail. This is called a *bounced* e-mail message. Reasons for bounced mail include (in order of likelihood)

- *User unknown* (incorrect address in the username portion of the address).

- *Host unknown* (incorrect address in the domain or top-domain portion of the address).

- *Network unreachable* (gateway limitations or problems with the network backbone).

- *Connection timed out* (software problem on the destination mail server).

- *Connection refused* (problem with the destination mail server).

The important point here is, if your e-mail message is undeliverable—for whatever reason—it will be bounced back to you. Many first-time e-mail users waste countless hours worrying if their messages are delivered, often following e-mail transmissions with faxes and phone calls to the effect of "Did you get my e-mail?" As a general rule, assume that your e-mail efforts are successful rather than figuring they don't work at all.

E-Mail Etiquette & Courtesy

Electronic mail eliminates a lot of subtle impediments to effective communication. Judgments based on appearance, voice or social position are impossible in electronic communications. E-mail's asynchronous nature—the ability to deal with a message when it's most convenient for all parties involved—is truly a boon to communications among individuals and groups.

One of the most amazing things about e-mail is the immediacy of its delivery. When you click that Send button, your message is delivered in seconds. This is a great advantage in most cases, but can work as a disadvantage if you have a short fuse. Unlike a letter, which may sit on a desk for hours or days before being mailed, electronic communications are usually dashed off as soon as they're completed. If you've been using e-mail for a while, you'll notice that a lot of the messages you receive (and perhaps a few you've written) shouldn't have been sent. It pays to ponder the ramifications of an e-mail message before launching it into the electronic ether—once it's gone out, there's no way to get it back.

The price you pay for e-mail's convenience and speed is a fairly high potential for misunderstanding. The best way to avoid e-mail misinterpretations and mixed signals is to follow three simple, commonsense rules of e-mail etiquette and courtesy.

- *Don't send anything via e-mail that you wouldn't want to read in your hometown newspaper.* Invariably, that juicy e-mail message is read by the one person who was never meant to read it. There are lots of stories about the politics of e-mail, and until the law catches up with the technology, you're better off playing it safe. Assume your e-mail messages are available to anyone who wants to read them. Some companies even have a policy making e-mail the property of the company, not the individual correspondents. In early 1993, the Georgia Institute of Technology announced that it would no longer consider e-mail delivered to any of its systems on the Internet to be private. Already, landmark legal cases about trade secrets, corporate espionage and e-mail are filtering through the courts. E-mail *should* enjoy all the rights and securities of paper mail, but don't make the mistake of assuming that it *does*.

- *Facial expressions and body language don't fit through the narrow bandwidth of e-mail.* Statements that you intend as pithy may come across as condescending or sarcastic. Some people approach e-mail as conversational; others don't. Some people never take e-mail personally, others always do. Unless you're close friends with an e-mail recipient, never expect that he or she will understand your sense of humor, wry wit or playful repartee.

■ *You can't control when your message will be delivered, so assume it will arrive at the worst possible time.* Be careful with your wording. What may seem funny or cute today may be inappropriate or rude when e-mail is read tomorrow. Just because e-mail is delivered at warp speed doesn't mean it's read at the same rate. Lots of people get more e-mail than they can keep up with; keep that in mind as you compose your missive. If you only read three e-mail messages a day, you'll probably remember them all for a few days. But people who receive dozens of messages need reminders (or forwarded messages) to help clue them in to the context of previous correspondence.

Auto-advice from EmilyPost.

If you think you get some perplexing junk paper mail, consider receiving this automated e-mail message:

Dear Net-Mail User [o EweR-635-78-2267-3 aSp]:

Your mailbox has just been rifled by EmilyPost, an autonomous courtesy-worm chain program released in October 2036 by an anonymous group of Net subscribers in western Alaska. [o ref: sequestered confession 592864 -2376298.98634, deposited with Bank Leumi 10/23/36:20:34:21. Expiration-disclosure 10 years.] Under the civil disobedience sections of the Charter of Rio, we accept in advance the fines and penalties that will come due when our confession is released in 2046. However we feel that's a small price to pay for the message brought to you by EmilyPost.

In brief, dear friend, you are not a very polite person. EmilyPost's syntax analysis subroutines show that a very high fraction of your Net exchanges are heated, vituperative, even obscene.

Of course you enjoy free speech. But EmilyPost has been designed by people who are concerned about the recent trend toward excessive nastiness in some parts of the Net. EmilyPost homes in on folks like you and begins by asking them to please consider the advantages of politeness.

For one thing, your credibility ratings would rise. (EmilyPost has checked your favorite bulletin boards, and finds your ratings aren't high at all. Nobody is listening to you, sir!) Moreover, consider that courtesy can foster calm reason, turning shrill antagonism into useful debate and even consensus.

We suggest introducing an automatic delay to your mail system. Communications are so fast these days, people seldom stop and think. Some Net users act like mental patients who shout out anything that comes to mind, rather than as functioning citizens with the human gift of tact.

More ▸

If you wish, you may use one of the public-domain delay programs included in this version of EmilyPost, free of charge.

Of course, should you insist on continuing as before, disseminating nastiness in all directions, we have equipped EmilyPost with other options you'll soon find out about....

—From David Brin's *Earth* (Bantam, 1990).

E-Mail Privacy

If I took a paper letter from your mailbox, opened it and read it, I'd be guilty of a federal offense. If I did the same thing by intercepting or retrieving your e-mail, chances are I would not be committing a crime.

Electronic communications are not given the same protection as first-class mail. As the rapid rate of change outpaces the social and legal conventions that govern how we use technology, we continue to suppose that we have freedoms and rights that simply do not exist. For example, in the past, wiretapping had to be physically carried out. A spook had to be near the person under surveillance. A tape recorder had to be in the immediate vicinity of persons recorded. With advancements in telephone switching technology, this is no longer the case. Anyone can now easily eavesdrop on conversations simply by sending the proper signal tones down the telephone wire—from anywhere.

In 1986, President Ronald Reagan signed into law the Electronic Communications Privacy Act (ECPA). The act is designed to expand the scope of telecommunications covered under the protection of the 1968 federal wiretapping laws. The ECPA protects electronic mail, cellular telephones, pagers and electronic data transmission. It also requires government agencies to obtain a court order before intercepting electronic communications.

The ECPA, as currently written, has two main goals:

■ Protecting all electronic communications systems, including e-mail, from outside intrusion.

■ Protecting the privacy of certain messages transmitted over public-service e-mail systems.

The ECPA makes it a federal crime to intercept certain electronic communications, but makes a distinction between public and internal electronic communications systems. Most importantly, electronic mail messages transmitted within internal e-mail systems that are used solely for interoffice communications are not subject to the privacy provisions of the ECPA. That means that a company can read such messages without invading the privacy of employees. Electronic mail messages transmitted within internal e-mail systems that allow outside access can be read by a company if either the sender or receiver grants permission. Reading electronic mail messages exchanged over public e-mail systems by anyone other than the sender and receiver is a felony under the ECPA. To make matters more confusing, it's not clear whether the Internet is considered a public e-mail system under the ECPA.

If this all seems a little vague and you're wondering how it relates to you as an e-mail user, a poll conducted by *Macworld* magazine might bring the issue into clearer focus. In its July 1993 issue, *Macworld* published the results of a nationwide poll of top corporate managers from 301 businesses of varying sizes. The poll found that 21 percent of respondents have "engaged in searches of employee computer files, voice mail, electronic mail or other networking communications." The figure was even higher—30 percent—among large companies.

E-mail horror stories.

Linda Ellerbee's infamous Associated Press e-mail incident didn't so much involve eavesdropping or invasion of privacy as it did the simple misrouting of electronic communications. Ellerbee, so the story goes, sent a note to a friend through the Associated Press e-mail system. The note included some very nasty comments about her boss and the Dallas city council, as well as other Texas luminaries. An accident in the network caused the message to be distributed to every AP outlet in four states. Ellerbee lost her job over the incident, and the potential for legal action by everyone involved—including Ellerbee, her boss and the AP—was gigantic.

In the summer of 1990, the members of the city council of Colorado Springs became outraged when they discovered the mayor was secretly reading their private e-mail messages.

In August of 1990, Alana Shoars, a network administrator in charge of electronic mail at Epson America, Inc., filed a lawsuit against the company. Shoars's lawsuit alleged that her supervisor, Robert Hillseth, manager of data communications for Epson, had intercepted her MCI Mail mes-sages on a regular basis as they were passing through the company's network gateway. Shoars claims that when she complained about Hillseth's activities, he fired her. Shoars filed an individual suit for wrongful termination and also filed a class action suit with 2,500 other current and former Epson employees, asking for unspecified damages of up to $3,000 per violation. That's $3,000 for each message that was intercepted. The class action suit was filed as an invasion of privacy under Section 631 of the California Penal Code.

Secret Service Director John Simpson admitted in a letter to California State Representative Don Edwards that the United States government has been intercepting private e-mail and surreptitiously monitoring computer bulletin boards in order to track the activities of suspected hackers.

While there are various techniques for encrypting or otherwise protecting e-mail messages, they are not always practical or convenient, and no system is completely foolproof. So until specific laws are passed and sweeping policy changes are enacted by government and business alike, the lesson here is clear: assume that your e-mail messages are being read by people other than their intended recipients.

How to Send E-Mail Anywhere

You can do anything with e-mail that you can do with postal mail, except mail physical objects. With an Internet account, you can even send e-mail to people who have accounts on one of the commercial electronic mail or information services like MCI Mail or CompuServe.

Addressing e-mail on the Internet is standardized and simple, despite how arcane or inscrutable some Internet addresses seem.

Everyone's Internet e-mail address, as explained in Chapter 3, "Network Infrastructure," is formatted the same:

username@domain.top-domain

To send e-mail to someone on the Internet, just address the message to his or her Internet address.

The next six sections detail how to send and receive mail from most of the common commercial information services that provide an *e-mail gateway* to the Internet.

An e-mail gateway is software or hardware that connects networks that use different protocols. In effect, it translates between the protocols so that computers on the connected networks can exchange data. Be careful with the size of the files you send by e-mail. Most of the e-mail gateways provided by the commercial information services like CompuServe and America Online have severe file-size limitations, as indicated in Table 4-1.

E-mail addresses are not case-sensitive, and most people don't care how you capitalize their name or domain name, as long as their e-mail gets to them.

Internet to UUCP & Back

UUCP, the UNIX-to-UNIX Copy Program, is a protocol used by UNIX workstations to communicate with each other over telephone lines. UUCP is also commonly referred to as a network, because e-mail and files can be sent to any UUCP-capable computer by specifying which intermediate computers the e-mail must pass through to reach the final recipient. Since many UUCP sites are switching over to full domain-name registration, you might first check to see if your recipient has a standard Internet domain-name address.

To send e-mail to a UUCP user, use either of these formats:

user@host.uucp

user%host.uucp@gateway

For example, to send e-mail to Peter Piper (whose user ID is *ppiper*) at his Megacorp (*megacorp.uucp*) host, use this format:

ppiper@megacorp.uucp

Alternatively, if Megacorp uses the Performance Systems International (PSI) gateway to receive e-mail (check with Peter or his assistant if you aren't sure), use the following address format:

ppiper%megacorp.uucp@uu.psi.com

Sometimes UUCP users will provide you with what's called a *bang-path address*. Bang-path addresses are easily spotted because they contain exclamation marks (!):

...!uunet!megacorp!ppiper

The exclamation marks are pronounced as "bang." The above address would be pronounced as "from bang uunet bang megacorp bang ppiper."

You can always convert bang-path addresses to this format:

user%host.uucp@gateway

UUCP users with access to an e-mail gateway send e-mail messages to colleagues on the Internet using the standard domain-name addressing:

user@domain.top-domain

For example, UUCP users with access to a gateway address e-mail to my Internet address as follows:

mfraase@farces.com

UUCP users without access to a gateway must route Internet e-mail using whatever paths are appropriate to reach a computer that is connected to the Internet.

"Dear Sysadmin, Punish your user for what he said!"

In mid-April 1993, Carl Kadie asked a variety of system administrators how they respond to the above request from Internet users. The responses were very interesting:

- Ten respondents explained the value of free expression or replied that punishing users wasn't their job.

- Seven respondents told the accused to "cool it" (or else).
- Four respondents said the situation has never come up.
- Two respondents said they judge the article and punish the user if the posting is found to violate policy.
- One respondent removed the entire newsgroup in which the article was posted.
- One respondent told the complainer "we'll handle it," but didn't do anything to follow up.
- One respondent passed the complaint up the chain of command.

Internet to CompuServe & Back

CompuServe is a commercial information service that opened an e-mail gateway to the Internet in July 1989. CompuServe subscribers are assigned a unique identification number as a username, in this format:

71234,5678

To send e-mail to a CompuServe subscriber, use this format:

useridentification.number@compuserve.com

For example, to send e-mail to Peter Piper (whose CompuServe ID number is 71234,5678) use the following address format:

71234.5678@compuserve.com

Note that the comma in the recipient's user identification number is translated to a period.

You should also remember that there is a 50,000-character limit on e-mail messages that pass through CompuServe's Internet gateway.

CompuServe subscribers send e-mail to the Internet using the following format:

>Internet:user@domain.top-domain

For example, CompuServe subscribers address e-mail to my Internet address like this:

>Internet:mfraase@farces.com

Internet to MCI Mail & Back

MCI Mail is a commercial electronic mail service that has offered an experimental Internet gateway since the late 1980s; the gateway is no longer considered experimental. MCI Mail subscribers are assigned a unique MCI ID number, an MCI ID name and a full username, in the following respective formats:

557-4126

mfraase

Michael Fraase

To send e-mail to an MCI Mail subscriber, use any of the three following formats:

idnumber@mcimail.com

idname@mcimail.com

full_user_name@mcimail.com

For example, to send e-mail to any of the above three MCI Mail address formats, use one of the three following formats:

5574126@mcimail.com

mfraase@mcimail.com

michael_fraase@mcimail.com

Note that when you use the idnumber@mcimail.com format, the dash separating the numbers is eliminated. Also, spaces—like those between first and last names—are translated to the underscore (_) character.

There is no limit on the size of e-mail messages that pass through the MCI Mail Internet gateway.

MCI Mail subscribers send e-mail to the Internet with the following steps:

1. At the Command prompt, type **create** and press Return.
2. At the TO prompt, type the full name of the recipient followed by **(EMS)** and press Return.
3. At the EMS prompt, type **Internet** and press Return.
4. At the MBX prompt, type the recipient's Internet domain-name address in the format user@domain.top-domain and press Return.

For example, MCI Mail subscribers address e-mail to my Internet address as follows:

1. At the Command prompt, type **create** and press Return.
2. At the TO prompt, type **Michael Fraase (EMS)** and press Return.
3. At the EMS prompt, type **Internet** and press Return.
4. At the MBX prompt, type **mfraase@farces.com** and press Return.

Internet to America Online & Back

America Online is a commercial information service that maintains an e-mail gateway to the Internet. Each America Online subscriber has a unique "screen name" as a username, at least three and no more than ten characters long.

To send e-mail to an America Online subscriber, use this format:

screenname@aol.com

For example, to send e-mail to Peter Piper (PetePiper) use the following address format:

petepiper@aol.com

Note that there is a 27,000-character limit on e-mail messages that pass through America Online's Internet gateway.

America Online subscribers send e-mail to the Internet using the standard domain-name addressing:

user@domain.top-domain

For example, America Online subscribers address e-mail to my Internet address like this:

mfraase@farces.com

Internet to AT&T Mail & Back

AT&T Mail is a commercial electronic mail service that opened an e-mail gateway to the Internet in June 1990. Each AT&T Mail subscriber is assigned a unique username.

To send e-mail to an AT&T Mail subscriber, use this format:

username@attmail.com

For example, to send e-mail to Peter Piper (ppiper) use the following address format:

ppiper@attmail.com

AT&T Mail subscribers send e-mail to the Internet using the standard domain-name addressing:

user@domain.top-domain

For example, AT&T Mail subscribers address e-mail to my Internet address like this:

mfraase@farces.com

Internet to AppleLink & Back

AppleLink is a commercial information service that Apple Computer initially provided for developers, dealers and employees, but Apple now offer accounts to the general public as well. Each AppleLink subscriber is assigned a unique username.

Note that AppleLink subscribers have to specifically enable the Internet gateway for their account (see below). By default, all AppleLink accounts have the Internet gateway turned off. This means that if you send e-mail to an AppleLink subscriber who has not enabled the Internet gateway for his or her account, your e-mail will be returned as undeliverable. *The AppleLink service also carries a fifty-cent surcharge for each message either entering or leaving the AppleLink e-mail gateway to the Internet.*

To send e-mail to an AppleLink subscriber, use this format:

username@applelink.apple.com

For example, to send e-mail to Peter Piper (piper1) use the following address format:

piper1@applelink.apple.com

Note that there is a 32,000-character limit on e-mail messages that pass through AppleLink's Internet gateway.

Before an AppleLink subscriber can send e-mail to the Internet, he or she has to enable the Internet gateway for his or her account by sending an empty e-mail message to the following address:

TurnOn@Internet#

AppleLink subscribers send e-mail to the Internet using this format:

usernname@domain.top-domain@internet#

The entire address (not counting the *@internet#* portion) must be less than a total of 35 characters or the e-mail will be returned as undeliverable.

For example, AppleLink subscribers address e-mail to my Internet address like this:

mfraase@farces.com@internet#

"Dear Sysadmin, Punish your user for what he said!" revisited.

In mid-April 1993, Carl Kadie asked a variety of system administrators how they respond to the above request from Internet users. Here's one of the responses he received:

"I believe you need a short lesson in the operation of free speech. I have no particular opinions on the subject of this newsgroup, but I took the trouble to read some of the 'belligerent and harassing' postings of which you speak, and, frankly, they weren't."

"It seems to me that your attempt to characterize them as such stems from a desire to stifle ideas with which you disagree. I have no intention of cooperating with you in this. The remedy for speech with which you disagree is more speech, not a silencing (the rather low signal-to-noise ratio on USENET notwithstanding)."

"If these postings offend you, I suggest you find out how 'kill files' work, rather than wasting the time of overworked system administrators who aren't being underpaid to deal with this sort of childishness."

Cross-Network E-Mail Addressing Quick Reference

The addressing information presented in the previous six sections is distilled for quick reference in Table 4-1.

Table 4-1: Cross-network e-mail addressing at a glance.

Service	From Internet	To Internet
UUCP [1]	user@host.uucp user%host.uucp@gateway …!gateway!host!user	user@domain.top-domain [1]
CompuServe	user.number@compuserve.com [2]	>Internet:user@domain.top-domain
MCI Mail	idnumber@mcimail.com [3] idname@mcimail.com full_user_name@mcimail.com	TO: recipient's full name (EMS) EMS: Internet MBX: user@domain.top-domain
America Online	screenname@aol.com [4]	user@domain.top-domain
AT&T Mail	username@attmail.com	user@domain.top-domain
AppleLink [5]	username@applelink.apple.com [6]	usernname@domain.top-domain@internet# [7]

[1] Requires access to a gateway.

[2] The comma in the recipient's user identification number is translated to a period. There is a 50,000-character limit on e-mail messages that pass through CompuServe's Internet gateway.

[3] The dash separating the numbers is eliminated.

[4] There is a 27,000-character limit on e-mail messages that pass through America Online's Internet gateway.

[5] Before an AppleLink subscriber can send or receive Internet e-mail, he or she has to enable the Internet gateway for his or her account.

[6] There is a 32,000-character limit on e-mail messages that pass through AppleLink's Internet gateway.

[7] The entire address (not counting the *@internet#* portion) must be less than a total of 35 characters or the e-mail will be returned as undeliverable.

Quick Guide to Using Eudora

Eudora is an electronic mail program for the Macintosh that is fully compatible with the POP3 mail server offered by most Internet service providers. (If you're not sure whether Eudora is compatible with your mail server, ask your network administrator.) Originally written by Steve Dorner at the Urbana campus of the University of Illinois, Eudora is now supported by Qualcomm, Inc., and will likely become a commercial product in the near future.

The current release of the freeware version of Eudora is provided on *The Macintosh Internet Tour Guide Companion Disks,* and the latest version is always available from Ventana Online. Eudora is distributed via the express written permission of Steve Dorner and Qualcomm, Inc. It's a freeware product, and you are free to distribute it to others so long as the program is distributed in its entirety. For more information, please see the Read Me documents that accompany Eudora on the companion disks.

Qualcomm representatives have assured the Internet community that a free version of Eudora will remain available and will be updated from time to time. The company has stated that a reasonably priced commercial version will include enhancements ranging from MIME (Multipurpose Internet Mail Extensions—a new e-mail standard that supports graphics, styled text, audio, video and binary file transfers) to PEM (Privacy-enhanced Electronic Mail—a standard for e-mail encryption and authentication).

Configuring Eudora

Eudora must be properly configured before you can begin using it to send e-mail. To use Eudora, you must have an account on a computer that runs a POP3 (Post Office Protocol version 3) mail server. Use these steps to configure Eudora for use with your mail server.

1. Launch Eudora by double-clicking on its icon.

2. Select the Configuration command from the Special menu. The Configuration dialog box will be displayed, as shown in Figure 4-1.

Figure 4-1: Eudora
Configuration
dialog box.

| POP account: | |
| Real Name: | |

Connection Method: ● MacTCP   ○ Communications Toolbox   ○ Offline

SMTP Server:	
Return Address:	
Check For Mail Every	___ Minute(s)
Ph Server:	
Dialup Username:	

Message Window Width: ___   Application TEXT files belong to:
Message Window Height: ___   **TeachText**
Screen Font: Geneva   ☐ Automatically save attachments to:
Size: 9
Print Font: Courier
Size: ___   [Cancel] [OK]

3. Enter your user name in the POP account box in the format user@domain.top-domain.

   ■ For example, my login name is mfraase and the name of the computer that provides my e-mail service is mr.net. I would enter **mfraase@mr.net** in the POP account box.

4. Enter your full name in the Real Name box.

5. Click the MacTCP Connection Method radio button.

6. Enter the name of your mail server in the SMTP Server box, using the format domain.top-domain.

7. Enter your e-mail address in the Return Address box in the format user@domain.top-domain. This will likely be the same domain name address you entered in the POP account box, but not necessarily.

8. Click the OK button. You've completed the basic configuration process for Eudora.

TeX.

It's pronounced "tech," and if you're an academician, you probably already know about it. TeX is a very specialized typesetting software program. It's notoriously difficult to learn and painful to use, but for some things—like typesetting mathematical equations—it's indispensable. CMacTeX is a shareware port of the UNIX version of TeX 3.14 and METAFONT 2.7. It's available by anonymous FTP at math.tamu.edu and is located in the /pub/CMacTeX/ directory.

There are several other convenient features Eudora offers that you might want to take advantage of. Or you can begin using Eudora to compose and send e-mail messages. If you want to begin using Eudora without configuring Eudora for your own personal preferences, you can skip the rest of this section and advance to "Using Eudora."

Follow these steps to further customize Eudora to your own personal preferences.

1. Select the Configuration command from the Special menu. The Configuration dialog box will be displayed, as shown in Figure 4-1.

2. Enter how often (in minutes) you want Eudora to look in your mailbox for new mail in the Check For Mail Every box. If you want to check for mail manually, leave this box empty.

3. Enter the name of your e-mail address lookup server in the Ph Server box. Leave this box empty if your mail server doesn't provide a Ph server. (For more information on the Ph protocol and Ph servers, see the "Ph Servers" sidebar later in this chapter.)

4. Leave the Dialup Username box empty.

5. Enter the number of characters to display on each line of e-mail messages in the Message Window Width box. Leave the box empty to use the default value of 80 characters.

6. Enter the number of lines of each message you want Eudora to display at a time in the Message Window Height box. Leave the box empty to use the default value of 20 lines.

7. Select a font to use to display e-mail messages from the Screen Font pop-up menu.

8. Specify a font size to use to display e-mail messages in the Screen Font Size box.

9. Select a font to use to print e-mail messages from the Print Font pop-up menu.

10. Specify a font size to use to print e-mail messages in the Print Font Size box.

11. Click the button labeled TeachText to assign a new software program to open text files. A standard file dialog box will appear, from which you can make your choice.

12. Click the Automatically save attachments to check box if you want to save to a standard location any files that are attached to e-mail messages you receive.

13. Click the empty button to specify a drive or folder in which to save the attached files. A standard file dialog box will appear, from which you can make your choice.

14. Click the OK button. You've completed the basic customization process for Eudora.

A sample Eudora configuration is shown in Figure 4-2.

Figure 4-2:
Completed Eudora
Configuration
dialog box.

POP account:	mrfaase@mr.net
Real Name:	Michael Fraase
Connection Method:	● MacTCP ○ Communications Toolbox ○ Offline
SMTP Server:	mr.net
Return Address:	mfraase@farces.com
Check For Mail Every	10 Minute(s)
Ph Server:	
Dialup Username:	
Message Window Width:	80
Message Window Height:	100
Screen Font:	Geneva
Size:	9
Print Font:	Courier
Size:	

Application TEXT files belong to:
TeachText

☐ Automatically save attachments to:

Cancel   OK

At this point, you can further tweak Eudora's preferences to suit your individual needs, or you can simply start using it. If you want to use Eudora without further configurations, skip the rest of this section and advance to "Using Eudora."

The table below details the function of each option in the Switches dialog box. Use the information in the following table and execute these steps to finish configuring Eudora.

1. Select the Switches command from the Special menu. The Switches dialog box will be displayed, as shown in Figure 4-3.

Figure 4-3: Eudora Switches dialog box.

Composition:
- ☒ May use QP
- ☒ Word Wrap
- ☒ Tabs In Body
- ☐ Keep Copies
- ☒ Use Signature
- ☐ Reply to All
- ☐ Include Self

Send Attachments:
- ☐ Always As Mac Documents

Encode With:
- ○ AppleDouble
- ◉ BinHex

Checking:
- ☒ Save Password
- ☐ Leave Mail On Server
- ☒ Skip big messages

Sending:
- ☒ Send On Check
- ☒ Fix curly quotes
- ☒ Immediate Send

Get Attention By:
- ☒ Alert
- ☒ Sound
- ☒ Flash Menu Icon
- ☒ Open "In" Mailbox (Mail arrival only)

Switch Messages With:
- ☐ Plain Arrows
- ☒ Cmd-Arrows

Miscellany:
- ☐ Show All Headers
- ☐ Zoom Windows
- ☒ Easy Delete
- ☐ Mailbox Superclose
- ☒ Empty Trash on Quit
- ☒ Easy Open
- ☒ Show Progress
- ☐ Auto-Ok

[Cancel] [OK]

2. Based on the information presented in Table 4-2, check or uncheck the available boxes to suit your personal preferences.

Table 4-2: Eudora Switches settings.

Check Box	Function When Enabled
May Use QP	Uses MIME Quoted-Printable encoding to ensure that all characters stay intact when sending a message.
Word Wrap	Automatically wraps line endings in outgoing messages.
Tabs in Body	Inserts eight space characters each time Tab key is pressed.
Keep Copies	Leaves copies of outgoing messages in Out mailbox.
Use Signature	Signature file will be automatically attached to ourgoing messages.
Reply to All	Reply message addressed to sender and all recipients.
Include Self	Reply message includes your address.

Check Box	Function When Enabled
Always As Mac Documents	Keeps the Mac file structure intact when sending attachments.
Save Password	Saves login password between sessions.
Leave Mail On Server	Retains copies of mail messages on mail server after they have been received.
Skip big messages	Downloads only first few lines of very large messages.
Send On Check	Sends any queued messages when checking for new mail.
Fix curly quotes	Changes the curved typesetting quotes to straight quotes.
Immediate Send	Messages get sent as soon as they're queued.
Alert	Uses dialog boxes to get attention.
Sound	Uses sound to get attention.
Flash Menu Icon	Flashes icon in menu bar to get attention.
Open "In" Mailbox	Opens In mailbox when new e-mail is received.
Plain Arrows	Arrow keys can be used to navigate messages.
Cmd-Arrows	Command-Arrow keys can be used to navigate messages.
Show All Headers	Displays entire header, including routing information.
Zoom Windows	New mailbox and message windows open to zoomed size.
Easy Delete	Deletes messages without warning dialog box.
Mailbox Superclose	Closing mailbox window also closes messages from that mailbox.
Empty Trash on Quit	Empties trash mailbox when you quit Eudora.
Easy Open	Deleting or transferring topmost message opens next message.
Show Progress	Displays Progress window during network connections.
Auto-Ok	Network problem dialog boxes are automatically dismissed.

3. Click the OK button. The Switches settings will be saved.

4. Select the Signature command from the Special menu. An empty Signature window will be displayed.

5. Enter your signature in the Signature window.

  ■ A *signature* is a three- or four-line text file containing your contact information. An example is shown in Figure 4-4.

Figure 4-4: Example Eudora Signature window.

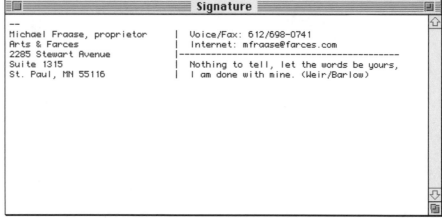

6. Click the Signature window's close box. You'll be asked if you want to save the changes you made to your signature.

7. Click the Save button.

You have now completely configured Eudora and are ready to use it to send and receive e-mail.

Internet/NREN Business Journal.
The *Internet/NREN Business Journal* is a new hardcopy newsletter from Michael Strangelove. Internet/Bitnet/NREN topics will include case studies of business ventures, legislation news, advertising strategy and ethics, Net-based public relations, university-industry activity, resource directories and emerging opportunities. Bimonthly, plus six annual special supplements, $75–$149. For information, contact 441495@acadvm1.uottawa.ca

Using Eudora

Eudora is a full-featured e-mail program comparable to many commercial products. In fact, by the time you read this, a reasonably priced commercial version of Eudora will probably be available. The following sections provide instructions for using Eudora's basic features.

The Mac Internet Tour Guide

Eudora's complete electronic documentation files would not fit on *The Mac Internet Tour Guide Companion Disks*. You can download complete documentation in Microsoft Word format from Qualcomm's FTP server—ftp.qualcomm.com (192.35.156.5) in the mac/eudora/ directory—or you can order a printed manual and distribution disk from the company for $30.

> Qualcomm, Inc.
> 10555 Sorrento Valley Rd.
> San Diego, CA 92121

You can always get the latest information about Eudora by sending e-mail to eudora-info@qualcomm.com.

Retrieving & Reading E-Mail With Eudora

Use these steps to log into your mail server and automatically retrieve any waiting e-mail.

1. Launch Eudora by double-clicking on its icon.

   ■ If you've configured Eudora to automatically check for mail, the program will automatically log into the server and download any e-mail addressed to you. The rest of this section assumes that you will be checking for e-mail manually.

2. Select the Check Mail command from the File menu. The Password dialog box will be displayed.

3. Enter your e-mail password and click the OK button. The Progress window will be displayed at the top of your screen, providing feedback about the status of your e-mail retrieval.

   ■ If your password is rejected you'll have to reselect the Check Mail command from the File menu and then reenter your password in the Password dialog box.

   ■ If there is a problem connecting to the mail server, a dialog box will inform you of the problem. Try selecting the Check Mail command from the File menu again; if Eudora still has problems establishing a connection, see your network administrator.

   ■ If you have no e-mail waiting on the server, the Progress window will disappear, and Eudora will return to its previous state. If you have waiting e-mail, it will be downloaded and the status will be updated in the Progress window. When all your waiting e-mail has been retrieved, you will be notified (based on the configuration settings you specified), and the In Mailbox window will automatically be displayed. Your new messages will be listed as shown in Figure 4-5.

Figure 4-5: Eudora In Mailbox window.

	In			
●	Rick Watson	10:32 PM 3/22/9...	2	re: 1.01b57 script problem
●	TELECOM Moderator	10:46 PM 3/22/9...	25	TELECOM Digest V13 #197
●	The Moderators	6:39 PM 3/22/9...	24	Info-Mac Digest V11 #63 1/5
●	The Moderators	6:39 PM 3/22/9...	24	Info-Mac Digest V11 #63 2/5
●	The Moderators	6:39 PM 3/22/9...	24	Info-Mac Digest V11 #63 3/5
●	The Moderators	6:39 PM 3/22/9...	24	Info-Mac Digest V11 #63 4/5
●	The Moderators	6:39 PM 3/22/9...	22	Info-Mac Digest V11 #63 5/5
●	TELECOM Moderator	11:25 PM 3/22/9...	19	TELECOM Digest V13 #198
●	andy	11:30 PM 3/22/9...	17	FutureCulture Digest #314
●	TELECOM Moderator	12:01 AM 3/23/9...	24	TELECOM Digest V13 #199 1/2
●	TELECOM Moderator	12:01 AM 3/23/9...	1	TELECOM Digest V13 #199 2/2
●	TELECOM Moderator	1:32 AM 3/23/9...	19	TELECOM Digest V13 #200
●	Cu-Digest (tkOjut2...	12:12 AM 3/23/9...	24	Cu Digest, #5.21 1/2
●	Cu-Digest (tkOjut2...	12:12 AM 3/23/9...	14	Cu Digest, #5.21 2/2
●	Adam C. Engst	9:54 PM 3/22/9...	24	TidBITS#169/22-Mar-93 1/2
●	Adam C. Engst	9:54 PM 3/22/9...	8	TidBITS#169/22-Mar-93 2/2
●	TELECOM Moderator	2:40 AM 3/23/9...	24	TELECOM Digest V13 #201
●	TELECOM Moderator	3:23 AM 3/23/9...	20	TELECOM Digest V13 #202
●	TELECOM Moderator	4:01 AM 3/23/9...	19	TELECOM Digest V13 #203
●	adam fast	3:17 AM 3/23/9...	5	Re: Squatters R Us
●	"Focus on 3 things...	8:45 AM 3/23/9...	2	Re: STC'S Electronic Bulletin Board
●	Peggy Thompson	8:58 AM 3/23/9...	2	Re: hyphenation breaks
●	Peggy Thompson	9:23 AM 3/23/9...	2	RE: More bloopers
●	Chet_Cady@OCLC.ORG	9:31 AM 3/23/9...	3	Reply to: Writing Across the Curr
●	aba@OC.COM	6:44 AM 3/23/9...	5	STC on the INTERNET (was STC's Electr
●	lpraderio	9:52 AM 3/23/9...	5	Re: Writing Across the Curriculum
●	Bruce B. Harper	10:05 AM 3/23/9...	7	RE: More bloopers
●	Eric Weiss-Altaner	10:16 AM 3/23/9...	2	Numeric keypads: Kensington or PlusWar
●	Joseph T Chew	7:31 AM 3/23/9...	2	Bitnet vs. Internet
●	Marc Posner	10:34 AM 3/23/9...	2	ExpressModem Software 1.0.1
●	Brian R Bezanson	9:40 AM 3/23/9...	2	Re: ExpressModem Software 1.0.1
31/380K/OK				

4. Double-click on the subject line of the message you want to read. The full message will be displayed, as shown in the example in Figure 4-6.

Figure 4-6: Eudora
e-mail message.

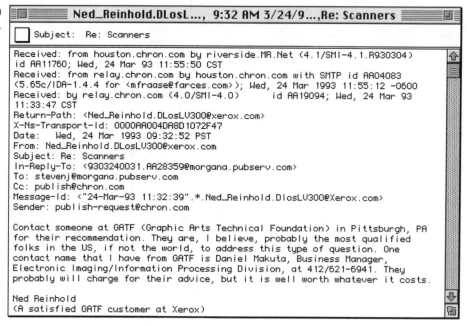

5. Close the message window by clicking in the close box.

6. Repeat steps 4–5 for each additional message you want to read.

E-mail messages are stored in the In mailbox until they are deleted or transferred to another mailbox. See "Managing E-Mail With Eudora" for more information.

Creating an E-Mail Message With Eudora

Use these steps to create an e-mail message with Eudora.

1. Launch Eudora by double-clicking on its icon.

2. Go to the Message menu and select the New Message command. A new Message Composition window will be displayed, as shown in Figure 4-7.

Figure 4-7: Eudora
Message
Composition
window.

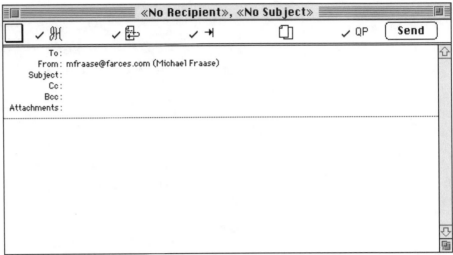

3. Enter the e-mail address of the recipient in the To field and press the Tab key.

4. Enter a short subject for the message in the Subject field and press the Tab key.

5. Enter the e-mail addresses of any recipients to whom you want to send a courtesy copy in the Cc field and press the Tab key. Tab through the field if you don't want to include any courtesy copies.

   ■ Courtesy copies are copies of your message sent to third parties *with* a notification to the addressee.

6. Enter the e-mail address of any recipients to whom you want to send a *blind* courtesy copy in the Bcc field and press the Tab key. Tab through the field if you don't want to include any blind courtesy copies.

   ■ Blind courtesy copies are copies of your message sent to third parties *without* a notification to the addressee.

Blind courtesy copies.

Courtesy copies used to be called carbon copies. But since we don't use carbon paper anymore, they're now called courtesy copies by the high-tech, in-the-know crowd. They're useful for distributing identical messages to a number of people.

Most people don't consider *blind* courtesy copies very nice, because they're secretive. They're generally used either by someone who is trying to cover a mistake or by someone who has something to hide. Privacy is a good thing. Secrecy isn't.

Blind courtesy copies are useful for large mailing lists because sending letters using the blind courtesy copy addressing feature prevents the names of all the recipients from appearing in the message header and overwhelming the actual message.

7. Press the Tab key to advance through the Attachment field.

8. Enter the body of your message. You can type or paste text into this field.

9. Click the Queue button. Your message will be stored on your hard drive and sent to the mail server when you select the Send Queued Messages command from the File menu.

   ■ If you've set Eudora's preferences to send mail immediately, there will be a Send button at the far right end of the Icon Bar instead of the Queue button.

Replying to E-Mail Messages With Eudora

Replying to an e-mail message is similar to creating a new message. Here's how to do it:

1. Double-click on the subject line of the message you want to read. The message will be displayed.

2. Go to the Message menu and select the Reply command. A new Message Composition window will be displayed with the original sender's e-mail address in the To field. In addition, all of the text from the original message will also be included, with a ">" preceding each line, as shown in Figure 4-8.

Figure 4-8:
Replying to an
e-mail message
with Eudora.

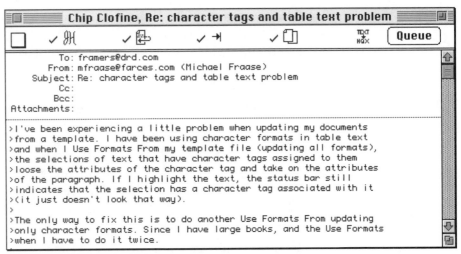

```
□  ✓ ℋ        ✓ 🗗      ✓ →|      ✓ ▢       TEXT   [ Queue ]
                                             HQX
        To: framers@drd.com
      From: mfraase@farces.com (Michael Fraase)
   Subject: Re: character tags and table text problem
        Cc:
       Bcc:
Attachments:

>I've been experiencing a little problem when updating my documents
>from a template. I have been using character formats in table text
>and when I Use Formats From my template file (updating all formats),
>the selections of text that have character tags assigned to them
>loose the attributes of the character tag and take on the attributes
>of the paragraph. If I highlight the text, the status bar still
>indicates that the selection has a character tag associated with it
><(it just doesn't look that way).
>
>The only way to fix this is to do another Use Formats From updating
>only character formats. Since I have large books, and the Use Formats
>when I have to do it twice.
```

Internet quoting conventions.

The ">" that precedes each line of a message is the Internet convention for quoted text. There are several variations, but ">" is the most common.

Second-hand quotes—quoted replies to quotes—are shown with a ">>" preceding each line.

This can soon get ridiculous. I've seen heated *flame wars* (vitriolic online debates) erupt into five or six levels of ">"s. It's not a pretty sight, and it's impossible to figure out who said what to whom.

A good rule of thumb when replying to e-mail or responding to a message posting is to quote only material that is necessary to further the understanding of the letter or message thread. Don't, for instance, quote a 300-line message in its entirety and add only "I agree" at the end.

3. Enter the body of your message. You can type or paste text into this field.

4. Click the Queue button. Your message will be stored on your hard drive and sent to the mail server when you select the Send Queued Messages command from the File menu.

   ▪ If you've set Eudora's preferences to send mail immediately, there will be a Send button (instead of the Queue button) at the far right end of the Icon Bar.

Sending E-Mail Messages With Eudora

Based on how you've configured Eudora, you can either send messages immediately or queue them to your hard drive for batch sending when you connect to the mail server. In general, it's a more efficient use of network resources to queue your e-mail messages for batch sending unless you maintain a constant connection to the Internet.

To send your queued e-mail messages,

1. Launch Eudora by double-clicking on its icon.

2. Select the Send Queued Messages command from the File menu. The Password dialog box will be displayed (unless you have configured Eudora to remember your password between sessions).

3. Enter your e-mail password and click the OK button. The Progress window will appear at the top of your screen, providing feedback about the status of your e-mail being sent.

   ■ If your password is rejected, you'll have to reselect the Send Queued Messages command from the File menu and then reenter your password in the Password dialog box.

   ■ If there is a problem connecting to the mail server, a dialog box will inform you of the problem. Try selecting the Send Queued Messages command from the File menu again; if Eudora still has problems establishing a connection, see your network administrator.

   ■ When the last e-mail message has been sent to the mail server, the Progress window will disappear, and Eudora will return to its previous state.

Managing E-Mail With Eudora

Eudora lets you organize your incoming e-mail by creating new mailboxes for storing and moving messages. To create new mailboxes,

1. Launch Eudora by double-clicking on its icon.

2. Select the New command from the Transfer menu. The New Mailbox dialog box will appear, as shown in Figure 4-9.

Figure 4-9: Eudora
New Mailbox
dialog box.

Name the new mailbox:

Untitled

☐ **Make it a folder**
☐ **Don't transfer, just create mailbox**

[Cancel] [OK]

3. Enter a name for the new mailbox.

4. Click the OK button. A new mailbox will be created with the name you specified in step 3.

   ■ Check the "Make it a folder" check box if you want to create a new folder within an existing mailbox.

   ■ Check the "Don't transfer, just create mailbox" check box if you want to create the new mailbox without transferring the selected message.

5. Repeat steps 2–4 to create any additional mailboxes you may need.

Mailbox strategies.

You can create mailboxes for any number of filing and organization strategies. Some people like to create mailboxes for each month or week, filing their messages by date. Others like to create a mailbox for each person they regularly correspond with, organizing messages based on contact.

The strategy that works best for me is to create mailboxes for various topics or projects I'm working on. When new e-mail messages come in, I sort them by content. As much as I like Eudora, I use TCP/Connect II (a commercial Mac Internet program) for most of my e-mail. It has intelligent *filters* that I can use to automatically sort my incoming e-mail based on a wide range of criteria I have set up. For more information on this technique, see "Managing E-Mail With TCP/Connect II."

To move e-mail messages between your mailboxes,

1. Launch Eudora by double-clicking on its icon.

2. Open the mailbox containing the message you want to move. You do this by selecting its entry from the lower portion of the Mailbox menu.

3. Select the subject line of the message you want to move. The subject line will be highlighted.

    ■ You can select a continuous range of messages by clicking on the first message and Shift-clicking on the last message. You can make multiple discontinuous selections by Command-clicking on the messages you want to select.

4. Select from the Transfer menu the new mailbox where you want to move the selected message, as shown in Figure 4-10.

Figure 4-10: Eudora Transfer menu with custom mailboxes.

Transfer
-> In
-> Trash
New...
-> FrameMaker
-> Information Politics
-> Internet Resources
-> Telecommunications

E-mail messages are stored in the In mailbox until they are deleted or transferred to another mailbox. To delete existing e-mail from any of your mailboxes,

1. Launch Eudora by double-clicking on its icon.

2. Open the mailbox containing the message you want to delete. You do this by selecting its entry from the lower portion of the Mailbox menu.

3. Select the subject line of the message you want to delete. The subject line will be highlighted.

    ■ As with transferring messages, you can select a continuous range of messages by clicking on the first message and Shift-clicking on the last message. You can make multiple discontinuous selections by Command-clicking on the messages you want to select.

4. From the Message menu, select the Delete command.

    ■ "Deleted" messages aren't actually erased; they're simply moved to a special Trash mailbox. Any message that has been "deleted" can be recovered by moving it out of the Trash mailbox before the Empty Trash command is chosen.

5. Select the Empty Trash command from the Special menu. (Don't confuse these Eudora commands and menus with those of the same names in the Mac's Finder.) The messages you "deleted" in step 4 will be erased when you quit Eudora.

Quick Guide to Using TCP/Connect II

TCP/Connect II is a commercial product (marketed by InterCon Systems Corporation) that integrates electronic mail, USENET news (also known as newsgroups), FTP (transferring or downloading files from remote sites) and telnet services (those services that require terminal emulation) in a single program. TCP/Connect II's e-mail module is extremely useful. The integrated nature of TCP/Connect II makes it easy to perform some tasks on the Internet that might not be possible with other programs, like forwarding (or responding to) USENET news articles by e-mail. I find that managing the various Internet resources I use most frequently is easier if all the tools I use are in a single program.

You can order TCP/Connect II from most of the Macintosh software mail order houses. The product carries a suggested retail price of $195.

> InterCon Systems Corporation
> 950 Herndon Parkway
> Herndon, VA 22070
> 703/709-5500 or 800/INTRCON
> 703/709-5555 (fax)
> info@intercon.com

Configuring the TCP/Connect II Mail Module

TCP/Connect II must be properly configured before you can begin using it to send e-mail. To use TCP/Connect II, you must have an account on a computer that runs a POP2 or POP3 (Post Office Protocol version 2 or 3; most sites use version 3) mail server. To configure TCP/Connect II for use with your network connection,

1. Launch TCP/Connect II by double-clicking on its icon. The Registration dialog box will be displayed, prompting you for name, organization and registration key information.

2. Enter the appropriate information in the Registration dialog box and click the Validate button. TCP/Connect II will automatically scan for the type of network connection you have

installed. Select Configure from the Edit menu. The Network
Configuration panel will appear, as shown in Figure 4-11.

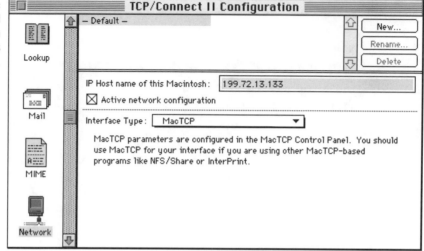

Figure 4-11:
TCP/Connect II
Configuration
dialog box's
Network panel.

3. Enter the IP host name of your Macintosh.

  ▪ If you're not sure of the appropriate IP host name of your
    Macintosh, see your network administrator or service provider.

4. Click on the Hosts icon in the scrolling list of configuration
   items. The Hosts Configuration panel will be displayed, as
   shown in Figure 4-12.

Figure 4-12:
TCP/Connect II
Configuration
dialog box's Hosts
panel.

TCP/Connect II Configuration

— Default —   culine.colorado.edu 862   New...
                                          Rename...
                                          Delete

General

IP Addresses:

Full Domain Name: culine.colorado.edu.862

Hosts

MTU: 1500   MSS: 1500   RWIN: 4096

IBM 327x

Paste Style: ● Full Speed ○ By Line ○ Blocked to

Lookup

Compressing space and time.

Ralph Brandi uses the Internet to compress space and time and to meet people that he would otherwise never encounter. Here is his story of how he uses the Internet:

"The Net demolishes the barriers of time and location. If you've got some kind of fairly obscure interest, you can be pretty sure there is someone else on the Net who shares it. The fact that they don't live in your neighborhood doesn't prevent you from carrying on an extended conversation. They can even live on the other side of the world and you don't have to worry about waking them up.

"The best thing about the Net that I've encountered in my six or so years connected has nothing to do with computers: it's the people. By communicating with people I share interests with, I've made a number of good friends.

"I had a Net.friend from New Zealand visit me for a week last year, after a couple of years of corresponding over the Net. I had a great time showing him New York City and the east coast, and he brought some books and records for me from New Zealand that I couldn't find for love nor money here in the U.S. I'm going to be visiting him in London—where he lives now— this summer.

"Some months ago, I was receiving a couple of low-powered radio stations from Australia on my shortwave radio. I had been trying to receive these stations literally for years, and they're highly sought-after targets among shortwave listeners. I posted a note to the rec.radio.shortwave newsgroup. The following morning, I had e-mail from a couple of people in Boston who had followed up on that tip and been rewarded with their first receptions of the stations. I later met them at a convention of shortwave enthusiasts and had a very enjoyable lunch with them and some of their friends.

"The common thread here is the interactions with *people*, not computers."

5. Click the New button. A dialog box will appear prompting you to enter the name of the host.

6. Enter the name of your mail server and click the OK button. A new entry will be created in the Hosts scrolling list.

7. Enter the IP address of your mail server in the IP Addresses box. Alternatively, enter the domain name of your mail server in the Full Domain Name box.

   ■ For instance, the IP address of my mail server is 137.192.2.5 and its domain name is mr.net.

8. Close the Configuration dialog box by clicking the close box.

To configure TCP/Connect II for use with your mail server,

1. Launch TCP/Connect II by double-clicking on its icon.

2. Select the Configure command from the Edit menu. The Configuration dialog box will appear.

3. Click on the Mail icon in the scrolling list of configuration items. The Mail Configuration panel will appear, as shown in Figure 4-13.

Figure 4-13: TCP/Connect II Configuration dialog box's Mail panel.

TCP/Connect II Configuration
Return Address:
Full Name:
Mail User ID:
Mail Server:
Connect to Server ○ Upon Request ● Every 10 minutes
POP Method: ○ POP2 ● POP3 ○ ACKS ● ACKD
☐ Allow mail to be received by SMTP (enable SMTP server)
Folder For Mail Files: Apps:Interne...:TCP/Connect II stuff ▼
Notification Sound: chika ▼

Lookup Mail MIME Network

4. Enter your e-mail address—using the format username@domain.top-domain—in the Return Address box.

5. Enter your real name (first and last) in the Full Name box.

6. Enter your e-mail account—using the format username@domain.top-domain—in the Mail User ID box. In most cases this is the same as your e-mail address, but not always.

7. Select your mail server from the Mail Server pop-up menu.

8. Click the appropriate POP Method radio button, representing the version of the Post Office Protocol used by your mail server. If you aren't sure which version your system uses, check with your network administrator.

9. Click the appropriate ACK radio button, depending on your needs:

- Click the ACKS radio button if you want to keep copies of your received e-mail on the mail server. This is useful for testing, but most system administrators prefer that you delete mail from the server once you have received and read it.

- Click the ACKD radio button to delete your e-mail messages on the server after they have been delivered and saved to your local hard drive.

10. Close the Configuration dialog box by clicking the close box.

Ph servers.

The Ph protocol was developed by Steve Dorner—author of the Eudora e-mail program—while he was at the Urbana-Champaign campus of the University of Illinois. Ph provides a way to look up e-mail addresses for colleagues and associates, usually at a single location.

In order for you to use the Ph lookup capabilities of either Eudora or TCP/Connect II, your mail server must also have a Ph server installed and properly configured.

Unfortunately, Ph servers are provided only for single locations—a large corporate site or a university, for example. Ph is useful only if you know the organization with which the person you want to contact is affiliated.

There are other methods—some relatively simple, others mind-numbingly sophisticated—to find e-mail addresses, and a few are covered elsewhere in this book. But the easiest way to find out someone's e-mail address is to call him or her on the telephone and ask. Sometimes the simplest methods are the best.

Using the TCP/Connect II Mail Module

The mail module of TCP/Connect II uses the Post Office Protocol (POP) to retrieve e-mail and the Simple Mail Transfer Protocol (SMTP) to send mail. All e-mail you send and receive with TCP/Connect II is handled automatically.

You can always get the latest information about TCP/Connect II by sending e-mail to info@intercon.com.

Retrieving & Reading E-Mail With TCP/Connect II

To log into your mail server and automatically retrieve any waiting e-mail,

1. Launch TCP/Connect II by double-clicking on its icon.

   ■ If you've configured TCP/Connect II to automatically check for mail, the program will automatically log into the server and download any e-mail addressed to you. The rest of this section assumes that you will be checking for e-mail manually.

2. From the Mail menu, select the Check Mailbox command. The Password dialog box will appear.

3. Enter your e-mail password and click the OK button. The Mail Status window will appear at the top of your screen, providing feedback about the status of your e-mail retrieval and any outgoing messages waiting in the queue.

   ■ If your password is rejected, you'll have to reselect the Check Mailbox command from the Mail menu and then reenter your password in the Password dialog box.

   ■ If there is a problem connecting to the mail server, a dialog box will inform you of the problem. Try selecting the Check Mailbox command from the Mail menu again; if TCP/Connect II still has problems establishing a connection, see your network administrator.

   ■ If you have no e-mail waiting on the server, the Mail Status window will disappear, and TCP/Connect II will return to its previous state. If you have waiting e-mail, it will be downloaded and the progress will be updated in the Mail Status window. When all your waiting e-mail has been retrieved, you will be notified based on the configuration settings you specified, and your In Box window will automatically be displayed, with your new messages listed as shown in Figure 4-14.

Figure 4-14:
TCP/Connect II In
Box window.

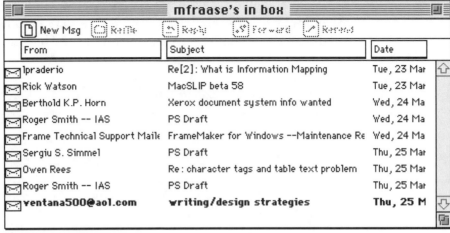

4. Double-click on the subject line of the message you want to read. The message appears, as shown in the example in Figure 4-15.

Figure 4-15:
TCP/Connect II
e-mail message.

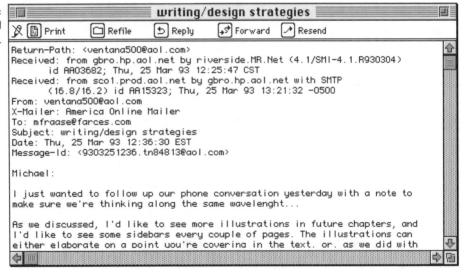

5. Close the message window by clicking in the close box.

6. Repeat steps 4 and 5 for each additional message you want to read.

7. Incoming e-mail messages are stored in the In Box until they are deleted or transferred to another mailbox. See "Managing E-Mail With TCP/Connect II" for more information.

Note: The only way to move mail between mailboxes is to use the menus or keyboard commands. There is no way to move it between mailboxes as you might move files from one folder to another from the Finder.

Creating an E-Mail Message With TCP/Connect II

To create an e-mail message with TCP/Connect II,

1. Launch TCP/Connect II by double-clicking on its icon.

2. Select the Create New Message command from the Mail menu. Alternatively, you can click the New Msg button in the upper left portion of the In Box window. A new Untitled Message window will appear, as shown in Figure 4-16.

Figure 4-16: TCP/Connect II Untitled Message window.

Untitled Message
Print   Save   Send   Post
Subject:
To:	Bcc:
Cc:	Archive: No Archive
	Signature: No Signature
	☐ Request Return Receipt
	☐ Archive Attachments

3. Enter the body of your e-mail message in the lower section of the window. You can type or paste text into this field.

4. Enter a short subject for the message in the Subject box.

5. Enter the e-mail addresses of the recipients—in the username@domain.top-domain format—directly in the To box.

6. Enter the e-mail addresses of the Cc recipients—in the username@domain.top-domain format—directly in the Cc box.

   ▪ Courtesy copies are copies of your message sent to third parties *with* a notification to the addressee.

7. Enter the e-mail addresses of the Bcc recipients—in the username@domain.top-domain format—directly in the Bcc box.

   ▪ Blind courtesy copies are copies of your message sent to third parties *without* a notification to the addressee.

   ▪ For more information on courtesy copies and blind courtesy copies, see the "Blind courtesy copies" sidebar earlier in this chapter.

8. If you want to archive a copy of the e-mail message you're sending, select an Archive mailbox from the Archive pop-up menu. You can archive mail in any of your existing mailboxes, or you can create a new mailbox.

   ▪ You can define a default archive mailbox by holding down the Option key while you select a mailbox from the Archive pop-up menu.

   ▪ You can obtain the same result by sending a Cc of the message to yourself. Using an archive is more efficient, however, because a Cc is delivered to you as a new (unread) e-mail message. Another nice touch of TCP/Connect II's mail feature is that the archive message isn't actually filed in the target mailbox until the actual message has been sent successfully.

9. Click the Send button. If you have an active network connection, your e-mail message will be sent to the specified recipients. If your network connection is inactive, the e-mail message will be saved in your Mail folder and automatically sent the next time you log into your mail server.

Replying to E-Mail Messages With TCP/Connect II

Replying to an e-mail message is similar to creating a new message, although it's partially automated. To use the e-mail module of TCP/Connect II to reply to an e-mail message,

1. Double-click on the subject line of the message you want to read. The message then appears.

2. Click the Reply button in the upper portion of the Message window. The Reply dialog box will appear, as shown in Figure 4-17.

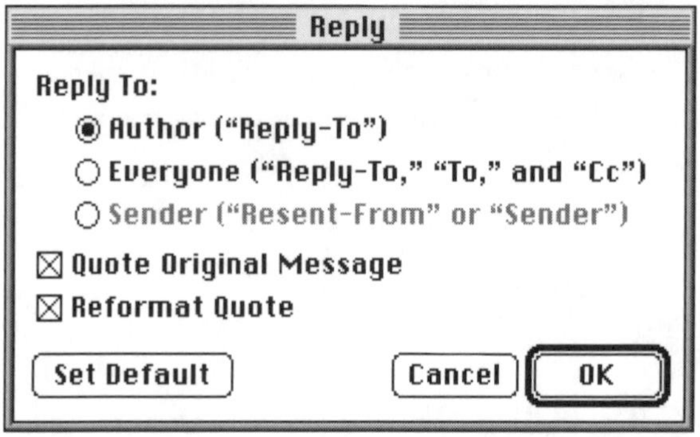

Figure 4-17:
TCP/Connect II
e-mail Reply
dialog box.

Reply

Reply To:
- ◉ **Author ("Reply-To")**
- ○ **Everyone ("Reply-To," "To," and "Cc")**
- ○ **Sender ("Resent-From" or "Sender")**

☒ **Quote Original Message**
☒ **Reformat Quote**

[**Set Default**]　　　　[**Cancel**] [**OK**]

3. Select the recipients of your reply from the Reply To radio buttons.

4. Click the Quote Original Message check box if you want to include quoted text from the original sender with a ">" preceding each line.

5. Click the Reformat Quote check box if you want to reformat the line endings of the quote to match SMTP's hard carriage returns, which occur after about every 78 characters.

6. Click the OK button. A new Message window will be displayed with the original sender's message, with a ">" preceding each line, as shown in Figure 4-18.

BBEdit.

BBEdit is a high-quality text editor that allows you to use the UNIX grep command to search for patterns of text across multiple files. The Claris XTND file translation system is supported, as are various plug-in modules (several are included with the distribution package and more are available in various FTP archives). The program is available by FTP from mac.archive.umich.edu in the /mac/util/text/ directory.

Figure 4-18: Replying to an e-mail message with TCP/Connect II.

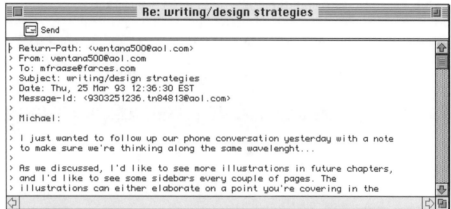

> ■ For more information on quoting existing messages, see the "Internet quoting conventions" sidebar earlier in this chapter.

7. Enter the body of your message. You can type or paste text into this field.

8. Click the Send button in the upper left portion of the Message window. The TCP/Connect II Send window will appear. Note that the Subject and To boxes have already been filled with the correct information.

9. Click the Send button in the Send window. If you have an active network connection, your e-mail reply will be sent to the specified recipients. If your network connection is inactive, the e-mail reply will be saved in your Mail folder and automatically sent the next time you log into your mail server.

Managing E-Mail With TCP/Connect II

TCP/Connect II lets you organize your incoming e-mail by creating new mailboxes for storing and moving messages. And TCP/Connect II is the only Macintosh e-mail product I'm aware of that you can use to set up *filters* to automatically sort your e-mail into the appropriate mailboxes. If you're a heavy e-mail user, this feature greatly stream-lines your e-mail activities.

To create new mailboxes,

1. Launch TCP/Connect II by double-clicking on its icon.

2. From the Mail menu, select the Mailboxes command. The Mail-boxes window will be displayed, like the example (with several mailboxes already created) shown in Figure 4-19.

Figure 4-19:
TCP/Connect II
Mailboxes
window.

Mailbox	Unread	Total
General Mail Archive	0	1
Internet Book Permissions	0	10
Internet Resources	0	18
kfraase's in box	0	0
Macintosh Internet Book	0	2
mfraase's in box	0	0

3. Click the New button in the Mailboxes window. A standard Save File dialog box will appear, prompting you to enter a name for the new mailbox.

4. Enter the name for the new mailbox.

5. Click the Save button. The new mailbox will be created and its name and status will be added to the Mailboxes window.

For more information on managing your e-mail with different mailboxes, see the "Mailbox strategies" sidebar earlier in this chapter.

Working With E-Mail Filters

Filing important e-mail messages after you've read them is a good way to manage incoming e-mail. But wouldn't it be wonderful if you could file incoming e-mail messages *before* you read them? Well, if you use TCP/Connect II, you can. TCP/Connect II's e-mail *filter rules* allow you to automatically manage your e-mail in a number of ways, including routing e-mail to specific mailboxes.

Filters can be thought of as "almost-intelligent processors" that look at all incoming e-mail messages and manipulate those messages based on a set of rules you've defined. If you don't want to use TCP/Connect II's filters, or if you want to experiment with e-mail a little before setting up filters, feel free to skip this section.

TCP/Connect II provides both local and global e-mail filter actions. Global filter actions apply to all mailboxes; local filter actions apply only to an individual mailbox. It's best to use local filters whenever possible, because global filters cause the program to run more slowly. I have noticed no performance degradation when I use quite a few local filters on my single incoming mailbox.

To create local filter actions to automatically highlight and route e-mail messages to appropriate mailboxes,

1. Launch TCP/Connect II by double-clicking on its icon.

2. From the Mail menu, Select the Open Mailbox command. A standard Open File dialog box will appear.

3. Double-click on your incoming mailbox in the Open File dialog box. The mailbox will be opened on your desktop.

4. Click within the mailbox to make it the active window.

5. Select the Mailbox's Local Actions command from the Mail menu. Note that this menu command will change to reflect the currently active mailbox window, as shown in the example in Figure 4-20.

Figure 4-20:
TCP/Connect II
Mail menu.

Mail

Open Mailbox...	⌘⇧O
Check Mailbox...	⌘M
Mailboxes...	⌘⇧P
Create New Message...	⌘⇧M
Send...	⌘⇧U
Send File...	⌘⇧E
Forward...	⌘⇧Y
Reply...	⌘⇧T
Resend...	⌘⇧I
Refile...	⌘⇧R
Select Messages...	
Global Mail Actions...	⌘⇧]
mfraase's in box's Mail Actions	⌘]
Address Book...	⌘⇧B
Lookup...	
Show Mail Status	

■ The Mail Actions dialog box for the currently active mailbox will appear, as shown in the example in Figure 4-21.

Figure 4-21:
TCP/Connect II
Mail Actions
dialog box.

6. Click the New Action button in the Mail Actions dialog box. The Edit Action dialog box will appear, as shown in Figure 4-22.

Figure 4-22:
TCP/Connect II
Edit Action
dialog box.

Edit Action

Action Rule:

Look In: **Message Header** ▼

For something that: **Contains** ▼

☐ Case-sensitive comparisons ☐ Use * and ? wildcards
☐ Disregard following actions

Highlighting for existing and new messages:

☐ Bold ☐ Underline Foreground
☐ Italic ☐ Outline Background

Operations performed on new messages only:

⦿ No marking, deleting, refiling, or copying
◯ Mark As Read ◯ Refile To: Archive: *No Archive* ▼
◯ Delete ◯ Copy To:

[Cancel] [OK]

7. Select the Message Header item from the Look In pop-up menu.
   This is the default selection and should appear automatically.

   ▪ The items on the Look In pop-up menu instruct TCP/Connect II
     where to search within e-mail messages for the word or phrase
     that you supply in the next field.

8. Select the Contains item from the "For something that" pop-up
   menu. This is the default selection and should appear automatically.

9. In the empty search box, enter the word or phrase for which you
   want the program to search.

10. Click the Case-sensitive comparisons check box if you want the
    search to be case-sensitive. Checking this box will match identi-
    cally the capitalization of the search word or phrase.

    ▪ If this box is checked and you entered **Internet** in the search
      box, *Internet* would be matched, but *internet* or *InterNet* would
      not.

11. Click the Use * and ? wildcards check box if you want the search
    to use simple pattern matching.

    ▪ An asterisk (*) represents any string of characters, and a ques-
      tion mark (?) represents a single character.

- For instance, if you want to find every e-mail message that pertains to the word *writing*, you could enter **writ*** in the search box. This would result in *write, writer, writing* and *written* all being matched.

- If you want to really get fancy, you could enter **wr?t*** in the search box. This would result in *write, writer, writing, written* and *wrote* all being matched.

12. Click the Disregard following actions check box if you want to ignore all of the following action items in the Edit Action dialog box.

13. Click any of the "Highlighting for existing and new messages" check boxes if you want the e-mail messages that meet the search criteria to be highlighted.

- If you have a black-and-white monitor, your highlighting options are any combination of Bold, Italic, Underline and Outline. If you have a color monitor, you can also select foreground and background colors.

14. Specify an action for those e-mail messages that meet the specified criteria by clicking one of the "Operations are performed on new messages only" radio buttons.

- Click the "No marking, deleting, refiling or copying" radio button to take no additional action on messages that match the criteria.

- Click the Mark As Read radio button to display an opened envelope icon next to messages that match the criteria, even though you have not read them.

- Click the Delete radio button to automatically delete messages that match the criteria.

- Click the Refile To radio button to automatically route messages that match the criteria to the mailbox you specify in the Archive pop-up menu.

- Click the Copy To radio button to automatically place a *copy* of all messages that match the criteria to the mailbox you specify in the Archive pop-up menu.

15. Click the OK button. The filter action will be added to the Mail Actions dialog box.

Filter action ideas.

TCP/Connect II's filter actions are invaluable to me, and I find it hard to justify ever using an e-mail product that doesn't have them. Here are a few ideas for putting filter actions to use.

Most of the employees at Ventana Press, the publisher of this book, use e-mail (you'd be amazed at the number of computer book publishing houses that don't). I created filter actions for various groups at Ventana. Messages from the marketing people got blue highlighting. Mail from the sales people was highlighted in green. E-mail from my editor got an orange highlight with bold type. Messages from the publisher were highlighted in red with bold and italic type attributes. All of the messages from the Ventana folks were refiled to a special mailbox.

I subscribe to a lot of electronic mailing lists (for more information on mailing lists, see the "Electronic Mailing Lists" section later in this chapter). All messages from a mailing list originate from the same e-mail address, even though they are written by lots of different people. I created a mailbox for each mailing list and created a filter action to refile each mailing list message to the appropriate mailbox.

The biggest problem with mailing lists is that some people insist on sending administrative requests (subscribe, unsubscribe, etc.) to the mailing list address rather than the *administrative* address. It's a simple matter to filter out these bozo messages with TCP/Connect II. Just search for subscribe, unsubscribe, signoff and the like in the message headers and click the Delete radio button.

One thing that I'd really like to see added to TCP/Connect II's e-mail module is the ability to automatically send out a message or file based on the results of the specifications of a filter.

Finding Addresses

If you work within a large corporation or university, finding the e-mail addresses of your colleagues is usually simple enough, because your site will probably have a Ph server. The problem is that the Ph server will probably only have addresses for people at your site or within your organization, which doesn't help you if you're trying to send e-mail to someone across the country or around the world.

The easiest way to find the e-mail address of someone is to call him or her on the telephone and ask for the e-mail address. It's a low-tech solution to a high-tech problem. Because of security and privacy concerns, and because there is no unifying standard for e-mail directories on disparate systems, there is no central directory for Internet e-mail addresses.

But even though no central Internet directory exists, there are a few tools you can use to try to find e-mail addresses.

Using Finger

Finger is a software utility that looks at the user login file on a UNIX system. Since most computers on the Internet run some variation of UNIX, Finger is probably the best place to start.

You can FTP (or transfer to your computer) a Macintosh version of Finger from the Sumex Info-Mac archive or the University of Michigan's Macintosh archive. For more information on using FTP to transfer files, see Chapter 6, "Transferring Files." Unfortunately, Finger requires you to know the name of the host machine where the person you are trying to locate has an account.

To use the Macintosh version of the Finger utility,

1. Launch Finger by double-clicking on its icon.

2. Select the Finger command from the File menu. The Finger dialog box will be displayed, as shown in Figure 4-23.

Figure 4-23: Finger dialog box.

Finger	
User	
Machine	
☐ **Whois Server ⌘S**	
[Cancel] [Set Default] [Finger]	

3. Enter the name of the person you are trying to locate and the name of the host machine using the domain-name format— username@domain.top-domain—in the User box. Alternatively, you can enter a valid IP address (the address that uses numbers instead of domain names) in the Machine box.

4. Click the Finger button. The results will be displayed in a window like the example shown in Figure 4-24. If the search is unsuccessful, a dialog box will appear, notifying you of the failure.

Figure 4-24: Finger
Results window.

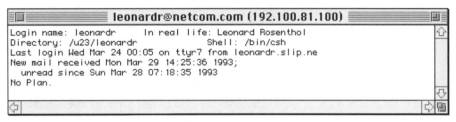

```
leonardr@netcom.com (192.100.81.100)
Login name: leonardr      In real life: Leonard Rosenthol
Directory: /u23/leonardr          Shell: /bin/csh
Last login Wed Mar 24 00:05 on ttyr7 from leonardr.slip.ne
New mail received Mon Mar 29 14:25:36 1993;
  unread since Sun Mar 28 07:18:35 1993
No Plan.
```

Using MIT's USENET User List

If the person you are trying to locate has ever posted a message to any of the USENET newsgroups, you may be able to locate him or her by using a specialized mail server at the Massachusetts Institute of Technology (MIT). The MIT server constantly monitors incoming USENET postings and extracts each poster's name and e-mail address.

To use MIT's USENET User List service,

1. Launch Eudora (or TCP/Connect II) by double-clicking on its icon.

2. Send an e-mail message consisting only of the single line "send usenet-addresses/*name*" (leave out the quotes), where *name* is the name of the person you are trying to locate. To search for my e-mail address, the line would be "send usenet-addresses/fraase."

3. Address the e-mail message to mail-server@pit-manager.mit.edu.

4. Send the e-mail message. You'll soon receive a responding message from the MIT mail server that looks something like the one shown in Figure 4-25.

Figure 4-25: MIT
USENET User List
example.

```
mail-server: "send usenet-addresses/fraase"
  Print      Refile      Reply      Forward      Resend

Return-Path: <daemon@athena.mit.edu>
Received: from bloom-picayune (BLOOM-PICAYUNE.MIT.EDU) by riverside.MR.Net
(4.1/SMI-4.1.R930326)
        id AA07361; Mon, 29 Mar 93 18:13:28 CST
Received:  by bloom-picayune (5.57/2.2JIK)
        id <AA23986@bloom-picayune>; Mon, 29 Mar 93 19:13:26 -0500
Date: Mon, 29 Mar 93 19:13:26 -0500
Message-Id: <9303300013.AA23986@bloom-picayune>
From: mail-server@pit-manager.mit.edu
To: Michael Fraase <mfraase@farces.com>
Subject: mail-server: "send usenet-addresses/fraase"
Reply-To: mail-server@pit-manager.mit.edu
Precedence: bulk

-----cut here-----
mfraase@mr.net (Michael Fraase)   (Jan 11 93)
mfraase@farces.com (Michael Fraase)    (Mar 11 93)
-----cut here-----
```

Using Whois

Whois is a directory that is maintained by the DDN Network Information Center. Unfortunately, it contains listings only for people who are responsible for the actual working of the Internet and is useless for most people in the real world.

You can use the Macintosh Finger utility mentioned in the previous section to access a Whois server with these steps.

1. Launch Finger by double-clicking on its icon.

2. Select the Finger command from the File menu. The Finger dialog box will be displayed, as shown in Figure 4-23.

3. Enter the name of the person you are trying to locate in the User box.

4. Check the Whois Server check box. The Finger button will change into a Whois button.

5. Click the Whois button. The results will be displayed in a window similar to the one shown in Figure 4-24.

Using the PSI White Pages

Performance Systems International (PSI)—an Internet service provider—offers a directory service that is accessible to Mac users with the PSIWP software program. You can FTP the software directly from the PSI archive at the address ftp.psi.com in the /pilot/ directory. Unfortunately, most of the listings seem to be for PSI clients or employees.

To access PSI's white pages service,

1. Launch the PSIWP program by double-clicking on its icon. The program's Watch window will be displayed. This window is used to translate your menu selections and dialog box actions into command lines that the server can understand.

2. Select the Find command from the White Pages menu. The program's Find dialog box will be displayed.

3. Enter the name of the person you want to locate in the box. Alternatively, you can enter a partial domain name so long as it is preceded with the @ symbol.

4. Click the OK button. The program will perform the search and display the results in a separate window, as shown in the example in Figure 4-26.

Figure 4-26: PSI
White Pages
search results
window.

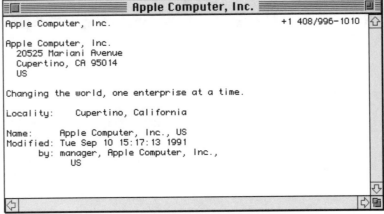

```
▤▤▤▤▤▤▤▤▤▤▤ Apple Computer, Inc. ▤▤▤▤▤▤▤▤▤▤▤
Apple Computer, Inc.                          +1 408/996-1010

Apple Computer, Inc.
  20525 Mariani Avenue
  Cupertino, CA 95014
  US

Changing the world, one enterprise at a time.

Locality:    Cupertino, California

Name:      Apple Computer, Inc., US
Modified: Tue Sep 10 15:17:13 1991
     by: manager, Apple Computer, Inc.,
         US
```

E-Mail Address Starter Kit

Lots of Macintosh-related companies and luminaries are accessible by
Internet e-mail. A starter kit of some e-mail addresses is provided in
Table 4-3.

Table 4-3:
Macintosh-related
e-mail addresses.

Company/Person	E-Mail Address
Apple Computer, Inc.	info@apple.com
Apple Developer Support	devsupport@applelink.apple.com
John Perry Barlow	barlow@well.sf.ca.us
Jerry Berman	jberman@eff.org
Steve Bobker	72511.45@compuserve.com
Stewart Brand	sbb@well.sf.ca.us
CPSR	cpsr-staff@csli.stanford.edu
Steve Dorner	sdorner@qualcom.qualcomm.com
Dan Farber	72511.124@compuserve.com
Ric Ford	72511.44@compuserve.com
Frame Technology	comments@frame.com
Hyde Park Software	info@hydepark.com

Company/Person	E-Mail Address
Andy Ihnatko	andyi@world.std.com
InterCon Systems, Inc.	info@intercon.com
Mitch Kapor	mkapor@eff.org
Guy Kawasaki	76703.3031@compuserve.com
Bob LeVitus	76004.2076@compuserve.com
Henry Norr	76117.1770@compuserve.com
Mitch Ratcliffe	coyote@well.sf.ca.us
Howard Rheingold	hlr@well.sf.ca.us
Kathleen Tinkel	76702.750@compuserve.com
Whole Earth Review	wer@well.sf.ca.us

And don't worry that you might be annoying these people by sending them mail—they've all published their e-mail addresses.

Electronic Mailing Lists

Electronic mailing lists have very little in common with their paper mail counterparts, even though they work in much the same manner.

- Electronic mailing lists actually serve a useful purpose.
- You have to specifically request to join an electronic mailing list.
- Electronic mailing lists don't overflow landfills.

Electronic mailing lists exist either as a forum for group discussions or as distribution lists. Currently, there are close to 3,000 publicly accessible mailing lists on the Internet. They cover a wide variety of subjects, and the number grows daily. You can find a mailing list for just about any subject of interest. If not, you can always start your own.

You can join a mailing list by sending e-mail to the list administrator. Once your name has been added to the list, you'll begin receiving messages from other members of the list, and you can read and respond to any of those messages. Your responses will automatically be forwarded to all the other subscribers on the list.

The quality of mailing lists is generally higher than in USENET newsgroups, because the "signal to noise ratio" is higher—there are generally more worthwhile messages in a day's mailing list message traffic than there are in a day's newsgroup message traffic. It's pretty rare to find an Ivy League freshman wanting to sell a microwave oven in a cyberpunk mailing list, but that's a pretty common happening in most any newsgroup (especially in early autumn).

You can download a list of current mailing lists from ftp.nisc.sri.com in the directory /netinfo/interest-groups/.

Subscribing to Mailing Lists

Most mailing lists are set up to automatically forward any message sent to the list to all members of the mailing list. You subscribe to an electronic mailing list by sending an e-mail request to the list's administrative address. The list's *administrative address* is almost always different from the list's *submission address*. Many mailing list administrative addresses can be recognized by the word "request" in the list address. Make sure you use the right address for the job.

In general, to subscribe to a mailing list you send a short message requesting a subscription to the mailing list's administrative address. Some mailing lists are automated and have specific subscription requirements.

For example, to subscribe to the Info-Mac Digest mailing list,

1. Launch Eudora (or TCP/Connect II) by double-clicking on its icon.

2. Send a message consisting only of the single line "subscribe info-mac *your name*" (leave out the quotes), where *your name* is your first and last name. For example, for my subscription, the line would be "subscribe info-mac michael fraase."

3. Address the e-mail message to listserv@ricevm1.rice.edu.

4. Send the e-mail message. You'll receive a response introducing you to the mailing list and instructions on how to use it.

The Info-Mac Digest is run by a *Listserv* automated mail server. A Listserv mail server is simply a computer program that accepts and responds to the commands you send it.

Use these steps to subscribe to a manual mailing list, like the Electronic Frontier Foundation's mailing list.

1. Launch Eudora (or TCP/Connect II) by double-clicking on its icon.

2. Send a brief message requesting to be added to the mailing list. Just a simple message like "please add me to the EFF mailing list, thanks" is enough.

3. Address the message to eff-request@eff.org.

4. Send the e-mail message. You'll receive a response from the list owner or the person administrating the mailing list.

Table 4-4 provides a general overview for some of the popular mailing lists.

Table 4-4: Electronic mailing list subscription information
Note: Addresses in this chart are too long to fit on a single line, but they should be entered as a single address, with no spaces or breaks.

Mailing List	Administrative Address	Subscription Instructions	Submission Address
EFF	eff-request@eff.org	send brief request	eff@eff.org
Eudora	listserv@vmd.cso.uiuc.edu	subscribe eudora your name in message	eudora@vmd.cso.uiuc.edu
FrameMaker	framers-request@drd.com	send brief request	framers@drd.com
Grateful Dead	dead-flames-request@fuggles.acc.virginia.edu	send brief request acc.virginia.edu	dead-flames@fuggles.acc.virginia.edu
Info-Mac	listserv@ricevm1.rice.edu	subscribe info-mac your name in message	info-mac@ricevm1.rice.edu
New Lists	listserv@vm1.nodak.edu	subscribe new-list your name in message	new-list@vm1.nodak.edu
PowerBook	listserv@yalevm.ycc.yale.edu	subscribe macpb-l your name in message	macpb-l@yalevm.ycc.yale.edu
TidBITS	listserv@ricevm1.rice.edu	subscribe tidbits your name in message	tidbits@ricevm1.rice.edu
University of Michigan Recent Files	mac-recent-request@mac.archive.umich.edu	Send brief request	mac-recent@mac.archive.umich.edu

Canceling Subscriptions to Mailing Lists

In general, to cancel your subscription to a mailing list you send a short message requesting to be removed from the list to the mailing list's administrative address. Some mailing lists are automated and have specific subscription cancellation requirements.

For example, use these instructions to cancel your subscription to the automated Info-Mac Digest mailing list.

1. Launch Eudora (or TCP/Connect II) by double-clicking on its icon.

2. Send a message consisting only of the single line "signoff info-mac *your name*" (leave out the quotes), where *your name* is your first and last name. For example, for my subscription, the line would be "signoff info-mac michael fraase."

3. Address the e-mail message to listserv@ricevm1.rice.edu.

Send the e-mail message. You'll receive a response acknowledging your subscription cancellation and removal from the mailing list.

Use these steps to cancel your subscription to a manual mailing list, like the Electronic Frontier Foundation's mailing list.

1. Launch Eudora (or TCP/Connect II) by double-clicking on its icon.

2. Send a brief message requesting to be removed from the mailing list. Just a simple message like "please remove me from the EFF mailing list, thanks" is enough.

3. Address the message to eff-request@eff.org.

Send the e-mail message. You'll receive a response from the list owner or the person administrating the mailing list acknowledging your subscription cancellation and removal from the mailing list.

E-Mail & Attached Files

In addition to sending *messages*, you can also use e-mail to send any sort of *file* through the Internet. Actually, most Macintosh files have to first be converted to a text document before you can send them through the Internet, but the good news is that the process is automatic and transparent. Both Eudora (which is included on *The Mac Internet Tour Guide Companion Disks*) and TCP/Connect II automatically convert any Macintosh file for transmission over the network.

The two programs take different approaches to sending files through e-mail, however. Eudora's implementation is more elegant, allowing you to *attach* a file to an e-mail message. This lets you describe the file for your recipient by providing a brief text note at the top of the e-mail message. TCP/Connect II's approach is to simply send the file without any notation.

Sending Files in E-Mail Messages

To attach a file to an e-mail message in Eudora,

1. Create an e-mail message as you ordinarily would, following steps 1–8 in the "Creating an E-Mail Message With Eudora" section earlier in this chapter.

2. Select the Attach Document command from the Message menu. A standard Open File dialog box will be displayed.

3. Select the file you want to attach to the e-mail message by double-clicking on its name in the Open File dialog box. The attached file's name and location will be added to the Attachments line in the message header, as shown in Figure 4-27.

Figure 4-27: Eudora message header with attached file.

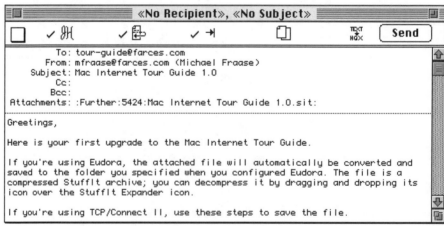

4. Click the Send button in the Message Composition window. The message will be sent immediately.

   ■ If you have set Eudora's preferences to queue mail, there will be a Queue button in far right end of the Icon Bar instead of the Send button.

To send a file through e-mail with TCP/Connect II,

1. Launch TCP/Connect II by double-clicking on its icon.

2. Select the Send File command from the Mail menu. A standard Open File dialog box will be displayed.

3. Select the file you want to send by double-clicking on its name in the Open File dialog box. TCP/Connect II's Send window will be displayed.

4. Address your file as you would any other e-mail message, using steps 5–9 in the "Creating an E-Mail Message With TCP/Connect II" section earlier in this chapter.

5. Click the Send button. Your file will be sent to the specified recipients if you have an active network connection. If your network connection is inactive, the file will be saved in your Mail folder and automatically sent the next time you log into your mail server.

Receiving Files in E-Mail Messages

Receiving files attached to e-mail messages is automatic in Eudora. The attached files of any e-mail message are automatically converted and saved in the folder you specified for received files when you configured Eudora.

If you're using TCP/Connect II, you have to manually save files that you receive by e-mail. The only exception to this is if the sender used TCP/Connect II to mail the file to you. In either case, the file is automatically converted into its original Macintosh file format.

To save files you receive by e-mail with TCP/Connect II,

1. Launch TCP/Connect II by double-clicking on its icon.

2. Retrieve your mail as you ordinarily would, following steps 2–7 in the "Retrieving & Reading E-Mail With TCP/Connect II" section earlier in this chapter.

3. Files sent to you by another TCP/Connect II user will appear in your In Box window with a document icon (instead of the regular envelope icon), as shown in Figure 4-28.

Figure 4-28:
TCP/Connect II In
Box window with
received file.

		mfraase's in box		
New Msg	Reply	Reply	Forward	Resend
From	Subject			Date
Michael Fraase	Mac Internet Tour Guide 1.0			Tue, 30 Mar

4. Double-click on the subject line of the received file. A standard Save File dialog box will appear.

5. Navigate to the folder where you want to save the received file and click the Save button. The file will be saved in the location you selected.

6. Drag the file over the StuffIt Expander icon and drop it onto the icon once it is highlighted. The file will be automatically decompressed.

Note that files sent to you by someone using any other e-mail program will appear as standard e-mail messages (with the familiar envelope icon) in your TCP/Connect II In Box window.

To save these files to your hard disk drive,

1. Double-click on the subject line of the message you want to read. The message will be displayed, as shown in the example in Figure 4-29.

Figure 4-29:
TCP/Connect II
Message window
with received file.

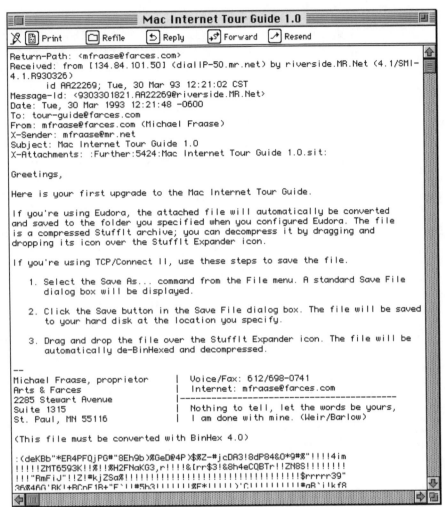

2. Select the Save As command from the File menu. A standard Save File dialog box will be displayed.

3. Navigate to the folder where you want to save the received file and click the Save button. The file will be saved in the location you selected.

4. Drag the file over the StuffIt Expander icon and drop it onto the icon once it is highlighted. The file will be automatically decompressed.

Files in E-Mail Caveats

From time to time, you may receive non-Macintosh files by e-mail. One of the hottest trends in cross-platform software is something called "binary compatibility." That's a software program that runs on different kinds of computer hardware and saves its documents in a format that is common to all the different kinds of computers. FrameMaker documents, for example, are binary compatible, regardless of the kind of computer used to create them. I can open NeXT, Windows or UNIX FrameMaker files on my Macintosh without converting them.

But since people often compress binary files before sending them, and there are different compression utilities for each kind of computer, you can imagine the problems that can arise. What do you do with UNIX files you receive that have been "tarred and compressed"? Or what about those goofy DOS files that have been "zipped"? This dilemma is covered in "A Primer on File Types" in Chapter 6, "Transferring Files."

Be careful with the size of the files you send by e-mail. Most of the e-mail gateways provided by the commercial information services like CompuServe and America Online have severe file-size limitations, as indicated in Table 4-1. TCP/Connect II allows you to specify a maximum size for e-mail messages and files, and it will automatically split the file into separate messages, as shown in Figure 4-30.

Figure 4-30:
TCP/Connect II In Box window with file received in split segments.

From	Subject	Date
Michael Fraase	Mac Internet Tour Guide 1.1 (part 1 of 8)	Tue, 30 Mar
Michael Fraase	Mac Internet Tour Guide 1.1 (part 2 of 8)	Tue, 30 Mar
Michael Fraase	Mac Internet Tour Guide 1.1 (part 3 of 8)	Tue, 30 Mar
Michael Fraase	Mac Internet Tour Guide 1.1 (part 4 of 8)	Tue, 30 Mar
Michael Fraase	Mac Internet Tour Guide 1.1 (part 5 of 8)	Tue, 30 Mar
Michael Fraase	Mac Internet Tour Guide 1.1 (part 6 of 8)	Tue, 30 Mar
Michael Fraase	Mac Internet Tour Guide 1.1 (part 7 of 8)	Tue, 30 Mar
Michael Fraase	Mac Internet Tour Guide 1.1 (part 8 of 8)	Tue, 30 Mar

mfraase's in box

New Msg   Delete   Reply   Forward   Resend

You can use TCP/Connect II to save a multi-part file by double-clicking on the first segment, specifying the folder where you want to save the complete file, and clicking the Save button. TCP/Connect II will automatically convert and reconstitute the file segments into the image of the original file.

Moving On

This chapter has given you a thorough overview of electronic mail, from the nuts and bolts of how to send and receive it to the subtleties of e-mail courtesy and etiquette.

E-mail is most useful for communicating with individuals or small groups of people. But what if you want to exchange information with large groups of people, all over the world? That's what network news is for, the topic of the next chapter. So let's stop the tour bus at that newsstand just ahead and take a break to learn about reading and posting USENET news articles.

CHAPTER 5

NETWORK NEWS & NEWSGROUPS
Broadsheets of the Broadband

the text around the outside reads:
"When reality is contained, we all are biblical. Just believe."

As our tour through the Internet continues, it's easy to become overwhelmed with the size and scope of all that it offers. But one of the most important resources on the Net is easy to overlook: people. Network news and newsgroups are valuable because of the insights and information that people bring to them.

For instance, wouldn't it be great if you could poll all the most knowledgeable folks on the Internet for answers to technical questions, or advice on everything from buying the best VCR to cooking the perfect pot roast? While electronic mail is useful for communicating with another individual or small workgroup, you can't send e-mail to thousands of people you don't know, asking questions about topics that don't interest them. (Well, I suppose you *could*, but it probably wouldn't be very productive. And if you think it sounds like it might be a good idea, put this book down and go outside for a walk. A long walk.) But with network news, there's a better way.

What Is Network News & What Are Newsgroups?

Think of network news as a worldwide collection of automatically updated electronic bulletin boards. Except these aren't bulletin boards like the single-line systems set up by thousands of hobbyists in small towns across America. Network news messages are seen by millions of people who generate as much as 40mb of network news information every day.

Electronic bulletin boards are like the cork bulletin boards you see at your local grocery store. You know, where you can find a great deal on a 1955 Buick or a litter of prize poodle puppies. Network news on the Internet is the same concept, only it's all electronic and much more extensive. Imagine the electronic equivalent of 9,000 different grocery store cork bulletin boards, and you've got a pretty good grasp of the thousands of newsgroups that make up network news.

If you've used CompuServe or America Online, you're probably familiar with the concept of forums or bulletin boards. Each newsgroup is roughly equivalent to a message area on America Online or CompuServe, except that network news newsgroups are seen by many more people, and on the Internet, highly specialized newsgroups are available for just about any topic.

You'll see everything from announcements for new software products to in-depth technical discussions to candid—and sometimes heated—conversations. These super-heated discussions are called *flame wars*; each individual message in a flame war is called a *flame*. Flames are considered to be in bad taste (except in newsgroups set up just for flames), and starting a flame war will win you lots of enemies with long memories. Each message within an individual newsgroup is called a *post* or an *article*. Articles can be cross-posted to several newsgroups, but this practice is considered bad form unless the article is especially relevant to several newsgroups.

Articles within each newsgroup are arranged in *topics*. Topics within a newsgroup about laptop computers, for instance, may include battery conservation tips, problems with a specific model's keyboard or comparisons between different available configurations. Initial queries or informational articles will likely generate several responses. This patchwork of queries and responses forms a *message thread* within a specific topic. The software you use to read network news will automatically piece together the various queries and responses in logical order. The original article will appear first, followed by any available *follow-up* (response) articles in the message thread.

E-mail blind courtesy copies that aren't.

There is a troublesome fluke with most mail servers on the Internet that could prove to be as embarrassing for you as it was for me. If you send an e-mail message to a group of people, with each recipient sent a blind courtesy copy, make sure you also e-mail a copy to at least one address in the To field. If you send an e-mail message with the To field empty, most mail servers will insert "Apparently-To" addresses, neatly listing every recipient of your blind courtesy copies.

Network news is actually not even part of the Internet—although, to the uninitiated, it is probably perceived as being the most easily recognizable part of the Internet. Network news is transmitted on USENET, a network of about 3 million people (mostly UNIX users). USENET is even more disjointed and anarchic than the Internet. Just about the only thing USENET sites have in common is that they communicate using the UNIX-to-UNIX Copy Protocol (UUCP). Some USENET sites have connections to the Internet, which is how network news—and other USENET traffic—gets to the Internet.

Internet sites that provide a network news server use the Network News Transfer Protocol (NNTP) to provide a database for local news clients and to transfer news between servers. In order to read network news on the Internet, you must use NNTP client software or use the archaic UNIX commands for navigating and reading newsgroups.

Network news is divided into *newsgroups*. Each newsgroup is devoted to a single topic (at least hypothetically; most newsgroups sort of cross-pollinate one another). Each newsgroup article is received and stored on each participating USENET computer. Unlike e-mail, where the messages are actually sent to your computer and stored on your own hard drive, newsgroup articles are stored on a *news server*, at the site that services your account. The newsgroup articles you read are stored on the news server, not on your own computer.

The network news—or USENET—newsgroups are organized in a hierarchy. Each newsgroup has a name with periods in it, similar to the Internet domain-name system. The periods (read as "dots") separate the various hierarchical levels. For example, comp.sys.mac.system is read as "comp-dot-sys-dot-mac-dot-system" or "comp-sys-mac-system" and reflects the hierarchy shown in Figure 5-1.

Figure 5-1:
Network news
newsgroups
hierarchy.

comp.sys.mac.system

translates in the newsgroup hierarchy to:

Computers

Systems

Macintosh

System Software

There are several top-level newsgroup categories in the hierarchy, as shown in Table 5-1.

Table 5-1:
Network news
newsgroups top-
level categories.

Category	Topic Explanation
alt	Alternative discussions; not carried by all sites. The newsgroups found here range from the bizarre to the useful. The most useful "alt" newsgroups were created in this top-level hierarchy to avoid going through the bureaucratic hassle of forming a certified newsgroup.
bionet	Biology discussions.
bit	Discussions that originate from Bitnet Listserv mailing lists.
biz	Business discussions. Commercial articles are permitted only in this top-level hierarchy.
comp	Computer discussions.
misc	Miscellaneous discussions—topics that don't fit in any of the other top-level hierarchies.
news	Discussions related to network news and the software used to transmit, read and create articles.

Category	Topic Explanation
rec	Recreation discussions and topics related to the arts.
sci	"Hard" science discussions.
soc	Discussions related to social issues.
talk	Argumentative discussions.

An Overview of Newsgroups

There are more than 9,000 active newsgroups covering virtually every conceivable topic. Some network-savvy observers in mainstream media hypothesize that the Internet will eventually replace most sources of news. It simply won't happen—at least not for another 10 years or so. Computer news and Grateful Dead concert dates travel faster on the Net than they do through other news channels, but that's about it.

There was one case of "pseudo-news" on the Internet. In April 1992, an area developed on IRC (Internet Relay Chat—similar to a wide-open international conference call using keyboards instead of phones) that carried news relays of the Los Angeles riots following the first Rodney King verdict. Of course, most of the information came from people who were simply relaying what they had received from local television coverage.

You can always find a regularly updated list of all available newsgroups by reading the news.list newsgroup.

Interesting Newsgroups

Interesting newsgroups exist for just about any topic you can think of. A listing of some is provided in Table 5-2. Remember, this is just a tiny sample of the thousands of newsgroups you can access via the Internet.

Table 5-2:
Interesting
newsgroup
descriptions.

Newsgroup	Description
comp.archives	Listings and descriptions of public-access archives (moderated) [1]
comp.dcom.isdn	Discussions related to the Integrated Services Digital Network (ISDN)
comp.dcom.telecom	Telecommunications digest (moderated)
comp.infosystems.gopher	Discussions related to Gopher
comp.newprod	Computer product announcements (moderated)
comp.org.acm	Discussions related to the Association for Computing Machinery (ACM)
comp.org.eff.news	Electronic Frontier Foundation (EFF) news (moderated)
comp.org.eff.talk	Discussions related to the Electronic Frontier Foundation (EFF)
comp.risks	Discussions related to the risks of computers (moderated)
comp.society.cu-digest	Computer Underground Digest (moderated)
comp.society.privacy	Discussions related to computers and privacy in society (moderated)
comp.text.desktop	Discussions related to desktop publishing
misc.consumers	Discussions related to consumer interest
misc.entrepreneurs	Discussions related to running a business
misc.invest	Discussions related to investing
misc.jobs.contract	Postings of work-for-hire contract availability
misc.jobs.offered	Listings of positions available
misc.jobs.offered.entry	Listings of entry-level positions available
misc.jobs.resumes	Listings of resumes and position queries
news.announce.important	Announcements of general interest (moderated)
news.announce.newgroups	Announcements of new newsgroups (moderated)

[1] Moderated newsgroups are best described as read-only newsgroups. Don't send articles directly to the newsgroup; instead, follow the instructions available in each moderated newsgroup. In general, you send articles to the group's moderator, who posts them as appropriate.

Newsgroup	Description
news.announce.newusers	Announcements for new users (moderated)
news.newusers.questions	Questions and answers for new users
rec.arts.movies	Discussions related to film
rec.arts.movies.reviews	Movie reviews (moderated)
rec.mag	Discussions related to magazines
rec.music.bluenote	Discussions related to jazz and blues
rec.music.dylan	Discussions related to Bob Dylan's music
rec.music.gdead	Dead-head discussions
rec.music.reggae	Discussions related to reggae music
rec.sport.baseball	Discussions related to baseball
soc.culture.japan	Discussions related to Japan and Japanese culture
soc.politics.arms-d	Political discussions (moderated)
soc.rights.human	Discussions related to human rights and activism

Macintosh Newsgroups

Several newsgroups cater specifically to the Macintosh community. A partial listing of these newsgroups is provided in Table 5-3.

Table 5-3: Macintosh newsgroup descriptions.

Newsgroup	Description
comp.sources.mac	Macintosh software sources (moderated)
comp.sys.mac.advocacy	Macintosh flame wars
comp.sys.mac.announce	Important Macintosh-specific announcements (moderated)
comp.sys.mac.apps	Discussions related to Macintosh software programs
comp.sys.mac.comm	Discussions related to Macintosh communications
comp.sys.mac.databases	Discussions related to Macintosh database software
comp.sys.mac.digest	Discussions related to general Macintosh use; includes listings of additions to major archive sites (moderated)
comp.sys.mac.games	Discussions related to Macintosh game software

Newsgroup	Description
comp.sys.mac.hardware	Discussions related to Macintosh hardware
comp.sys.mac.hypercard	Discussions related to HyperCard
comp.sys.mac.misc	Discussions related to the Macintosh that don't fit in any of the other comp.sys.mac newsgroups
comp.sys.mac.oop	Discussions related to Macintosh object-oriented programming
comp.sys.mac.programmer	Discussions related to programming on the Macintosh
comp.sys.mac.system	Discussions related to the Macintosh system software
comp.sys.mac.wanted	Macintosh-specific for sale (and items wanted) articles
misc.forsale.computers.mac	Macintosh-specific items for sale

A Primer on Newsgroup Etiquette

The USENET news system is a remarkable beast. By nature, it is a wide open terrain with absolutely no restraints on freedom of expression. Each author assumes the responsibility for his or her articles, and the uncensored environment of network news is widely appreciated.

News article posting etiquette is based pretty much on the kind of behavior you'd expect in a college dormitory: don't hit anyone, and clean up your own messes. The sole overriding principle is that just about anything is allowed, as long as it does not put the network itself in jeopardy. While you're pondering what that really means, here are a few tips to get you started:

- I remember asking one of my teachers how long an essay I had been assigned should be; her response simultaneously answered my question and taught me about metaphor. She told me the essay should be like a woman's skirt: short enough to be interesting but long enough to cover the subject. Her advice is appropriate for news articles as well.

- Lots of people on the Internet read hundreds of messages each day. You can't reasonably expect someone to remember what has been said in every previous message. Include appropriate background material that will help the reader understand the context of your message.

■ By the same token, don't provide 50 lines of background about a message if you're only responding to a small part of it. Don't, for example, quote a 1000-line article only to add "I agree!"

Evangelizing the Internet.

Paul Jacoby is a consultant with David Mitchell & Associates, on assignment with 3M. He's been working long and hard to introduce 3M employees to the Internet:

"I've been in the process of evangelizing the Internet to the folks I work with here at 3M. The main response I get from people who begin to delve into the depths of the Internet is, 'Wow, I had no idea this existed!' Followed closely by 'You mean it's *free*?'

"People are continually amazed at the concepts of software archives ('... filled with *free* software?') and the near instantaneous access to points across the globe. Most are tickled to death to find associates with Internet addresses, exchanging e-mail with turn-around time in the sub-minute range.

"In presenting a summary of the Internet and trying to describe how it works, I boiled all the technical stuff down to one important phrase: It's *automagic*; i.e., don't worry, be happy, use and learn without worrying about the fine points. Most people are quite happy to operate this way :-)"

■ Limit your lines to lengths of 80 characters or less.

■ Don't use long, rambling signatures or include ASCII graphics— keep it to four lines or less.

■ Don't post "me too!" follow-up articles unless you have a worth-while comment to add.

■ Use the right newsgroup for the job. Some newsgroups are in-tended for discussions while others are intended for announce-ments. Don't engage in discussions in newsgroups intended for announcements.

■ Newsgroups are called newsgroups—not bulletin boards, boards or bboards.

■ Don't post private e-mail correspondence in a network news article without the permission of the author. While it may be technically legal to do so, it's rude and could be a copyright violation in some circumstances. (Besides, would you want some-one plastering your private e-mail on a network where 10 million people could read it?)

- Don't ask what ":-)" means (tilt your head 90 degrees to the left, and see Table 5-4 later in this chapter).

- Don't post flames outside a newsgroup labeled specifically for flames. (See the "Flames, Flame-Bait & Flaming" section later in this chapter.)

- Don't end your post with a snooty comment like "Please send e-mail, because I don't read this newsgroup." If you don't read a newsgroup, why would you be posting messages there?

- Don't use excessive CAPITALIZATION & PUNCTUATION!!!!!!!!!!

- Don't cross-post to multiple newsgroups unless it's completely relevant and absolutely necessary.

- If you ask for help with a software program, make sure you state what kind of computer you're using. Not everyone uses a Macintosh. Also, include specific details like which model Mac you have, how much RAM you have, what version of the system software you're using and so on.

- Keep a sense of humor. There's little room for self-righteous stuffed shirts in the world of network news.

- Don't post articles about what kind of computer is better. Similarly, don't respond to articles arguing the issue.

- Before posting a question in a newsgroup, read its Frequently Asked Questions (FAQ) file. These files contain answers to— you guessed it—the most frequently asked questions. Most newsgroups post the FAQ file to the newsgroup on a regular basis. The FAQ files for most newsgroups are available by FTP from pit-manager.mit.edu.

- Understand that you're going to make mistakes, and as sure as grits is groceries, some jerk's going to let you know about it when you do. Try to keep a thick skin about it. See the sidebar about my first network news mistake for an example.

My first network news mistake.

Less than a month after I started using the Internet, I asked a stupid question in the comp.sys.mac.misc newsgroup. I had accumulated quite a few PostScript files—mostly documentation—some of them very large.

I didn't want to waste paper by printing these files out if I could view them on the screen. My assumption was that if there were all these wonderful Macintosh-specific Internet software tools, there was probably a PostScript viewer somewhere. I had checked every archive I knew about, but I couldn't find one.

Timidity is not usually one of my more defining qualities, but I timidly—*yes, timidly*—posted a very short query on comp.sys.mac.misc. Something on the order of "Does anyone know where I can find a PostScript viewer for the Mac? This is for multi-page, raw PostScript files, not EPS documents."

Within hours I received 10 e-mail responses. The more polite of the bunch were to the effect of, "You ignorant *?!)&$. Why don't you read the *$?)#!* FAQ??!!" I didn't have the slightest idea what a FAQ was, and I sure wasn't going to ask.

A day or so later the comp.sys.mac.misc FAQ was posted and, of course, my question was answered:

IS THERE A UTILITY TO VIEW POSTSCRIPT FILES ON THE MAC? (11.1)
Net godhood awaits the first person to write a shareware or freeware solution to this problem. The payware products Canvas 3.0 and TScript allow viewing PostScript files on the Mac, but both are large packages with other purposes and cost over $50 each.

I drew some strange consolation from knowing that the FAQ file is at least partially wrong. I've never heard of TScript, but Canvas can't deal with multi-page, raw PostScript files.

What continues to confound me is that every one of the pinheads that responded to my original question at length could have saved themselves a lot of trouble with a simple, two-letter, one-word response: "No."

I think it's either a network culture thing ("let's jump the newbie") or these guys have canned messages that they automatically send out as one of their few means of entertainment.

Since then, a PostScript viewer for the Macintosh—GhostScript—has been released. It's available in the Info-Mac and Michigan archives, if you're interested, but it's useless for multi-page documents.

Flames, Flame-Bait & Flaming

You'll hear a lot about *flames* while reading network news. A flame is an inflammatory message, usually posted for no other reason than to start an argument. It's pretty common for someone to log into one of the comp.sys.mac newsgroups (strongholds of Macintosh advocates) and post a message with a title like, "Macs suck, buy a PC!" The best response to this sort of wasted bandwidth is to ignore it. Unfortunately, the message always gets answered and a *flame war* erupts, with vile epithets hurled in all directions.

Emotion is hard to communicate on the network. Irony and sarcasm are easily misinterpreted without verbal cues or body language. Similarly, terseness can come across as rudeness. And until we can add italics and bold type to our messages, things are even worse—we're limited to ASCII text as the lowest common denominator.

In general, use of capital letters is considered shouting, so be careful how you use them. You can show emphasis by setting off a word or phrase with asterisks: That's *not* what I said. This is considered more polite and respectful than: That's NOT what I said.

Another result of the difficulty of communicating with only ASCII text is the *smiley*. Tilt your head 90 degrees counterclockwise and look at this:

:-)

Remember those yellow "Have a Nice Day" smiley faces? Well, a smiley, like the one shown above, is the electronic equivalent. A smiley is used to convey emotion within an electronic message, and you'll find them widely used throughout the Internet. I hate them, and I almost never use them (in fact, I can't think of a single time I've used one). But they are everywhere, and you'd better learn to decode them. The following table includes a few of the more common smileys you're likely to encounter.

Table 5-4: Basic smiley decoder.

Smiley	Meaning
:-)	basic smiley; connotes cheer or a grin, sometimes tongue-in-cheek sarcasm
;-)	wink; connotes light sarcasm
:-I	indifference
:->	devilish grin; connotes heavy sarcasm
:-(	frown; connotes anger or displeasure
@:-)	curly hair
8-)	eye-glasses
:-D	shock or surprise
:-/	perplexed
:-P	tongue sticking out

Abbreviation mysteries.

There is a set of abbreviations that are commonly used as shorthand in network communications. Don't worry too much about decoding abbreviations you see. You'll find that they're pretty self-explanatory in context; sort of like reading real-estate listings or personal ads in the newspaper. Here are some of the abbreviations in widest use.

Abbreviation	Meaning
IMHO	in my humble opinion (it very rarely is)
BTW	by the way
ROTFL	rolling on the floor laughing
TANSTAAFL	there ain't no such thing as a free lunch
OBO	or best offer
RTFM	read the "funny" manual
FYI	for your information

Now that you know a little about the politics and etiquette of using network news, you can start reading and posting on your own. But first, you'll need a first-class utility for navigating newsgroups and composing and posting articles.

Selecting a News Reader

A news reader is a software program that runs on your Mac that simplifies the process of navigating and reading network news articles. You use this program to select which newsgroups you want to monitor on a regular basis and which articles you want to read. You also use the news reader to post new articles or reply to existing ones. It's important that you choose a news reader that you can live with—one that lets you quickly navigate through the thousands of pages of articles available—to target the information you need.

There are several good news readers available for the Macintosh, and new ones under development. One of the most popular Macintosh news readers is Peter Speck's Nuntius, included on the companion disks at the back of this book. The latest version of Nuntius is always available from Ventana Online. Nuntius is distributed as *freeware*; you can use it free of charge, but the author reserves copyright. The news reader I prefer is the news module of TCP/Connect II, which is a commercial product.

In this chapter, we'll walk through the steps for configuring and using both of these products for reading network news.

Configuring Nuntius

To configure Nuntius for use with your news server,

1. Launch Nuntius by double-clicking on its icon. The News server dialog box will appear as shown in Figure 5-2.

Figure 5-2: Nuntius News server dialog box.

News server

Please specify the name of your news server (something like nohost.nowhere.moon or 127.0.0.1)

[Quit] [OK]

2. Enter the domain-name or IP address of your news server in the box. (If you don't know the address, check with your network administrator or commercial service provider.)

3. Click the OK button.

■ Nuntius will retrieve and build a list of all available news-groups on your news server. This may take a while. This process occurs only the first time you configure Nuntius, and whenever you manually choose to rebuild the list of all available newsgroups.

■ When Nuntius is finished building the list, two windows will be displayed on your screen—a list of available newsgroups and an empty, untitled group list—as shown in Figure 5-3.

Figure 5-3: Nuntius windows: All Groups (left) and empty Untitled group list (right).

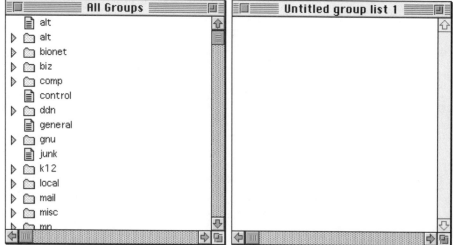

4. Pick a top-level newsgroup category in the All Groups window that interests you, and double-click on its folder icon.

■ The folder will open, displaying a list of available newsgroups, and any subfolders representing subcategories in the newsgroup hierarchy. For example, the comp.sys.mac newsgroups are located inside of the sys folder, which itself is inside the comp folder. Some of the newsgroups are nested deep within multiple subcategories.

5. Click and hold on the newsgroup to which you want to subscribe.

■ Select multiple newsgroups within the same category by Shift-clicking on each newsgroup you want to select, just as you choose files or folders in the Finder. Note that you can only use this technique to select newsgroups within the same category.

6. Drag your selection into the empty Untitled group list window, as shown in Figure 5-4.

Figure 5-4: Nuntius partially expanded All Groups hierarchy (left) and Untitled group list window with subscribed newsgroups (right).

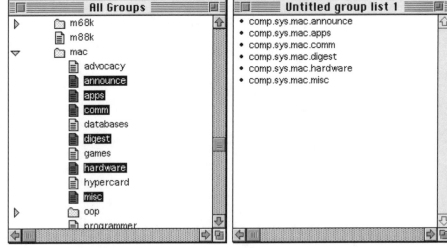

7. From the File menu, select the Save As command. A standard Save File dialog box will appear.

8. Enter a name for the group list. Obviously, it helps to choose a name that relates to the subject matter of the newsgroups in that list, so don't name it something like "My Newsgroups."

Meckler Publishing.

Meckler Publishing (Westport, CT) is aggressively developing Internet guides for librarians, researchers and information professionals. Contact meckler@jvnc.net for notification of coming books on Internet basics, electronic scholarship, Internet directories, WAIS and Gopher servers, citation of electronic sources, Internet/NREN policy, etc. Meckler's quarterly *Electronic Networking* will now be *Internet Research: Electronic Networking, Applications, and Policy.*

9. Click the Save button. The newsgroup list will be saved to your hard drive at the location you specified.

10. From the Prefs menu, select the Your Name command. The Preferences: Your name dialog box will appear, as shown in Figure 5-5.

Figure 5-5:
Nuntius
Preferences: Your
name dialog box.

Preferences: Your name

Your real name :

Your e-mail address :

Name of your organization :

Cancel   OK

11. Enter your full name in the Your real name box.

12. Enter your e-mail address (using the username@domain.top-domain format) in the Your e-mail address box.

13. Enter the name of your organization (if appropriate) in the Name of your organization box.

14. Click the OK button. You've configured Nuntius appropriately for basic news reading tasks.

Managing network news and newsgroups can quickly become an overwhelming task. A good approach is to begin by selecting only those newsgroups you are especially interested in. Later, if you find you have enough time to read more articles, you can create additional lists or add more newsgroups to existing lists. It's much easier to add newsgroups later than to wade through massive amounts of information you may not be interested in.

Nuntius does not have a built-in editor (a program that you can use to compose and format responses), which is fine if all you want to do is read other people's postings. But who wants to be just a spectator? It's easy to specify an editor using these steps:

1. From the Prefs menu, select the Editing Articles command. The Preferences: Editor dialog box will appear, as shown in Figure 5-6.

Figure 5-6: Nuntius
Preferences: Editor
dialog box.

Preferences: Editor

Editor of choice:

[Select new...]

Articles folder:

[Select new...]

☐ **Use signature as default**
Signature file...

[Select new...]

☐ **Edit signature when editing articles**
☐ **Edit headers (for wizards)**

Auto wrap width: 75

[Cancel]   [OK]

2. Click the "Editor of choice: Select new" button. A standard Open File dialog box will appear.

3. Locate the text editor or word processor you want to use to write your news articles.

   ■ Note that you can select any text editor or word processor for use with Nuntius. But you will probably want to choose a small, quick-opening editor, because Nuntius launches the editor automatically whenever you reply to an existing news article or create a new post. TeachText or SimpleText would be a good choice if you don't have a text editor you prefer.

4. Click the Open button.

5. Click the "Articles folder: Select new" button. A standard Open File dialog box will be displayed.

6. Navigate to the folder you want to use for your outgoing news articles. This folder will be used to hold temporary copies of the articles you create.

7. Click the Select Folder button.

8. Click the "Use signature as default" check box if you want your signature to be attached to each article you post. A signature is a three- or four-line text file containing your contact information.

9. Click the "Signature file… Select new" button. A standard Open File dialog box will be displayed.

10. Navigate to the signature file you want to use. (If you don't have a signature file prepared, you can cancel and create one, then select it later when you're working in Nuntius again. For more on signatures, see the "Internet signatures" sidebar later in this chapter.)

11. Click the Open button.

12. Click the OK button in the Preferences: Editor dialog box. You've completely configured Nuntius for all network news tasks.

Configuring the TCP/Connect II News Module

I prefer TCP/Connect II's news module for reading and posting network news. Although it's a commercial product, it provides an integrated environment for replying to news articles via e-mail. I especially like its article filtering capabilities—called "bozo filters" in UNIX-speak—which I use to automatically delete postings from certain individuals and automatically highlight postings from people whose opinions I don't want to miss.

To configure TCP/Connect II for use with your news server,

1. Launch TCP/Connect II by double-clicking on its icon.

2. From the Edit menu select the Configure command. The TCP/Connect II Configuration dialog box will appear.

3. Click on the News icon in the scrolling list of configuration items. The News Configuration panel will appear, like the configured example shown in Figure 5-7.

Barney the Dinosaur.

I don't know about you, but I just don't understand this Barney the Dinosaur phenomenon. At the April Fools Day 1993 Grateful Dead concert, Barney appeared on stage. Everyone there except the kids thought it was bassist Phil Lesh in a purple suit. The kids knew it was Barney.

And on the Internet there are dozens of savvy adults, wise to Barney's global conspiracy to brainwash kids into spewing a mindless doctrine of vapid grins and hyperkinetic world-glee. In fact, one guy even started a newsgroup, alt.barney.dinosaur.die.die.die, to help rally opposition against the "Great Evil Purple One."

Figure 5-7:
TCP/Connect II
Configuration
dialog box's
News panel.

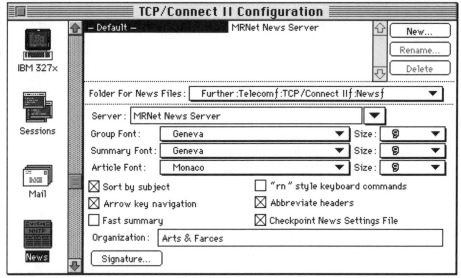

4. Enter the domain-name or IP address of your NNTP server in the Server box. Alternatively, if you have already configured the server information for your news server, you can select its entry from the Server pop-up menu.

5. From the Folder For News Files pop-up menu, choose the Select Another Folder item. This will specify a folder on your hard drive where news settings will be stored.

6. Customize the news display characteristics using the following criteria:

▪ From the Group Font pop-up menus, select an available font and size for displaying newsgroups.

▪ From the Summary Font pop-up menus, select an available font and size for displaying news article summaries.

▪ From the Article Font pop-up menus, select an available font and size for displaying news articles.

▪ Check the Sort by subject check box if you want news article summaries to be displayed in alphabetical order, rather than the order in which they were received by your news server.

▪ Check the Arrow key navigation check box if you want to navigate through available news articles with the arrow keys on the keyboard.

- Check the Fast summary check box if you want to display only the Subject line of news articles within the news article summaries. This can be useful if you use SLIP or PPP to access the Internet. Note that when using this setting is that you can't use some of the more powerful news article filtering capabilities of TCP/Connect II.

- Check the "rn" style keyboard commands check box if you want to torture yourself with the UNIX news reading commands. Actually, many long-time Internet users like the rn (read news) commands. I suspect it's because they got used to using them before there were news readers with a Macintosh interface, and their brains have been permanently imprinted with the appropriate commands. I've never been able to remember the commands, but TCP/Connect II provides them if you want them.

- Check the Abbreviate headers check box if you want the header of each article to display only the subject, author, organization, summary, keywords and newsgroup information. This will eliminate a lot of the arcane network addressing information about where the message has been that works its way into article headers.

- Check the Checkpoint News Settings File check box if you want the current news settings to be saved whenever you switch newsgroups or modify your subscription list. This setting helps preserve the read/unread status of news articles in the event of a network error, software crash or power failure.

7. Enter the name of your organization (if appropriate) in the Organization box.

8. If you want your postings to include a signature, click the Signature button. The Signature dialog box will be displayed.

9. Enter your optional signature in the box. A signature is a three- or four-line text file containing your contact information.

10. Click the OK button.

11. Click the close box of the Configuration dialog box. You've configured TCP/Connect II for network news tasks. All that's left now is to subscribe to the newsgroups you want to read. Subscribing to newsgroups via TCP/Connect II is covered in "Reading News With TCP/Connect II" later in this chapter.

Internet signatures.

Electronic communications—both e-mail and network news postings—are usually much less formal than the typical business letter. Formal salutations are rarely called for and are generally considered something of a waste of bandwidth.

Similarly, formal closings are almost never seen. Instead, most networkers end their messages with a *signature*. A signature is a short—four lines or less—identification tag that includes your full name, organization and contact information.

Signatures range in style from the strictly functional to the almost rococo-like. The function of a signature is to provide identification and contact information in case the address header is incorrect or incomplete.

The best signatures usually include a quote that tells you something about the person writing the message. Quotes are fine, but should be kept short and pithy.

In creating a signature, remember that ASCII text is still the lowest common denominator for Internet communications. Use a monospaced font and keep the length of each line under 80 characters.

Sometimes, signatures carry a disclaimer stating that the comments represent the views of the individual posting the message, but not necessarily the views of that person's employer, company or organization. Sometimes, these disclaimer lines are even written with a sense of humor:

```
"Opinions this ludicrous are mine. Reasonable opinions will
cost you."
```

Here are some of the better signature tag lines I've come across lately:

```
"I need some indication that all of this is real now."
"Slipping into madness is good for the sake of comparison."
"Tens of thousands of messages, hundreds of points of view. It
was not called the Net of a Million Lies for nothing." -Vernor
Vinge
"Spread peanut butter, not AIDS."
"Fear is a little darkroom where negatives are developed."
"Stop yawning. Start yearning."
"Bandwidth expands to fit the waste available."
"Practice random kindness and senseless acts of beauty."
"I stand behind all of my misstatements." — Dan Quayle
```

How to Read, Post & Reply to Articles

In a graphical environment like the Macintosh, each news article is represented by an individual icon, regardless of the news reader you use. You read an article by clicking on its icon. You can reply to an article by selecting the range of text to which you want to respond and using your news reader's Reply command. Sometimes you'll want to create a completely new topic within a newsgroup. To do this, simply create a new message using the appropriate Create New Message command in your news reader. This section shows you how to read, post and reply to network news articles using two popular Mac news readers, Nuntius and TCP/Connect II.

Using Nuntius

Nuntius is one of the most popular newsreaders in the Macintosh community, probably because it's free and offers an intuitive interface. Newsgroups are represented as folders in windows, and articles are represented as documents. This is similar to how you already sort files on your Macintosh using the Finder, so using Nuntius will probably be second nature to experienced Mac users.

Reading News With Nuntius

Use the following steps to read network news articles with Nuntius. This section assumes that you have already properly configured Nuntius and selected the newsgroups you want to monitor. The examples provided here use the comp.sys.mac series of newsgroups, but Nuntius works the same for all available newsgroups.

1. Launch Nuntius by double-clicking on its icon. The All Groups window and the newsgroup set window you previously configured will be displayed, as shown in Figure 5-4.

2. Double-click on the newsgroup within the Group List window that you want to read. A window for the selected newsgroup will appear, with a list of all message *threads* in the newsgroup, as shown in Figure 5-8.

Figure 5-8:
Nuntius
newsgroup
window.

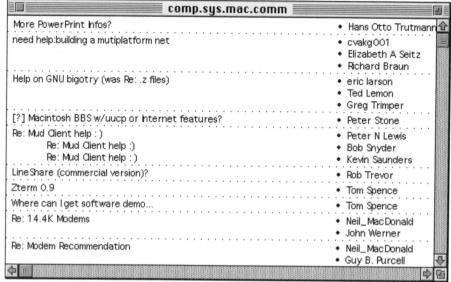

■ A message *thread* is a collection of a group of articles that are all related to the same topic. They sometimes—but not always—evolve around an original question and a collection of responses and discussions. Often, the message threads evolve far afield of their original topic.

3. Double-click on the message thread that interests you. A window for the selected thread will appear, showing a list of all news articles contained in the thread, as shown in Figure 5-9.

Figure 5-9: Nuntius
message thread
window.

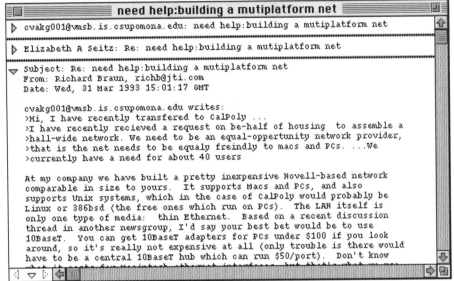

4. Click the Closed article button (it's a little triangle) next to the article you want to read. The article button will change to its Open state (the triangle will point down instead of to the right), as shown in Figure 5-9. If you're familiar with using System 7's hierarchical Finder view, this stuff will be nothing new.

5. Click the Page down button to scroll the window one full window at a time.

6. Click the Next thread button to advance to the next sequential message thread.

7. Click the Previous thread button to move to the previous sequential message thread.

8. Repeat steps 3–7 for each newsgroup you are interested in.

   ▪ Each article in the Nuntius message thread window may have one of two symbols next to the author's name—or the area to the left of the message may be blank—indicating the status of each message. These symbols are illustrated in Table 5-5.

Table 5-5:
Nuntius message
thread symbols.

Symbol	Meaning
●	You have not seen the article and the article is a new posting since the last time you browsed this newsgroup.
—	You have not seen the article and the article is not a new posting in this newsgroup.
	You have seen the article.

Posting a News Article With Nuntius

Reading news articles is only half the point of participating in newsgroups. To get the most out of your time with network news, you also have to know how to post original articles and responses to existing articles. To post a news article with Nuntius,

1. Launch Nuntius by double-clicking on its icon. The All Groups window and the newsgroup set window you previously configured will be displayed, as shown in Figure 5-4.

2. From the Threads menu, select the "Post article in new thread" command. The Creating article dialog box will appear, as shown in Figure 5-10.

Figure 5-10:
Nuntius Creating
article dialog box.

Creating article

Subject: [   ]

Newsgroups: [comp.sys.mac.comm   ]

Distribution: [world   ]

☐ Add signature

[Cancel] [**Edit it**]

■ To reply to an existing news article, select the range of text within the article that you specifically want to reply to, and select the "Post follow-up article" command from the Article menu.

3. Enter a short description for your article in the Subject box. The current newsgroup will be automatically reflected in the Newsgroups box.

4. Enter the level of distribution for the article in the Distribution box. The default is worldwide distribution and is indicated by the word "world."

   ■ This setting determines how widely your article is distributed, and you should set it with some caution. If you're posting an article that has little or no interest outside of your geographic location, specify a narrower level of distribution. If you're selling a large monitor, for example, you may want to limit your distribution to your local area.

How fast can UFOs go?

There are all sorts of strange newsgroups available on the Internet. Here's a sample exchange—the message title is "How fast can UFOs go?"—from the alt.alien.visitors newsgroup.

Original post:

"Putting aside the energy requirements for accelerating to c, how far is 'far into space'? Assuming that their solar system is constructed similarly to ours, and the time spent in 'hyper-space' is effectively none, that would imply a 3.5 hour trip to the jump point on each side of the hyper-flight. I vaguely recall my high school astronomy teacher telling me that Pluto is 5 lighthours from the sun. So in order to reach a point at which the light speed drive can be used, our insystem drive needs to reach 1.4c? I'm available to these guys as an efficiency consultant."

Follow-up post:

"When I think of the problem of needing to get some distance from a gravitational source—Earth, Moon, Sun, whatever—I would not head towards Pluto. I would head straight up the Y-axis. Cartoon analogy: When a truck is headed towards Daffy Duck, he runs away down the road in-stead of going left or right to get off the road. The solar system is sort of flat, the universe is not."

5. Click the Edit it button. The text editor or word processor you specified when you configured Nuntius will launch automatically.

6. Enter your article in your text editor.

7. Save your article.

8. Close the window in your text editor or word processor. The Nuntius Article to post dialog box will appear, as shown in Figure 5-11.

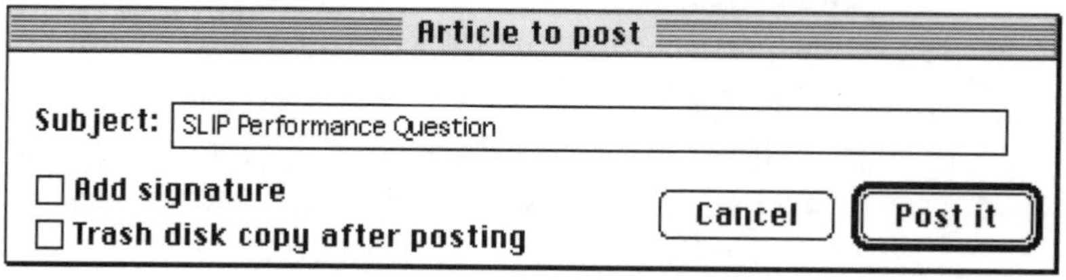

Figure 5-11:
Nuntius Article to
post dialog box.

Article to post

Subject: | SLIP Performance Question |

☐ **Add signature**
☐ **Trash disk copy after posting**   [Cancel]   [**Post it**]

9. Check the Add signature check box if you want to attach your signature file to the end of your article.

 ▪ For more information on signatures, see the "Internet signatures" sidebar earlier in this chapter.

10. Check the "Trash disk copy after posting" check box if you want the file your text editor saved to disk to be deleted after your article has been posted.

11. Click the Post it button. Your article will be posted to the open newsgroup.

12. If you have second thoughts about a posting, click the Cancel button. You can always open your saved copy, edit it and post it later.

Using the TCP/Connect II News Module

It's hard to beat the bargain you get with a piece of quality freeware like Nuntius, but I generally use TCP/Connect II to read and post network news articles. TCP/Connect II lacks Nuntius's expandable message threading capabilities, but I can navigate between the few newsgroups I read more quickly using TCP/Connect II.

Reading News With TCP/Connect II

Before you can actually use TCP/Connect II to read network news articles, you have to subscribe to the newsgroups you want to monitor on an ongoing basis. The subscription process is as simple as dragging items between panes in a window.

To subscribe to newsgroups with TCP/Connect II,

1. Launch TCP/Connect II by double-clicking on its icon.

2. From the News menu, select the Connect command. The Open a news session dialog box will appear, as shown in Figure 5-12.

Figure 5-12: TCP/Connect II Open a news session dialog box.

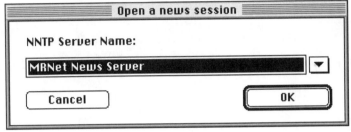

3. Select your news server from the pop-up menu. Alternatively, you can enter the domain-name or IP address of any available NNTP server in the box.

4. Click the OK button. The News Browser window will appear, as shown in Figure 5-13.

Figure 5-13: TCP/Connect II News Browser window.

```
MRNet News Server
2 groups with news          Subject              From        Date
news.announce.newusers
news.newusers.questions
```

- The first time you log into your news server, only two newsgroups appear in the News Browser window: news.announce.newusers and news.newusers.questions.

5. From the News menu, select the Edit Newsgroups command. The News Groups dialog box will be displayed, as shown in Figure 5-14.

Figure 5-14:
TCP/Connect II
News Groups
dialog box.

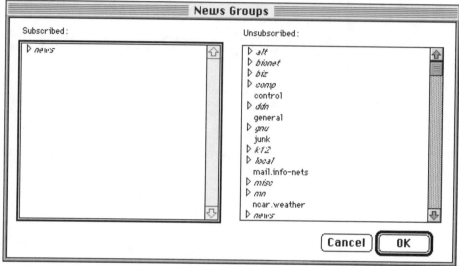

6. In the Unsubscribed panel of the News Groups dialog box, click on the triangle icon next to the top-level newsgroup category that interests you.

- The newsgroup category will expand, displaying a list of available newsgroups and any subcategories in the newsgroup hierarchy. For example, the comp.sys.mac newsgroups are located under of the sys subcategory, which itself is under the comp category. Some newsgroups are nested deeply within multiple subcategories.

7. Click on the newsgroup to which you want to subscribe.

- Select multiple newsgroups within the same category by Shift-clicking on each newsgroup you want to select. Note that you can only select newsgroups within the same category with this technique.

8. Drag your selection into the Subscribed panel to the left, as shown in the example of several comp.sys.mac newsgroups in Figure 5-15.

Figure 5-15: TCP/Connect II News Groups dialog box with comp.sys.mac subscriptions.

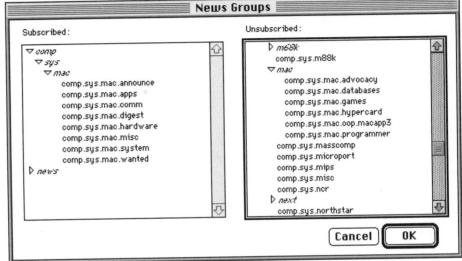

9. Repeat steps 6–8 for additional newsgroups to which you want to subscribe.

10. Click the OK button. The newly subscribed newsgroups will be added to the News Browser window, as shown in Figure 5-16.

Figure 5-16:
TCP/Connect II
News Browser
window with
subscribed
newsgroups.

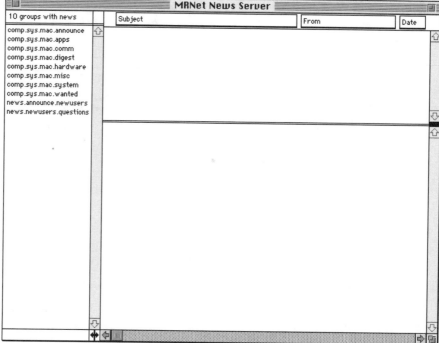

You can add newsgroups to your subscription list at any time. But now that you've got at least a few newsgroups lined up for reading, we'll learn how to read news articles with TCP/Connect II.

1. Launch TCP/Connect II by double-clicking on its icon.

2. From the News menu, select the Connect command. The Open a news session dialog box will be displayed, as shown in Figure 5-12.

3. Select your news server from the pop-up menu. Alternatively, you can enter the domain-name or IP address of any available NNTP server in the box.

4. Click the OK button. The News Browser window will be displayed, as shown in Figure 5-13.

5. In the Newsgroups panel of the News Browser window, click the newsgroup containing articles you are interested in reading. A list of messages will appear in the Summary panel of the window.

6. In the News Browser window's Summary panel, click on the message summary you want to read. The text of the news article will appear in the Article panel as shown in Figure 5-17.

Figure 5-17:
TCP/Connect II
News Browser
window with
open news
article.

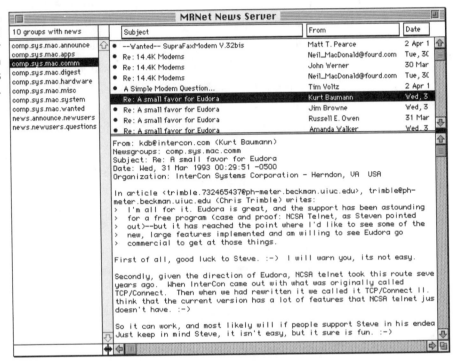

7. Repeat steps 5–6 for each newsgroup containing articles you are interested in reading.

I use TCP/Connect II to read network news because it is the only news reader I've found that offers filtering capabilities. I use TCP/Connect II's filtering capabilities to highlight articles from people whose opinions I value. I also use it as a "bozo filter," automatically deleting articles posted by individuals whose postings are invariably useless.

The filtering capabilities in TCP/Connect II's news module work almost the same as the mail module's filter actions (with the exception that you can't reroute a message to a specified mailbox).

The Mac Internet Tour Guide

Posting a News Article With TCP/Connect II

Reading news articles is only half the point of participating in news-groups. To get the most out of your time with network news, you also have to know how to post original articles and responses to existing articles. To post a news article with TCP/Connect II,

1. Launch TCP/Connect II by double-clicking on its icon.

2. From the News menu, select the Connect command. The Open a news session dialog box will appear, as shown in Figure 5-12.

3. Select your news server from the pop-up menu. Alternatively, you can enter the domain-name or IP address of any available NNTP server in the box.

4. Click the OK button. The News Browser window will appear, as shown in Figure 5-13.

5. Click the newsgroup where you want to post a new article. A list of messages in that newsgroup will be displayed in the Summary panel of the window.

6. From the News menu, select the Create New Article command. An empty Article window will appear, as shown in Figure 5-18.

Figure 5-18:
TCP/Connect II
empty Article
window.

Untitled Article
Post

7. Enter the text for your article.

8. Click the Post button in the Article window. The Post dialog box will appear, as shown in Figure 5-19.

Figure 5-19:
TCP/Connect II
Post dialog box.

Post

Subject:

Newsgroups:
> *comp*
> *alt*
> *biz*
> *comp*
ddn.newsletter
local.general
> *misc*
mn.general
> *news*
rec.music.gdead

Followup-To: ◉ **Newsgroups** ○ **Poster**

Distribution: ▼

Keywords:

Summary:

References:

Archive: *No Archive* ▼ [**Mail a copy...**] [**Cancel**] (Post)

9. Enter a short subject description for the article in the Subject box.

10. Click and drag the names of the newsgroups in which you want to post the article from the scrolling list in the right portion of the dialog box. Note that the default newsgroup is the one that is currently open.

MOOGopher.

MOOGopher is an object-oriented, multi-user dimension that uses an integrated Gopher client. Objects in the environment can contain Gopher items, and you navigate the GopherSpace as if you're exploring a game. You can try it by pointing your TurboGopher program at theory.cs.mankato.msus.edu port 1709. (For more on Gopher and TurboGopher, see Chapter 7, "Using Gopher.")

11. Click the "Followup-To: Newsgroups" radio button.

12. Select the level of distribution for the article from the Distribution pop-up menu. The default is worldwide distribution.

   ■ This setting determines how widely your article is distributed, and you should set it with some caution. If you're posting an article that has little or no interest outside your geographic location, specify a narrower level of distribution. If you're selling a large monitor, for example, you may want to limit your distribution to your local area.

13. Optionally, enter any keywords for your article in the Keywords box.

14. Optionally, enter a very short summary of your article in the Summary box.

15. Leave the References box empty. This box is filled in automatically when you are posting a reply, or follow-up, to an existing article within the newsgroup.

16. Select a mailbox from the Archive pop-up menu if you want to e-mail a copy to yourself for archival purposes.

17. Click the Mail a copy button if you want to send a copy of your article to someone by e-mail. The standard e-mail Send dialog box will be displayed. (For more information, see "Creating an E-Mail Message With TCP/Connect II" in Chapter 4, "Electronic Mail.")

18. Click the Post button. Your article will be posted to the newsgroup.

Moving On

Now you're ready to venture into the thousands of newsgroups on the Internet. But be careful: you can waste a lot of time trolling through network news looking for nuggets of useful information. Unfortunately, there are no proven secrets to tracking down worthwhile articles. I've found that the best information tends to cluster within the smaller newsgroups and those that are moderated. Also, it's usually a better idea to carefully read a few newsgroups than to try to skim scores of them. There are more newsgroups available than anyone can possibly read, so pick your targets wisely.

If hunting for truly informative newsgroups can be a challenge, then finding great Mac shareware files is a cakewalk. As our tour bus cruises through the next chapter, you'll learn how to effectively use the Internet's File Transfer Protocol (FTP) and two of the most popular Macintosh FTP clients (software that simplifies transferring files) to mine these information-rich resources.

CHAPTER 6

TRANSFERRING FILES
The Mother Download

Part of the fun of visiting any distant place is taking snapshots and collecting souvenirs to take back home. Our tour through the Internet is no exception. There are plenty of strange and wonderous curios—as well as practical items you'll use every day—nestled throughout the Net. And you don't have to hop a steamer or board a plane to collect them all. Thanks to the Internet's File Transfer Protocol (FTP), it takes only a few mouse clicks to download a shareware program or text file from a computer halfway around the world. But perhaps the most satisfying thing about using the Internet's FTP to download files is that you get exactly the information you want without wading through a lot of stuff you don't want.

Depending on how relevant it is to you as an individual, information has a level of density. E-mail is usually information-dense on one level, because it is of unique concern to you. Network news, on the other hand, is comparatively information-sparse, because there are a lot of useless messages you must plow through to get to the information that's important to you. Files that you download and use on your Macintosh are information-dense, perhaps more than anything else you will encounter on the Internet.

In this chapter, we'll cover the basics of the File Transfer Protocol itself, and we'll also go over the details of using two popular software programs that let you transfer files across the Internet: Fetch, by Jim Matthews of Dartmouth College, and InterCon's TCP/Connect II. So sit back, get your cameras ready and fish out those traveler's checks— we're going souvenir hunting.

What Is FTP?

FTP is an acronym for File Transfer Protocol, but nobody says File Transfer Protocol; everyone says FTP, as in "you can FTP that file from the Sumex archive" or "that file is available by FTP from the Michigan archive."

People use FTP as a noun when they refer to the actual File Transfer Protocol, but they also use it as a verb when describing the process of transferring files on the Internet. Technically, FTP is a full-fledged data-transfer protocol, like Z-Modem or Kermit. It allows files to be transferred between different kinds of computers, without regard to the operating system used by the computers, or even how they are connected.

As you explore this chapter, keep in mind that while different examples are used for Fetch and TCP/Connect II, you can use either program to access any FTP archive on the Internet.

Why Would You Want to Transfer Files?

You can use Macintosh applications (like Fetch and TCP/Connect II) that employ FTP to send and receive files between your Macintosh and any other computer on the Internet that supports FTP. There is a wealth of software available through the Internet by *anonymous FTP*. Anonymous FTP is an Internet service that allows anyone to enter publicly accessible file archives, practically anywhere in the world, without having an account on that archive. If an FTP server accepts anonymous logins (and there are thousands that do), you log in with the username *anonymous* and any text as a password. It is a generally accepted convention that anonymous FTP users enter their e-mail address—in the username@domain.top-domain format—as their password.

Hot news on the Net.
Savvy folks in public relations and publicity departments know that news travels fast along the Net. That's why you can count on the Internet to be one of the first places to offer news releases from all kinds of sources, ranging from the White House to Apple Computer. In short, you can see it on the Net today, or read about it in the paper tomorrow.

Resources available from anonymous FTP archives include fully-functional software programs (spreadsheets, text editors, telecommunications programs, databases, graphics programs, utilities and more) as well as graphic images, sounds, QuickTime movies and texts ranging from President Bill Clinton's speeches to *Macbeth*. Some of the most valuable software resources available on the Internet are updaters and bug fixes for commercially distributed software. Software companies distribute the updaters to the general public via the Internet and various online services. People who own a program that may not be compatible with a new hardware or software release can download the updater and run it on their outdated program to upgrade it to the newest version. It's a classic win-win situation: users get quick updates and the vendor gets inexpensive distribution and loads of good will within the community while at the same time keeping its installed base of users current and up-to-date.

Other valuable resources—information resources—are available by FTP. Developer notes, technical reports, technical support documents, electronic magazines, journals, templates and tutorials are all available. And then there are the thousands of "miscellaneous" resources that seem to find their way to FTP sites: things like musical notation and lyric sheets for just about any piece of music from the last 30 years, or full-text copies of classic literature ranging from *Alice in Wonderland* and *Peter Pan* to the complete works of Shakespeare.

A Primer on Software Resources

For the time being, there are three general types of software resources you can find on the Internet: information resources, software programs, and program-specific files for use with those software programs (templates and samples). Information resources—documents that were distributed as ink (or toner) on paper in the past—are widely available from numerous sources on the Internet. Software programs and files for use with those programs are generally less widely available, but plentiful nonetheless.

Dial "S" for software.

Just about the only kind of software resource you won't find on the Internet is commercially distributed software. And even that may change in the relatively near future. Imagine the benefit MondoCorp can reap if it can distribute within seconds a new version of its MondoWriter software to anyone on the Internet. Users could simply type in a credit card number and instantly download the software and documentation right to their hard drives. Look for this to happen soon, and look to see who the initial players are. Chances are, the first companies to distribute their software across the Internet will be the most forward-thinking in the industry.

There are three classifications for the software resources you will find on the Internet: public domain, freeware and shareware. Let's take a look at the differences between these three distribution methods.

Public Domain

Public domain resources are those that carry no copyright. The author or developer has created the resource for the good of the community and has released it for any and every use. There is no limit on redistribution or sale of public domain resources, and it can be modified or transformed by anyone.

Freeware

Freeware resources are those that carry the author's copyright. The author retains copyright but allows you to use the resource free of charge. There are generally some restrictions on freeware resources, most often regarding distribution and modification. The usual case with freeware is that you can give it away, but you can't sell it. Eudora—the e-mail program included on *The Mac Internet Tour Guide Companion Disks*—is an example of freeware. You can use it free of charge, but you can't sell it, and the author retains copyright.

Shareware

Shareware resources are those that are distributed on a "try-before-you-buy" basis. The author retains copyright and allows you to use the resource on a trial basis for a short evaluation period. At the end of the evaluation period, you must either pay the author for the resource or destroy all the copies of the resource in your possession. You are encouraged to make copies for your friends, but you can't charge for them. Shareware resources carry a relatively low price because the author doesn't have to pay distribution or advertising costs. The author cuts out the middlemen like distributors and resellers, dealing with you—the user—directly.

Fetch—the FTP program included on the companion disks—is an example of shareware. Actually, it's a freeware-shareware hybrid. If you're a non-commercial Internet user, you can use Fetch free of charge; it's freeware. But if you're a commercial Internet user, Fetch is distributed as shareware, and you must pay a $25 fee to the author.

Freeware PPP software.

PPP software allows you to log into the Internet using a high-speed modem and ordinary telephone lines. SLIP is more common right now than PPP, but PPP will probably surpass SLIP in the near future because it offers more features and better throughput during interactive sessions where small bits of information are passed in both directions. MacPPP is available by anonymous FTP at merit.edu in the /pub/ppp/mac/ directory.

Making Shareware Work

If shareware is to remain a viable way to distribute and sell software, people who use it must pay the shareware authors. If you regularly use a piece of shareware, it's in your own best interest to pay the shareware fee. Some of the programs included on the companion disk are shareware products and are included for evaluation purposes only. If you continue to use these programs, you must pay the software authors directly. See the documentation for each program for details.

A Primer on File Types

Files on the Internet are usually going to have names that look different than what you're used to seeing. Most Macintosh files that you find will be listed in this file-name format: filename.ext.hqx.

The "ext" part of a file's name represents the compression tool used to create the file. The most common options are sit, cpt and sea. The "hqx" extension indicates that the file has been placed on the FTP server in BinHex format. BinHex is a standard format that allows files to be accessed by virtually any computer, regardless of the hardware or software it uses.

You'll also probably find a lot of files that end with a "txt" or "ps" extension. These are ASCII text and PostScript files respectively and are intended for use on all kinds of computers. ASCII text can be read by any word processor and PostScript files can be printed—fully formatted—by any PostScript-capable output device.

Fetch will automatically determine the transfer mode to use based on the type of file you download. TCP/Connect II can also automatically determine the transfer mode to use, but it's not as reliable as Fetch.

Aladdin's StuffIt Expander utility—included on the companion disks—will automatically decode (convert from BinHex format) and decompress files created with the most popular Macintosh compression programs: StuffIt Lite (and previous versions of the shareware StuffIt program), StuffIt Deluxe and Compact Pro. To use StuffIt Expander, simply drag and drop the files you download onto the StuffIt Expander icon. StuffIt Expander will automatically launch, decode and decompress the file and quit.

Note that StuffIt Expander will not work with compressed files that have been split into multiple segments. You must have whatever program was used to create the compressed file segments to decompress and join the files.

Table 6-1 lists the file extensions and file types handled by StuffIt Expander.

Table 6-1:
StuffIt Expander
file-handling
capabilities.

Extension	Compression Program Used
bin	Native file formats created by various software programs (these files aren't actually processed by StuffIt Expander but are usually in BinHex format with an hqx extension)
hqx	BinHex 4.0
sit	StuffIt, StuffIt Lite or StuffIt Deluxe
cpt	Compact Pro
sea	Self-extracting archives created with StuffIt, Compact Pro, DiskDoubler or another program

If you stick to the major Macintosh FTP servers, you'll probably never see any other file-name extensions. But then you'd be missing out on most of the software resources available on the Internet. (For a list of the most popular Macintosh FTP sites on the Internet, see the "Famous Macintosh FTP archives" sidebar later in this chapter.)

Aladdin's StuffIt Deluxe is currently the best program for decompressing files created by computers other than the Macintosh. StuffIt Deluxe is also the best tool for compressing files you want to upload. Table 6-2 lists the file extensions and types handled by StuffIt Deluxe.

Table 6-2:
StuffIt Deluxe
file-handling
capabilities.

Extension	Compression Program Used
hqx	BinHex 4.0
sit	StuffIt, StuffIt Lite or StuffIt Deluxe
cpt	Compact Pro
sea	Self-extracting archives created with either StuffIt or Compact Pro
seg	Compressed files saved in multiple segments with either StuffIt or Compact Pro
pit	PackIt (the original Macintosh compression software)
dd	DiskDoubler (Macintosh)
zip	PKZip (DOS)
lzh	LHarc (DOS)
arc	ARC (DOS)
z	Compress (UNIX)
tar	Tar (UNIX)

If you download files almost exclusively from the most popular Macintosh archives, you'll probably be able to decompress them with the free StuffIt Expander utility included on the companion disks. But if you're planning to wander the Net, sampling files from all over, you may need a compression utility that's a little more versatile. StuffIt Deluxe is a commercial product available from Aladdin Systems, Inc., 165 Westridge Drive, Watsonville, CA 95073, 408/761-6200. Other programs, including the shareware StuffIt Lite, are available from most large Macintosh archives.

A Disinfectant for Viruses

If you're going to download files from any FTP archive on the Internet, you run the risk of having your system infected with a *virus*. A virus (and similar files like trojan horses or worms) is actually a computer program imbedded within another file you download. It "infects" your computer in one of a number of different ways. Some viruses are merely annoying, but others can cause severe damage by erasing files on your hard disk, scrambling your disk's file catalog or a number of other malicious tricks.

Your computer can't get infected by a text file—only by binary files—but it's generally a good policy to consider any file you download to be a potential source of viruses. While viruses are relatively rare, the Internet is a fertile breeding ground for them. So many files are uploaded and transferred every day, it's impossible to check them all, especially since there's no single system for checking for viruses.

The best way to protect yourself is to download the current version of John Norstad's Disinfectant antivirus program. You can always find the latest version of Disinfectant at ftp.acns.nwu.edu in the /pub/disinfectant/ directory.

University of Michigan Macintosh archive.

The Macintosh archive maintained by the University of Michigan is one of the most popular archives on the Internet. Just about any public domain, freeware or shareware software for the Macintosh is available here. It's accessible with TurboGopher (as well as the traditional methods). Point your TurboGopher at gopher.archive.merit.net port 7055.

Alternatively, all files are available by anonymous FTP at mac.archive.umich.edu. You can download an index of descriptions of all available files in the /mac/00help/ directory.

Using Disinfectant

Disinfectant is probably the most frequently updated and widely used antivirus utility for the Macintosh. With it, you can periodically scan your hard drive for viruses, install an extension that detects viruses as soon as they appear, and eradicate most any virus you might find. To scan your hard drive for any known virus and disinfect the drive if a virus is found,

1. Launch the Disinfectant program by double-clicking on its icon. The Disinfectant window will be displayed, as shown in Figure 6-1.

Figure 6-1:
Disinfectant
window.

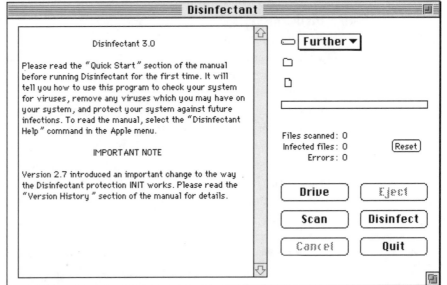

2. Select the disk you want to work with from the Disk pop-up menu. (You can scan and disinfect external drives as well as floppy disks.)

3. Click the Disinfect button. The program will scan the selected volume for viruses and attempt to remove any viruses it finds. The number of files scanned, the number of infected files and the number of errors will all be reported in the Disinfectant window during the process.

4. When the process is complete, click the Quit button.

Disinfectant contains extensive online help (select the Disinfectant Help command from the Apple menu). Refer to the Help file for further instructions on using Disinfectant, including installing the protective extension.

Using Fetch to Transfer Files

Fetch is a Macintosh File Transfer Protocol (FTP) program written by Jim Matthews of Dartmouth College. With Fetch, you can quickly and easily download (get) files from or upload (put) files to a remote host on the Internet. The file transfer speed will vary, based on the type of Internet connection you have. I use a Serial Line Internet Protocol

(SLIP) connection and a V.32bis modem with error correction and data compression. I almost always get throughput of about 1300 characters per second on compressed data files and significantly faster results on text files. Using a V.32bis modem with error correction and data compression, you can expect to download a 500k file in about five or six minutes. Of course, if you're fortunate enough to enjoy a direct connection to the Internet, you can transfer a 500k file in a few seconds (just a little bit longer than it takes to transfer the same amount of data from your local file server).

Fetch is an excellent, full-featured FTP program—in fact, it's the FTP tool I use most often. It is simple to use, providing an intuitive Macintosh interface for the FTP process. It automatically translates standard Macintosh file conventions into the required FTP commands.

A real Internet power user.

You thought being able to send e-mail to Australia made you a power user? Think again! There are people doing work on the Internet that boggles the mind of even the most arrogant Net gurus. One true power user writes:

"I'm an employee of the University of California and the US Department of Energy at Lawrence Livermore National Laboratory in California.

"The most interesting Internet usage I've ever participated in has been at the Supercomputing '92 conference in Minneapolis.

"We typically take one or more Macs with dual 16-inch monitors to the meeting and connect them to the show Net. Then, by way of MacX, we are able to open windows onto machines back at our home site in California, as well as at the vendor displays on the show floor, and even at the home sites of the vendors involved.

"For instance, at the Albuquerque conference in 1991, it wasn't unusual for us to have windows open on a Sun and a Cray at Livermore, an SGI machine on the show floor, and a Cray in Egan, Minnesota, all displayed and accessed from a Mac in Albuquerque."

A copy of Fetch is included on the companion disks that came with this book, and the latest version of Fetch is always available from Ventana Online. If you're on the Internet as a commercial user, the program is provided for evaluation purposes only. If you decide to continue to use Fetch, you must pay a $25 fee to the author. If you're a non-commercial user, you may use Fetch at no charge.

Fetch is licensed free of charge for use in educational and non-profit organizations. Users in for-profit enterprises may obtain an individual license by sending $25 to

Software Sales
Dartmouth College
6028 Kiewit Computation Center
Hanover, NH 03755-3523 USA

Site licenses are also available; please send inquiries to the above address, or e-mail to Fetch@dartmouth.edu.

Configuring Fetch

To configure Fetch to connect as an anonymous user to those FTP sites that allow connections without accounts,

1. Double-click on the Fetch icon to launch the program. The Connection dialog box containing the default connection information will appear.

2. Click the Cancel button in the Connection dialog box.

3. Select the Preferences command from the Customize menu. The Fetch Preferences dialog box will appear, as shown in Figure 6-2.

Figure 6-2: Fetch Preferences dialog box.

Fetch Preferences

Topic: [General ▼]

Default password (i.e. your e-mail address):

[user@host]

☒ Display server messages.

☐ Keep connection active.

☒ Show file sizes and dates (if possible).

[Cancel] [OK]

4. Enter the password to use as a default in the Default password box.

   ■ Note that it is common Internet convention and courtesy to use your full e-mail address—in the username@domain.top-domain format—as your password when you log into an FTP server as an anonymous user.

   ■ If you were logging into an FTP server on which you had an account, you would enter your login name and your password for that account in the appropriate boxes.

5. Select the other items from the Topic pop-up menu in the Preferences dialog box, and customize the Fetch settings to suit your purposes.

   ■ These additional settings are usually best left in their default state until you have more experience using Fetch and FTP.

6. Click the OK button. Your customized settings will be saved in the Fetch Preferences file on your hard disk drive.

You have successfully configured Fetch for use with those FTP servers that are preconfigured in Fetch. Included in the group of Fetch's preconfigured servers are the Dartmouth College archive, the Stanford University Mac archive (Info-Mac), the University of Texas archive, the University of Michigan archive, Apple's general file archive, the NCSA archive and the Washington University archive (which includes mirrors of the most popular archives). If you are anxious to begin downloading files, you can skip to the next section. The remainder of this section covers how to add additional FTP server connection information to Fetch.

Locating FTP servers.

Can't get enough of downloading files via FTP? Don't worry, it's not likely you'll run out of files or FTP sites. A list of publicly accessible FTP sites is available by FTP from pilot.njin.net in the /pub/ftp-list/ directory.

Any FTP site listed allows anonymous logins. It's Internet courtesy to supply your e-mail address—in the username@domain.top-domain format—as your login password.

Use these steps to configure Fetch for use with additional FTP servers. This tutorial provides information on configuring access to the University of Minnesota software distribution FTP server. This Fetch configuration will be used later in this chapter in another example.

1. Launch Fetch by double-clicking on its icon. The Connection dialog box containing the default connection information will be displayed.

2. Click the Cancel button in the Connection dialog box.

3. From the Customize menu, select the Edit Shortcuts command. The Shortcuts dialog box will appear, as shown in Figure 6-3.

Figure 6-3:
Fetch Shortcuts
dialog box.

Shortcuts

✓**Dartvax**
Info-Mac Archives (sumer
U. Texas Archives (rascal)
U. Michigan archives
Apple Archives
NCSA Archives
Info-Mac mirror

New

Change

Remove

Cancel

OK

Make Default

4. Click the New button to create a new FTP server entry. The New Server Entry dialog box will appear, as shown in Figure 6-4.

Figure 6-4: Fetch
New Server Entry
dialog box.

Shortcut:

Host:

User ID:

Password:

Directory:

Cancel   OK

5. Enter **U of M (Boombox)** in the Shortcut box. This entry is used only as a display reference; it has no effect on the server address.

6. Enter **boombox.micro.umn.edu** in the Host box.

7. Enter **anonymous** in the User ID box.

   ■ Note that if you were configuring Fetch for use with an FTP server on which you have an account, you would enter your login name *at the remote host* in the User ID box. Most public FTP servers will accept anonymous users.

8. Leave the Password box empty. The e-mail address you entered when you initially configured Fetch will be used as a password.

   ■ Note that if you were configuring Fetch for use with an FTP server on which you have an account, you would enter your password *at the remote host* in the Password box. Most public FTP servers will accept (some even require) an e-mail address for anonymous users.

9. Leave the Directory box empty. The New Entry Server dialog box for the U of M (Boombox) entry should look like the example shown in Figure 6-5.

Figure 6-5: Fetch New Entry Server dialog box for the U of M (Boombox) entry.

Shortcut: **U of M (Boombox)**

Host: **boombox.micro.umn.edu**

User ID: **anonymous**

Password:

Directory:

Cancel   OK

   ■ Note that you can add a default directory—in the format /directory/subdirectory/sub-sub-directory—if you want to log into a specific directory. Most publicly accessible FTP servers that accept anonymous logins restrict anonymous access to the /pub/ directory.

10. Click the OK button in the New Server Entry dialog box.

11. Repeat steps 4–10 to add additional FTP server entries. All you need to know to add an additional FTP server to the Shortcuts list is the domain-name or IP address of the site and whether the site will allow anonymous logins.

12. Click the OK button in the Shortcuts dialog box to save your FTP server entries to the Fetch Preferences file.

You can further customize Fetch to automatically process files compressed with the most popular Macintosh compression utilities, including Compact Pro, StuffIt Lite and StuffIt Deluxe. To configure Fetch to automatically expand certain compressed files,

1. Make sure the StuffIt Expander program is installed on your hard drive.

2. Launch Fetch by double-clicking on its icon. The Connection dialog box containing the default connection information will appear.

3. Click the Cancel button in the Connection dialog box.

4. Select the Post-Processing command from the Customize menu. The Post-Processing Configuration dialog box will appear, as shown in Figure 6-6.

Figure 6-6: Fetch Post-Processing Configuration dialog box.

File Type	Opening Application	
GIF Files	Giffer	**Add**
Compact Pro Archives	Compact Pro	Change
StuffIt Archives	StuffIt Expander	Remove
StuffIt SEAs		
		Enable
		Disable
		Cancel

NOTE: Automatic file-opening requires System 7.0.   **OK**

Pass the Popcorn.
Popcorn is a freeware QuickTime viewer developed by Leonard Rosenthal at Aladdin Systems. It's a simple, no-nonsense player that offers a clean interface. Multiple QuickTime movies can be displayed and edited. It's available by FTP from mac.archive.umich.edu in the /mac/graphics/quicktime/ directory.

5. Click on the grayed-out Compact Pro Archives item in the scrolling list.

6. Click the Change button. The Post-Processing Program Selection dialog box will appear, as shown in Figure 6-7.

Figure 6-7: Fetch Post-Processing Program Selection dialog box.

Automatically open a type of file with the specified application:

File Description: | Compact Pro Archives |

Type: | PACT | Creator: | CPCT | (Choose Example...)

Application: | Compact Pro |

Signature: | CPCT | (Choose Application...)

(Cancel)   [OK]

7. Click the Choose Application button. A standard Open File dialog box will appear.

8. Navigate to the folder containing StuffIt Expander, and double-click on its name in the scrolling list. The Post-Processing Program Selection dialog box will be updated to reflect your change.

9. Click the OK button in the Post-Processing Program Selection dialog box.

10. Click the Enable button in the Post-Processing Configuration dialog box. The Compact Pro Archives item in the scrolling list will appear as an enabled item, with black type instead of gray.

11. Repeat steps 5–10 for both the StuffIt Archives and StuffIt SEAs items in the Post-Processing Configuration dialog box's list.

12. Click the OK button in the Post-Processing Configuration dialog box to save your changes to the Fetch Preferences file.

Downloading Files With Fetch

An important information-browsing tool—TurboGopher—is discussed in the next chapter. TurboGopher brings a simple but very powerful interface to the Internet, and it's a program every Mac Internet user should have. The current version of TurboGopher is included on the companion disks at the back of this book, and the latest version is always available from Ventana Online. The following steps illustrate the process of downloading any file with Fetch, using the TurboGopher program and the University of Minnesota's software distribution FTP server as an example.

1. Launch Fetch by double-clicking on its icon. The Connection dialog box containing the default connection information will appear, as shown in Figure 6-8.

Figure 6-8: Fetch Connection dialog box.

> **Enter host name, user name, and password (or choose from the shortcut menu):**
>
> Host: `dartvax.dartmouth.edu`
>
> User ID: `anonymous`
>
> Password:
>
> Directory: `/pub`
>
> Shortcuts: ▼   [Cancel]   [OK]

2. Select the U of M (Boombox) item from the Shortcuts pop-up menu. The Connection dialog box should look like the example in Figure 6-9.

   ▪ Note that this step assumes that you added the University of Minnesota's software distribution FTP server to your Fetch Shortcuts configuration, as explained in the previous section. If you skipped that section, enter **boombox.micro.umn.edu** in the Host box, and **anonymous** in the User ID box.

Figure 6-9: Fetch
Connection dialog
box with entry for
the University of
Minnesota soft-
ware distribution
FTP server.

Enter host name, user name, and password
(or choose from the shortcut menu):

Host: `boombox.micro.umn.edu`

User ID: `anonymous`

Password:

Directory:

Shortcuts: ▼ [Cancel] [OK]

3. Click the OK button. Fetch will establish an FTP connection with the University of Minnesota's software distribution FTP server, log you in as an anonymous user, and update the File Browser dialog box to reflect the current directory.

   ▪ In this case, the directory you log into is the *root* directory (called the root directory because it is the lowest level directory), as shown in Figure 6-10.

Figure 6-10:
Fetch File
Browser
dialog box.

Fetch: boombox.micro.umn.edu

Fetch Copyright © 1992
Trustees of Dartmouth College

[**Close Connection**   ⌘W]

/ ▼

🗀 bin	-	Oct 6 1992
🗀 etc	-	Oct 6 1992
🗀 pub	-	Apr 1 18:17

[**Put File...**]

[**Get File...**]

● **Automatic**
○ **Text**
○ **Binary**

Status
Connected.

File

Transfer

2.1

4. Navigate through the folder hierarchy on the remote FTP server by double-clicking on the appropriate folder icons within the scrolling list at the left side of the Fetch window.

■ In this example, double-click on the pub folder, then double-click on the gopher folder and finally, double-click on the Macintosh-TurboGopher folder. This hierarchy of folders is known as a *pathname*, and is written like this: /pub/gopher/Macintosh-TurboGopher/. The root directory is indicated by the first slash (/).

5. Locate the most recent version of the TurboGopher file. As of fall 1994, the current version is 1.08b4, and the complete pathname is /pub/gopher/Macintosh-TurboGopher/TurboGopher.1.08b4.hqx. The File Browser dialog box should look like Figure 6-11.

Figure 6-11: Fetch File Browser dialog box with TurboGopher file highlighted.

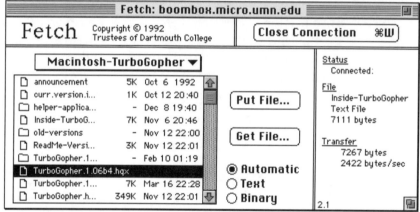

6. Click the Get File button. The file transfer will begin, and its progress will be reported in the lower right portion of the File Browser dialog box, as shown in Figure 6-12.

Figure 6-12: Fetch File Browser dialog box with file transfer in progress.

Fetch: boombox.micro.umn.edu		
Fetch Copyright © 1992 Trustees of Dartmouth College		Close Connection ⌘W

Macintosh-TurboGopher ▼

announcement	5K	Oct 6 1992
curr.version.i...	1K	Oct 12 20:40
helper-applica...	-	Dec 8 19:40
Inside-TurboG...	7K	Nov 6 20:46
old-versions	-	Nov 12 22:00
ReadMe-Versi...	3K	Nov 12 22:01
TurboGopher.1...	-	Feb 10 01:19
TurboGopher.1.06b4.hqx		
TurboGopher.1...	7K	Mar 16 22:28
TurboGopher.h...	349K	Nov 12 22:01

Put File...

Get File...

● Automatic
○ Text
○ Binary

Status
Getting file...

File
TurboGopher.1.06b4.H
BinHex
409638 bytes

Transfer
20032 bytes
2225 bytes/sec

Cancel ⌘.

2.1

7. When the file transfer is complete, you can download additional files from the same FTP server by repeating steps 4–6 for each file. Feel free to browse the files available at this site and download any that interest you.

8. When you are finished transferring files, click the Close Connection button. Your connection to the remote FTP server will be severed.

File extensions.

Every file you download from the Internet will probably have at least one—and perhaps several—*file-name extensions*. This is a method used to identify the types of files (and the software program used to create the files). File-name extensions have become a veritable alphabet soup and often end up confusing people more than they inform.

The file-name extension will give you a clue about which transfer mode (ASCII or binary) to use in your FTP program. The good news is, if you're using Fetch, all this is automatically handled for you; just click the Automatic radio button in the File Browser dialog box.

If you're using another FTP program, such as TCP/Connect II, files that end with hqx, txt or ps extensions are the *only* files that can be downloaded in ASCII mode. All other types of files *must* be downloaded in binary (also called image) mode. Chances are that if you get errors during file decompression indicating that your file is corrupt, it's because you used ASCII mode when you should have used binary mode.

StuffIt Expander will automatically handle most Macintosh-format files you download from the Internet. Unfortunately, most of the files on the Internet aren't Macintosh files.

Uploading Files With Fetch

Downloading files is just one side of the file transfer coin. You can also *upload*, or send, files to a remote FTP server using Fetch. If you have a file that you want to share with the rest of the world, consider uploading it (as long as there are no restrictions on its distribution) to your favorite FTP site. To upload files to a remote FTP server with Fetch,

1. Launch Fetch by double-clicking on its icon. The Connection dialog box containing the default connection information will be displayed.

2. From the Shortcuts pop-up menu, select the remote FTP server to which you want to upload a file. Alternatively, enter the domain-name or IP address for the remote FTP server in the Host box.

3. Enter **anonymous** in the User ID box.

   ■ Alternatively, if you have an account on the remote FTP server, enter your login name *at the remote host* in the User ID box. Most public FTP servers will accept anonymous users.

4. Leave the Password box emtpy. The e-mail address you entered when you initially configured Fetch will be used as a password.

   ■ Alternatively, if you have an account on the remote FTP server, enter your password *at the remote host* in the Password box.

5. Click the OK button. Fetch will establish an FTP connection with the remote FTP server, log you in and update the File Browser dialog box to reflect the current directory.

6. Navigate through the folder hierarchy on the remote FTP server by double-clicking on the appropriate folder icons within the scrolling list.

7. Create a new directory, if necessary, by selecting the Create New Directory command from the Directories menu. You'll be prompted for a name for the new directory.

   ■ Note that you must have the appropriate permissions on the remote FTP server in order to create a new directory. It's generally not a good idea to try creating new directories at remote FTP sites without clearing it first with that site's network administrator.

   ■ Note also that your new directory will be created as a subdirectory within the current directory.

8. Click the Put File button in the File Browser dialog box. A standard Open File dialog box will appear.

9. Double-click on the name of the file you want to upload.

10. The file transfer will begin, and its progress will be reported in the lower right portion of the File Browser dialog box.

11. When the file transfer is complete, you can upload additional files to the same FTP server by repeating steps 6–10 for each file.

12. When you are finished transferring files, click the Close Connection button. Your connection to the remote FTP server will be severed.

Etiquette for uploaders.

Here's a quick checklist of things to keep in mind when you upload files to remote FTP sites:

- Make sure you include all relevant documents.

- Compress your files using either a member of the StuffIt family or Compact Pro (these are the two "standard" file compression utilities in the Macintosh community).

- Check your files for viruses before uploading them.

- Upload your file to the appropriate directory.

- Provide a brief but accurate description for your uploaded file.

Using TCP/Connect II to Transfer Files

TCP/Connect II provides a fully functional FTP module—as well as an FTP server—but I don't find myself using it as much as Fetch. It offers some niceties that Fetch doesn't have (it beeps when file transfers are finished and it automatically lists host selections in alphabetical order), but it's not as intuitive to use on some remote FTP servers. Nonetheless, TCP/Connect II's FTP module is powerful and the product's developer, InterCon Systems, is responsive, so its few shortcomings will almost surely be addressed.

Configuring the TCP/Connect II FTP Module

As mentioned in the previous section, TCP/Connect II includes an FTP server implementation. This allows you to provide remote FTP service to other users on the Internet. For example, if you were a shareware author, you could set up a few directories where others on the Net could download your shareware and upload their questions, comments or favorite files of their own. Be careful with this capability; you can easily leave your Macintosh wide open to electronic intruders who will take great pleasure in browsing through your hard drive.

Use these steps to configure TCP/Connect II's FTP module, including the FTP server.

1. Launch TCP/Connect II by double-clicking on its icon.

2. Select the Configure command from the Edit menu. The Configuration dialog box will appear.

3. Click on the File Transfer icon in the scrolling list of configuration items at the left side of the window. The File Transfer Configuration panel will appear, as shown in Figure 6-13.

Figure 6-13:
TCP/Connect II
File Transfer
Configuration
panel.

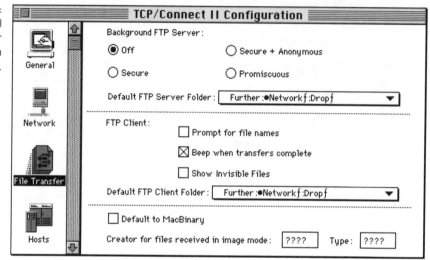

4. To define to what extent (if at all) others may connect to your Macintosh as an FTP server, click one of the Background FTP Server radio buttons based on the following criteria:

■ Click the Off radio button to completely deactivate the FTP server options in the program. This will prevent anyone from connecting to your Macintosh via remote FTP.

■ Click the Secure radio button to allow connections by only those users for whom you have defined access privileges.

Commercial software updates.

The University of Michigan archive (as well as Stanford University's Info-Mac archive) maintains a directory for commercial software updates on its FTP server. Updater programs for AfterDark, Canvas, FileMaker Pro, Now Up-to-Date, Now Utilities, PageMaker additions, QuarkXPress (and XTensions), Photoshop, QuicKeys, SoftPC and StuffIt are only a few of those you can download and use completely free. They're available by FTP from mac.archive.umich.edu in the /mac/misc/update/ directory.

■ Click the Secure + Anonymous radio button to allow connections by users for whom you have defined access privileges as well as anonymous users. Anonymous users will be restricted to a single folder (and any subfolders it contains) and will be unable to upload or delete files on your Macintosh.

■ Click the Promiscuous radio button to allow connections from anyone. Be aware that if you select this option, *anyone will be able to log into your Macintosh and upload or download any file without an account or password*. Think at least twice before you choose this option.

5. If you turned Off TCP/Connect II's Background FTP Server capabilities, skip this step and advance to step 6. If you're going to allow others to connect to your Macintosh and transfer files, define a set of privileges for each user with this procedure:

■ Click on the Users icon in the scrolling list of configuration items. The Users Configuration panel will be displayed, as shown in the preconfigured example in Figure 6-14.

Figure 6-14: TCP/Connect II Users Configuration panel.

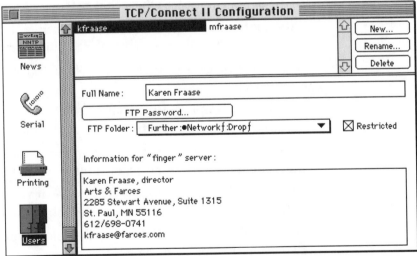

■ Click the New button. You'll be prompted to enter a name for the user.

■ Enter a name for the user. This will be used for display reference purposes only, and will have no effect on the user's privileges.

- Enter the user's full name in the Full Name box.

- Click the FTP Password button. You will be prompted to enter a password for the user.

- Enter the user's password. Remember that passwords should never be someone's first name, and a good password includes both numbers and letters and mixes upper- and lowercase letters.

- Click the OK button.

- Specify a default folder for the user with the FTP Folder pop-up menu.

- Check the Restricted check box if you want to restrict the user's access to the specified FTP folder. *If this check box is unchecked, the remote user could conceivably access any files and folders on your hard drive.*

- Enter any information you want to be displayed when a remote user on the Internet uses *finger* to contact your Macintosh. Finger is a UNIX command that lets remote users search for someone's login name and e-mail address if they know the name of the computer where that person has an account.

- Click on the File Transfer icon in the scrolling list of configuration items. The File Transfer Configuration panel will appear.

6. To configure the general preferences of the FTP client portion of the software,

- Check the Prompt for file names check box if you want to be asked for the destination file names for all file transfers.

- Check the Beep when transfers complete check box if you want the System beep to sound when a file transfer is complete.

- Check the Show Invisible Files check box if you want to display in the file transfer window those files that are normally invisible.

- Select a folder for saving downloaded files from the Default FTP Client Folder pop-up menu.

- Check the Default to MacBinary check box if you want the MacBinary file format to be used when you transfer files in TCP/Connect II's image mode. It's rare to find an FTP archive on the Internet that has native MacBinary files (as opposed to regular binary files), so this option should usually be left unchecked.

The Beauty of ZTerm.

ZTerm is one of the most popular Macintosh shareware programs. It provides terminal emulation, ANSI support and a built-in phonebook. ZTerm was the first Macintosh communications program that provided the Z-Modem file transfer protocol. X-Modem and Y-Modem protocols are also supported. But the real beauty of ZTerm is its sublime combination of power and simplicity. It's available by FTP from mac.archive.umich.edu in the /mac/util/comm/ directory.

- Specify a Creator for files received in image mode. You do this by entering the four-character creator code of the program you want to use to open and edit files received in image mode. This option is useful for specifying a program to use for opening downloaded files that your Mac can't recognize. Again, since it's rare to find an FTP archive on the Internet that has native Macintosh files, it's best to leave this option in its default state of four question marks (????).

- Specify a Type for files received in image mode by entering the four-character type code. This option is useful for specifying a file type for downloaded files that your Mac can't recognize. Because it's rare to find an FTP archive on the Internet that has native Macintosh files, it's best to leave this option in its default state of four question marks (????).

7. Click in the Configuration dialog box's close box to close the dialog box and save your changes to the TCP/Connect II preferences file.

You may want to configure a few of your favorite FTP servers before you begin to transfer files with TCP/Connect II. To configure the Info-Mac archive at Stanford University as one of TCP/Connect II's hosts,

1. Launch TCP/Connect II by double-clicking on its icon.

2. From the Edit menu, select the Configure command. The Configuration dialog box will appear.

3. Click on the Hosts icon in the scrolling list of configuration items at the left side of the window. The Hosts Configuration panel will appear, as shown in the preconfigured example in Figure 6-15.

Figure 6-15:
TCP/Connect II
Hosts Config-
uration panel.

```
┌─────────────────── TCP/Connect II Configuration ═══════════════════┐
│ ☐                                                                   │
│  ┌─────┐  ⬆ ─ Default ─              Appalachian State CWIS (Telnet)⬆  ┌─────────┐
│  │ 🖥  │    Apple (A/UX Support)      Apple (Bric-a-Brac)           │  New...  │
│  └─────┘    Apple (Cambridge)         Apple (General Archive)       ├─────────┤
│  General    Baseball Schedules (Telnet) Biosphere Newsletter        │ Rename...│
│             Bucknell (Telnet/Knowbot) ⬇ CARL (Telnet)              ⬇├─────────┤
│  ┌─────┐                                                             │ Delete   │
│  │ 🖥  │   IP Addresses : ┌────────────────────────────────────────┐│└─────────┘
│  └─────┘                  └────────────────────────────────────────┘ │
│  Network   Full Domain Name : ┌───────────────────────────────────┐  │
│                               └───────────────────────────────────┘  │
│            Operating System : ┌──────────┐   CPU Type : ┌──────────┐  │
│                               └──────────┘              └──────────┘  │
│                                                      RWIN : ┌──────┐  │
│  ┌─────┐                                                    └──────┘  │
│  │ 📄  │   ─────────────────────────────────────────────────────────  │
│  └─────┘   Paste Style :  ○ Full Speed  ◉ By Line  ○ Blocked to      │
│ File Transfer Paste Delay : ┌─┐ ticks (60ths of a second)            │
│                            │1│                                        │
│                             └─┘                                       │
│  ┌─────┐   FTP Client :                                              │
│  │ 📱  │                                                             │
│  └─────┘   ☒ Automatically log in     ☒ Automatically show file list │
│  Hosts     ☒ Use PORT commands        ☐ Transfer unknown file types as ASCII │
│         ⬇                                                            │
└──────────────────────────────────────────────────────────────────────┘
```

4. Click the New button. A dialog box will appear, prompting you to enter the name of the host.

5. Enter **Macintosh (Info-Mac)** and click the OK button. A new entry will be created in the Hosts scrolling list.

6. Enter **sumex-aim.stanford.edu** in the Full Domain Name box. Alternatively, enter **36.44.0.6** in the IP Addresses box. The entry for the Macintosh archive at Stanford University should look like the illustration in Figure 6-16.

Figure 6-16:
TCP/Connect II
host entry for
Stanford Univer-
sity's Macintosh
archive (Info-Mac).

```
┌─────────────────── TCP/Connect II Configuration ═══════════════════┐
│ ☐                                                                   │
│  ┌─────┐  ⬆ Macintosh (Info-Mac)        Macintosh (Sounds/Rochester)⬆ ┌─────────┐
│  │ 🖥  │    Macintosh (Univ. Maryland Archive) Macintosh (Univ. Maryland)│ New...  │
│  └─────┘    Macintosh (Univ. Mich.)      Macintosh (Univ. Minn.)    ├─────────┤
│  General    Macintosh (Univ. Texas Rascal) Macintosh (Univ. Texas)  │ Rename...│
│             Mars Hotel (Telnet)         ⬇ Media Lab                ⬇├─────────┤
│  ┌─────┐                                                             │ Delete   │
│  │ 🖥  │   IP Addresses : ┌────────────────────────────────────────┐│└─────────┘
│  └─────┘                  │ 36.44.0.6                               ││ │
│  Network                  └────────────────────────────────────────┘ │
│            Full Domain Name : ┌───────────────────────────────────┐  │
│                               │ sumex-aim.stanford.edu            │  │
│                               └───────────────────────────────────┘  │
│            Operating System : ┌──────────┐   CPU Type : ┌──────────┐  │
│                               └──────────┘              └──────────┘  │
│                                                      RWIN : ┌──────┐  │
│  ┌─────┐                                                    └──────┘  │
│  │ 📄  │   ─────────────────────────────────────────────────────────  │
│  └─────┘   Paste Style :  ○ Full Speed  ◉ By Line  ○ Blocked to      │
│ File Transfer Paste Delay : ┌─┐ ticks (60ths of a second)            │
│                            │1│                                        │
│                             └─┘                                       │
│  ┌─────┐   FTP Client :                                              │
│  │ 📱  │                                                             │
│  └─────┘   ☒ Automatically log in     ☒ Automatically show file list │
│  Hosts     ☒ Use PORT commands        ☐ Transfer unknown file types as ASCII │
│         ⬇                                                            │
└──────────────────────────────────────────────────────────────────────┘
```

7. Close the Configuration dialog box by clicking the close box.

Downloading Files With TCP/Connect II

The previous chapter described how to configure and use Nuntius to read network news. The current version of Nuntius is included on the companion disks at the back of this book, and the latest version is always available from Ventana Online. The following steps illustrate the process of downloading any file with TCP/Connect II, using the Nuntius program and Stanford University's Macintosh archive (Info-Mac) as an example.

1. Launch TCP/Connect II by double-clicking on its icon.

2. Hold down the Option key and select the Anonymous Connect command from the FTP menu. The Open FTP session dialog box will be displayed, as shown in Figure 6-17.

Figure 6-17:
TCP/Connect II
Open FTP session
dialog box.

Open FTP session
Host name: Macintosh (Info-Mac) ▼
User name: anonymous
Password: ••••••••••••••••••
Host type: Automatic
(Cancel) [OK]

3. Select the Macintosh (Info-Mac) item from the Host name pop-up menu.

   ▨ Note that this step assumes that you added the Info-Mac FTP server to your Hosts configuration, as explained in the previous section. If you skipped that section, enter **sumex-aim.stanford.edu** in the Host name box and **anonymous** in the User name box.

Internet Cruise.

Internet Cruise is an interactive animation that provides an excellent overview of the Internet and the various Internet services. Internet resources are available, including ways to access them listed by state. The software program is available by FTP from mac.archive.umich.edu in the /mac/misc/documentation/ directory.

4. Click the OK button. You will be logged in to the root directory and the FTP window will appear, as shown in Figure 6-18.

Figure 6-18:
TCP/Connect II FTP
window.

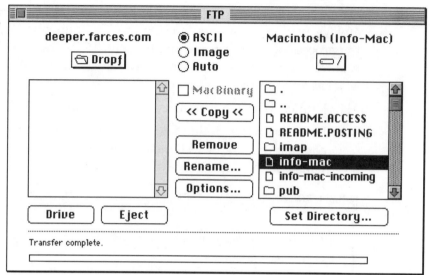

5. Click on the info-mac directory icon.

6. Click the Set Directory button. The Set directory to dialog box will appear, with the directory you selected in step 5 (info-mac in this example) shown in the text box, as seen in Figure 6-19.

Figure 6-19:
TCP/Connect II Set
directory to dia-
log box with info-
mac directory.

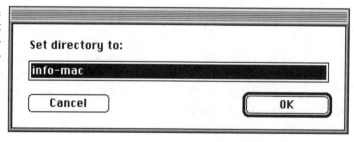

7. Navigate through the folder hierarchy on the remote FTP server by double-clicking on the appropriate folder icons within the scrolling list in the right portion of the window.

   ▪ In this example, double-click on the comm folder. This hierarchy of folders is known as a *pathname* and is written like this: /info-mac/comm/. The root directory is indicated by the first slash (/) character.

8. Locate the most recent version of the Nuntius file. As of fall 1994, the current version is 1.1.1d17 and the complete pathname is /info-mac/comm/nuntius-111d17.hqx. The FTP window should look like the example shown in Figure 6-20.

Figure 6-20: TCP/Connect II FTP window with Nuntius file highlighted.

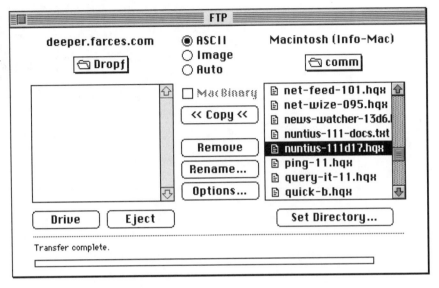

9. Click the << Copy << button. The file transfer will begin and its progress will be reported in the lower portion of the FTP window, as shown in Figure 6-21.

Ventana Online.

The latest versions of all of the software included on *The Mac Internet Tour Guide Companion Disks* can be downloaded via anonymous FTP from Ventana Online's FTP server at ftp.vmedia.com. See Appendix A for more information on the variety of resources available from Ventana Online's FTP and World Wide Web servers.

Figure 6-21:
TCP/Connect II
FTP window with
file transfer
in progress.

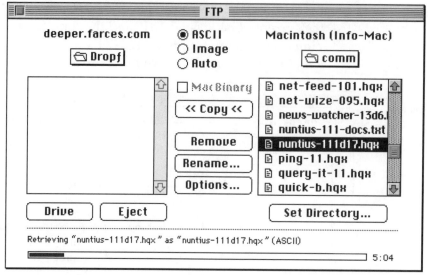

10. When the file transfer is complete, you can download additional files from the same FTP server by repeating steps 5–9 for each file. Feel free to browse among the other files available at this site and download any that interest you.

11. When you are finished transferring files, click the FTP window's close box. Your connection to the remote FTP server will be severed.

TCP/Connect II lacks the integrated ability to automatically un-decode BinHex files and expand compressed files that makes Fetch so painlessly easy to use. Thanks to the wizards at Aladdin Systems, you can automatically massage the Macintosh files you download using TCP/Connect II by simply dragging their icons over the StuffIt Expander icon until it is highlighted and then dropping them. It's almost painless and certainly easy to use, but not nearly as elegant as Fetch.

Famous Macintosh FTP archives.

Here are the most popular Macintosh-specific FTP sites. All accept anonymous logins, but be sure to use your full e-mail address—in the username@domain.top-domain format—as a password.

Domain Name	Directory
sumex-aim.stanford.edu	/info-mac/
mac.archive.umich.edu	/mac/
ftp.apple.com	/dts/
microlib.cc.utexas.edu	/microlib/mac/
ftp.funet.fi	/pub/mac/
ftp.lu.se	/pub/mac/
ezinfo.ethz.ch	/mac/

Here are the most popular Macintosh mirror FTP sites. A mirror site is an exact copy of another site. They are designed to relieve the heavy traffic in the major FTP sites. If you find that you can't log into one of the sites in the above listing, try one of these mirror sites.

Domain Name	Directory
archie.au	/micros/mac/
ftp.lth.se	/mac/
ftp.uni-kl.de	/pub/mac/
utsun.s.u-tokyo.ac.jp	/mac/info-mac/
wuarchive.wustl.edu	/systems/mac/
shark.mel.dit.csiro.au	/info-mac/

More information on these and other FTP sites is provided in Chapter 10, "Hot Spots on the Net."

Uploading Files With TCP/Connect II

Downloading files is just one side of the file transfer coin. You can also *upload*, or send, files to a remote FTP server using TCP/Connect II. If you have a file that you want to share with the rest of the world, consider uploading it (as long as there are no restrictions on its distribution) to your favorite FTP site. To upload files to a remote FTP server with TCP/Connect II,

1. Launch TCP/Connect II by double-clicking on its icon.

2. Hold down the Option key and select the Anonymous Connect command from the FTP menu. The Open FTP session dialog box will be displayed.

3. Select the FTP server where you want to log in from the Host name pop-up menu.

4. Click the OK button. You will be logged in to the root directory and the FTP window will be displayed.

5. Navigate through the folder hierarchy on the remote FTP server by double-clicking on the appropriate folder icons within the scrolling list in the right portion of the FTP window.

6. Locate the file you wish to upload by navigating through the folder hierarchy on your Macintosh by double-clicking on the appropriate folder icons within the scrolling list in the left portion of the FTP window.

7. Click on the name of the file you wish to upload in the scrolling list in the left portion of the FTP window.

8. Click the >> Copy >> button. The file transfer will begin and its progress will be reported in the lower portion of the FTP window.

9. When the file transfer is complete, you can upload additional files to the same FTP server by repeating steps 5–8 for each file.

10. When you are finished transferring files, click the FTP window's close box. Your connection to the FTP server will be severed.

Moving On

There are huge repositories of very interesting files scattered through-out the thousands of FTP servers available on the Internet. With a little perseverance—and more importantly, knowing where to look—you can use FTP to find files on just about any topic. There is an important Internet resource that can help you navigate many of the available FTP servers—its name is Archie, and you'll learn about it in Chapter 9, "Other Internet Resources."

One of the best ways to navigate quickly and effectively through the Internet is to use the University of Minnesota's Gopher, covered in the next chapter. When it comes to touring the Net, Gopher is a knowing native, helpful concierge and savvy travel agent, all rolled into one.

CHAPTER 7

USING GOPHER
Burrowing for Information

So far, our tour has covered the many strange languages and customs of the Internet, but we've barely scratched the surface of the vast resources the Net has to offer. And when navigating unexplored territories, even pioneers need all the help they can get. It's always a relief to find an amicable cab driver or savvy concierge who can clue you in to those great out-of-the-way spots where most tourists never venture. In this chapter, we'll explore how to use Gopher—the Internet's most sociable, well-connected pathfinder—to browse aimlessly or search specifically for everything from Russian poetry to local weather reports.

What Is Gopher?

Network news, e-mail, and FTP are great tools for specific tasks. As you've seen, it's simple enough to use a program like Eudora to dash off an e-mail message to someone, and it's a snap to use Nuntius to look for Macintosh-specific information in someplace like the comp.sys.mac newsgroups. Even finding and downloading a specific file from an FTP archive is a cinch if you're using Fetch. These programs and Internet resources are all specific tools for specific jobs.

But what if you don't know exactly what you're looking for, or only have a broad idea about a topic of interest? What if you just want to surf through the oceans of information available on the Internet? That's where Gopher comes in.

Gopher is one of the most powerful resources available to Internet users, and TurboGopher for the Macintosh is one of the most powerful implementations. Written by a team of programmers at the University of Minnesota, Gopher puts a menu-based interface on many of the Internet's resources, making moving from spot to spot on the Net as easy as picking options from a numbered list—and often easier.

Whole Earth 'Lectronic Link (WELL) Gopher.
The Whole Earth folks have put some of the best articles from the *Whole Earth Review* in a Gopher server. You'll find articles by Bruce Sterling, Stewart Brand and many others. This is one of the best information resources on the Internet. Access it by pointing your TurboGopher program at nkosi.well.sf.ca.us port 70.

If Gopher had been developed in California, instead of on the far edge of Minnesota, it might have been called Surfer. It's name comes from the University of Minnesota's mascot, the Golden Gopher. Information servers on the Internet that support access with the Gopher software are always called *Gopher sites*, *Gopher servers* or *Gopher holes*. The software's actual communication and database protocol is also referred to as *Gopher*. The program you run on your Mac to browse through Gopher holes is called *TurboGopher*.

What Can I Use Gopher For?

Gopher (the protocol) lets you burrow through information resources using a series of easy-to-navigate menus that appear as numbered lists. TurboGopher (the Mac program) lets you navigate through Gopher information resources using standard Macintosh file folders and icons. You can use TurboGopher on the Macintosh to navigate huge "dataspaces" by simply double-clicking the mouse button.

Gopher is best used as a browsing tool. It doesn't matter where an information resource you find with Gopher is physically located. As long as it is compatible with Gopher, it simply appears as another folder or icon in the hierarchy. You don't have to worry about IP addresses or even domain names with Gopher—when you find a resource you want to browse, just double-click on its folder.

Extensions to the Gopher protocol allow you to browse through different kinds of information resources—pictures, sounds, video, computer files—as well as text. Instead of groping around blindly through a series of interconnected servers, connecting and disconnecting each one in turn, you can use Gopher to wander aimlessly without worrying about the process of connecting and disconnecting. This chapter also explains how you can wander around through *Gopher-Spaces* (those areas that support the Gopher protocol) purposefully, as if you had a well-trained research librarian helping out.

Why Should I Use Gopher Instead of FTP?

Gopher is a *stateless* software program, making the most efficient possible use of network resources. Instead of keeping a connection to a remote site continuously open, Gopher opens a connection to initiate your request, closes the connection, and then reopens a connection to receive the host's response. By comparison, FTP maintains a continuous connection while you are browsing directories and transferring files. Many of the best archive sites restrict FTP access, while allowing unrestricted Gopher access. You can be a good Internet citizen by using Gopher whenever you can. Most of the major FTP archives also support Gopher access, and more Gopher servers are continually being added. Some sites support only FTP access, though, so it's important that you use the right tool for the job.

Using TurboGopher

The elegant simplicity of Gopher is that its developers didn't reinvent the wheel. They configured Gopher, and the TurboGopher software you use from your Mac, to take advantage of existing network conventions. When you use the TurboGopher application to log into a Gopher server and double-click on a network resource, TurboGopher automatically determines the right tool for the job. If you're accessing a computer file, it will be sent to you using FTP. If you double-click on an icon that represents a login resource, TurboGopher will automatically open a telnet session. It's all handled transparently.

Configuring TurboGopher

A copy of TurboGopher is included in on the companion disks that came with this book. The program is provided for evaluation purposes only. If you decide to continue to use TurboGopher, you must pay a $25 fee to the Regents of the University of Minnesota. The latest version of the TurboGopher software is always available from Ventana Online, as well as a number of FTP sites throughout the Internet.

International technical support in a flash.

North Americans take technical support for granted because the vast majority of software developers are based in the United States and Canada. International users are faced with a host of problems when they have technical questions. Many use the Internet as their sole avenue of support. Zviki Cohen of Israel is a good example:

"I'm from Israel, and I work and study at the Technion—Israel Institute of Technology. I use the Internet as an important tool to get support for my Macs. Last month, I was interested in buying some products. In America or Europe you can pick up a phone, dial a toll-free number and hear all about it. But here, when you are interested in a product the local salesman hasn't heard of (and there are plenty), you can forget about it.

"Well, not with the Internet. A few e-mail messages to the companies sorted out the problem, and I got a few suggestions for the products I needed. When I found a serious bug in a software program I bought, I didn't wait for the tech support people here to get me the answer. I got it myself the next day from the company's headquarters in the USA."

To configure TurboGopher,

1. Launch TurboGopher by double-clicking on its icon. Turbo-Gopher comes preconfigured for use with the University of Minnesota's Gopher server, and the program will automatically log into the "mother" Gopher and display both a Bookmarks window and a Home Gopher Server window, as shown in Figure 7-1.

Figure 7-1:
TurboGopher
initial display.

```
                           Bookmarks
              ════════════ Home Gopher Server ════════════
▼       Internet Gopher ©1991-1993 University of Minnesota.
   🗀  Information About Gopher                                  ⇧
   🗀  Computer Information
   🗀  Discussion Groups
   🗀  Fun & Games
   🗀  Internet file server (ftp) sites
   🗀  Libraries
   🗀  News
   🗀  Other Gopher and Information Servers
   🗀  Phone Books
   [?] Search lots of places at the U of M
   🗀  University of Minnesota Campus Information
                                                               ⇩
```

2. From the Setup menu, select the Configure TurboGopher command. The TurboGopher Configuration dialog box will be displayed as shown in Figure 7-2.

Figure 7-2:
TurboGopher
Configuration
dialog box.

```
                    TurboGopher Configuration

            Server name                        Port
        ┌──────────────────────────┐      ┌──────────┐
        │ gopher.tc.umn.edu        │      │ 70       │
        └──────────────────────────┘      └──────────┘
        ┌──────────────────────────┐      ┌──────────┐
        │ gopher2.tc.umn.edu       │      │ 70       │
        └──────────────────────────┘      └──────────┘

                         ( Cancel )   (   OK   )
```

3. If you want to continue to use the University of Minnesota's Gopher server as your home Gopher server, click the Cancel button, and skip to step 6.

   ■ There are other Gopher servers you can choose as your home server. Chances are your organization, campus or service provider offers a home server for your use.

- Some of the other Gopher servers are probably geographically closer to you and are less crowded than the University of Minnesota server.

- A list of popular Gopher servers is provided in Table 7-1 later in this chapter.

4. Enter the domain name of your home Gopher server in the upper Server name box, following the format shown in Figure 7-2.

5. Delete the domain-name entry in the lower Server name box.

- All Gopher servers use Port 70, so you should never need to change the Port settings in the TurboGopher Configuration dialog box.

6. Click the OK button. Your settings will be saved in a TurboGopher Settings file in the Preferences folder within your System Folder.

You've now configured TurboGopher for use with your home Gopher server. You can customize some aspects of TurboGopher with the following steps.

1. Launch TurboGopher by double-clicking on its icon. The program will automatically log into the home Gopher server you specified in the previous set of steps, and the Home Gopher Server and Bookmarks windows will be displayed.

2. From the Setup menu, select the Options command. The Options dialog box will appear, as shown in Figure 7-3.

Figure 7-3:
TurboGopher
Options dialog
box.

TurboGopher Options

- ☐ **Single Directory Window**
- ☐ **ISO Latin-1 characters**
- ☐ Extended Directory Listings

[Set...] Save text documents for: MacWrite II

Gopher Helper Applications

Gopher+ View	Mac Application	Mac Filetype
Application/mac-binhex40	DownLine	TEXT
Application/MacWriteII	MacWrite II	MW2D
Application/MSWord	Microsoft Word	WDBN
Application/PDF	Acrobat™ Exchange 1...	TEXT
Application/Postscript	MacWrite II	TEXT
Application/RTF	Microsoft Word	TEXT

[Change...] [Cancel] [OK]

3. Check the Single Directory Window check box if you want to prevent TurboGopher from using multiple windows. This is usually a good option only for users with very small screens or beginning users who might be confused by multiple windows.

4. If you want to use a text editor or word processor other than MacWrite II, click the Set button. A standard Open File dialog box will be displayed.

5. Double-click on the application file of the text editor or word processor you want to use to open text files downloaded with Gopher.

6. Modify the Gopher Helper Applications list to suit your needs by double-clicking on an item in the scrolling list. A modified Open File dialog box will be displayed, like the example for BinHex files shown in Figure 7-4.

Figure 7-4: TurboGopher Helper Applications selection dialog box.

Choose an application and Macintosh file type for Gopher File/hqx items.

[====] Desktop ▼

- ⊂ **Further**
- ⊂ **Intrepid**
- ☐ *Dropf*
- ◈ *Finger*
- ◈ *Netstat*
- ◈ **Stuff**
- ◈ **StuffIt Expander™**
- 🗑 Trash

[☐ ** ▼]**

⊂ **Further**

[Eject]

[Desktop]

[Cancel]

[**OK**]

[Clear]

7. Click on the program you want to use for the type of file you double-clicked. In this example, we double-clicked on the BinHex option, so in the new dialog box, we'll choose the StuffIt Expander icon. (StuffIt Expander is included on *The Mac Internet Tour Guide Companion Disks* and automatically decodes and decompresses files in BinHex format.)

StuffIt Lite.
StuffIt Lite is the shareware version of Aladdin Systems's commercial StuffIt Deluxe file compression utility. It's much less powerful than its commercial cousin, but it's still quite useful. With StuffIt Lite, you can create self-extracting archive files and segment files that are too large to fit on a single floppy disk. The program is available by FTP from mac.archive.umich.edu in the /mac/util/compression/ directory.

8. From the pop-up menu in the upper-right corner of the dialog box, select a file type for the Gopher helper application to recognize. In this case, accept the StuffIt Expander default selection.

9. Click the OK button.

10. Repeat steps 6–9 for each additional type of Gopher helper application you want to define.

   ■ If you don't have a favorite set of programs that you use to display graphics files, view QuickTime movies and read various word processor files, you can download from the "mother" Gopher server at the University of Minnesota some shareware TurboGopher helper applications that will perform these functions adequately.

11. Click the OK button in the Options dialog box. Your settings will be saved in the TurboGopher Settings file in the Preferences folder within your System Folder.

Browsing Information With TurboGopher

If you know how to use a Macintosh, you already know how to use TurboGopher. Navigate GopherSpace—that is, browse through those resources accessible via the Gopher protocol—by double-clicking on anything that looks interesting. It's as simple as that. Really!

■ Double-clicking on a folder opens that folder and displays its contents.

■ Double-clicking on a text file's icon displays the text of that document on your screen. If the file is larger than about 32k, you'll be prompted to save the file to disk.

- Double-clicking on a disk icon downloads that software resource to your Macintosh; you'll be prompted to save the file to disk.

- DOS-specific software resources are displayed with a PC icon.

- UNIX-specific software resources are displayed with a UX icon.

- Star icons represent graphics files—usually either GIF, JPEG or PICT format. Double-clicking on a star icon downloads the graphic image to your Macintosh and, optionally, launches a graphics program to display the image.

- Double-clicking on a terminal icon causes TurboGopher to open a telnet session using NCSA Telnet.

- To open a telnet session via TurboGopher, you must be running System 7 or higher and have NCSA Telnet installed on your hard drive. For more information, see "Using NCSA Telnet" in Chapter 9, "Other Internet Resources."

- Double-clicking on a question mark allows you to search within a database.

- Double-clicking on a phonebook icon allows you to search within a phonebook.

The politics of Gopher.

As the Internet changes from a network of networks dominated by research and education institutions to one populated by a mixture of commercial and academic users, the Internet community itself is experiencing great stress.

Nowhere has this stress been more apparent recently than with Gopher and the University of Minnesota's Gopher development team.

Gopher, like most other Net resources, had always been made available for use by anyone, free of charge. In March 1993, however, the Gopher team decided it was time to recover some of their expenses and issued a policy statement that requires commercial sites to pay an annual license fee for any Gopher servers they operate.

Under the new policy, the Gopher team is charging a first-year license fee of $5,000 per server ($2,500 license fee for succeeding years) to any commercial site accessible from the Internet that offers only free information. For commercial sites that sell their information or charge a fee for access, an additional license fee of 7.5 percent of receipts is required.

More▶

Needless to say, a firestorm erupted in the comp.infosystems.gopher newsgroup—the spot on the Net where users discuss Gopher-related issues. Charges of "greed killing Gopher" were fired off by angry Gopher users. People who had contributed to the development of Gopher publicly wondered how they would be compensated for their work. Others wondered how a taxpayer-supported University could attempt to turn a profit on something they had already been compensated for. A few days later, the University of Minnesota's Gopher development team posted an article stating that the Gopher server license fees would be "negotiable."

Within a month, a freeware Gopher-compliant server (software that would allow administrators to set up their own Gopher servers without using the University of Minnesota's software) was available on the Internet, with no license fee for commercial use. It was reportedly somewhat buggy, but it was available. The new software was provided by a consortium of programmers, in the spirit of the free flow of information that characterizes the Internet.

Should the University of Minnesota be able to charge license fees for what they used to give away free of charge? Sure. Gopher is theirs to do with as they please. That doesn't prohibit someone else from developing a competing product and giving it away. And in fact that's already happening.

Will greed kill Gopher? It's not very likely. Gopher has evolved and developed an identity of its own. Cream rises, and something as useful as Gopher isn't likely to fade away at this point.

But this "problem" isn't going to go away, and the commercialization of the Internet is something the researchers and academics are going to want to accept.

Downloading Files With TurboGopher

Some of the most popular FTP sites (especially archives rich with Mac software) on the Internet offer access to their files via Gopher. This means you can use TurboGopher instead of another program (like Fetch or TCP/Connect II) to download files from those sites.

To download files with TurboGopher,

1. Launch TurboGopher by double-clicking on its icon. It will automatically log into the home Gopher server you specified when you configured the program. The Home Gopher Server and Bookmarks windows will be displayed.

2. Navigate through GopherSpace by double-clicking on folder icons until you reach the Gopher server where you want to download files.

■ Stanford University offers Gopher access to its Info-Mac archive, and I'll use that Gopher server as an example for the rest of this section. The Info-Mac Gopher server is shown at the bottom of the window in Figure 7-5.

Figure 7-5:
TurboGopher window with Info-Mac Gopher server selected.

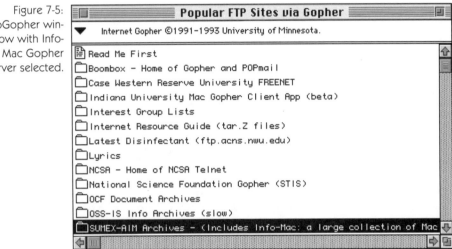

3. Double-click on the SUMEX-AIM Archives folder. TurboGopher will automatically log you into the Info-Mac Gopher server, and a new TurboGopher window will be opened, as shown in Figure 7-6.

Figure 7-6:
TurboGopher SUMEX-AIM Archives window.

■ The Info-Mac Gopher server offers a search function, as indicated by the first icon in the window. Not all Gopher servers provide a search function.

4. Double-click on the icon marked Search SUMEX-AIM archive titles. The Search dialog box will appear, as shown in Figure 7-7.

Figure 7-7:
TurboGopher
Search dialog box.

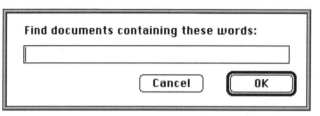

5. Enter a word or series of words contained in the name of the document or file you wish to download.

■ In this example, I'll search for a file that will allow me to turn my Macintosh into an FTP server. The name of the program I'm looking for is FTPd, so I'll enter that in the search box. (If I didn't know the exact name of the program, I could have entered just FTP, and TurboGopher would have displayed any files with FTP in their name, including FTPd.)

FTPd.

FTPd is a fully implemented FTP server and Gopher server for the Macintosh. Distributed as shareware, FTPd uses System 7's file sharing Users and Groups settings to restrict access to the server. MacBinary file transfer support is also provided. The program is also available by FTP from mac.archive.umich.edu in the /mac/util/comm/ directory.

6. Click the OK button. TurboGopher will search within the current Gopher server for documents and files matching the search words you specified. A new TurboGopher window will soon appear, displaying a list of the documents and files matching your search words, as shown in Figure 7-8.

Figure 7-8:
TurboGopher
window with
search results.

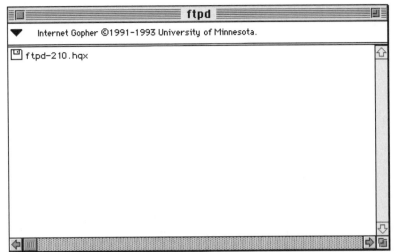

7. Double-click on the ftpd-210.hqx icon. Because it's a Macintosh file (indicated by the disk icon), a standard Save File dialog box will appear.

8. Navigate to the folder where you want to save the file, and click the Save button. As shown in Figure 7-9, TurboGopher will display a status window showing the progress of the download.

Figure 7-9:
TurboGopher
download status
window.

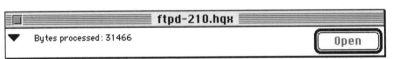

■ The status window will report when the download is complete, and the file will be automatically decoded from BinHex format and decompressed according to the helper application you specified when you configured TurboGopher.

9. Select the Quit command from the File menu.

Sometimes you just want to browse through a Gopher server, looking for interesting files and documents. This is a great way to keep up with what new software is available, and you'll often discover files and applications you might not have otherwise noticed.

To browse through the Info-Mac Gopher server,

1. Launch TurboGopher by double-clicking on its icon. It will automatically log into the home Gopher server you specified in the configuration process. The Home Gopher Server and Bookmarks windows will be displayed.

2. Navigate through GopherSpace by double-clicking on folder icons until you reach the Info-Mac Gopher server, as in Figure 7-5.

3. Double-click on the SUMEX-AIM Archives folder. TurboGopher will automatically log you into the Info-Mac Gopher server, and a new TurboGopher window will appear, as shown in Figure 7-6.

4. Double-click on the info-mac folder. A new TurboGopher window will appear, as shown in Figure 7-10.

Figure 7-10:
TurboGopher info-
mac Archive
window.

```
┌─────────────────────────────────────────────────┐
│ ▢       ══════════ info-mac ══════════        ▣ │
├─────────────────────────────────────────────────┤
│ ▼   Internet Gopher ©1991–1993 University of Minnesota. │
├─────────────────────────────────────────────────┤
│ 📄 00readme.txt                               ⬆ │
│ 📁 app                                        ▨ │
│ 📁 art                                          │
│ 📁 card                                         │
│ 📁 comm                                         │
│ 📁 cp                                           │
│ 📁 da                                           │
│ 📁 demo                                         │
│ 📁 digest                                       │
│ 📁 ex                                           │
│ 📁 fkey                                         │
│ 📁 font                                         │
│ 📁 game                                       ⬇ │
├─────────────────────────────────────────────────┤
│ ⬅ ▥                                         ➡ ▢ │
└─────────────────────────────────────────────────┘
```

5. Double-click on the folder icon that interests you, such as the comm (communications) folder, as shown in this example. A new TurboGopher window will appear, as shown in Figure 7-11.

Figure 7-11:
TurboGopher
/info-mac/comm
window.

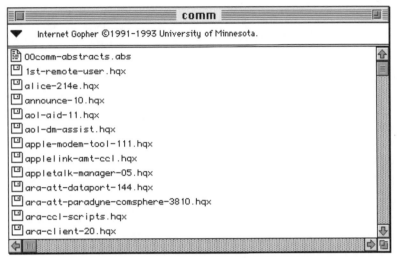

6. Double-click on the icon of any item that interests you. Short text files will be displayed in a window, while larger text files and application files will be transferred to your hard drive. For more information, see "Browsing Information With TurboGopher" earlier in this chapter.

7. Select the Quit command from the File menu.

Using TurboGopher Bookmarks

TurboGopher is great for browsing through lots of different kinds of information resources on the Internet. As you gain more experience prowling these resources, you'll probably start wishing for a way to leave a "crumb trail" to your favorite Gopher servers so you can easily find your way to them again. TurboGopher's Bookmark feature lets you define a trail to your favorite Gopher servers. This allows you to quickly and easily log into your favorite Gopher servers by double-clicking on a single icon.

To set Bookmarks within TurboGopher,

1. Launch TurboGopher by double-clicking on its icon. The program will automatically log into the home Gopher server. The Home Gopher Server and Bookmarks windows will appear.

2. Navigate through GopherSpace by double-clicking on folder icons until you reach the resource for which you want to create a Bookmark.

3. Select the resource's icon by clicking on it once. Figure 7-12 shows how you would select the Info-Mac archive before setting a book-mark for it.

Figure 7-12:
TurboGopher
window with
Info-Mac archive
selected.

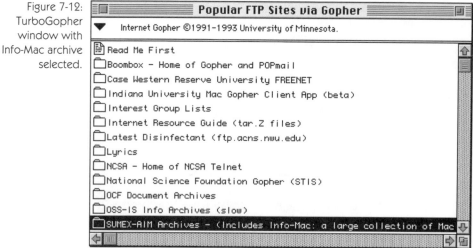

≡□≡	**Popular FTP Sites via Gopher**	≡▣

▼ Internet Gopher ©1991–1993 University of Minnesota.

📄 Read Me First
📁 Boombox – Home of Gopher and POPmail
📁 Case Western Reserve University FREENET
📁 Indiana University Mac Gopher Client App (beta)
📁 Interest Group Lists
📁 Internet Resource Guide (tar.Z files)
📁 Latest Disinfectant (ftp.acns.nwu.edu)
📁 Lyrics
📁 NCSA – Home of NCSA Telnet
📁 National Science Foundation Gopher (STIS)
📁 OCF Document Archives
📁 OSS-IS Info Archives (slow)
📁 SUMEX-AIM Archives – (Includes Info-Mac: a large collection of Mac

Chatting in real-time.

Two programs, Ircle and Talk, offer Mac users a couple of handy options for communicating on the Net in real-time.

Ircle is an Internet Relay Chat (IRC) client for the Macintosh that features a familiar Mac interface. Internet Relay Chat allows you to communicate with other individuals (or software agents) that are currently logged into an IRC server. All communication takes place in real-time.

Talk is a Macintosh implementation of the UNIX *talk* command. It allows you to communicate with UNIX users on the Internet in real-time. The best part is that they need never know you're using a Macintosh.

Both programs are available by FTP from mac.archive.umich.edu in the /mac/util/comm/ directory.

4. From the Gopher menu, select the Set Bookmark command. The Save Bookmark dialog box will appear, as shown in Figure 7-13.

Figure 7-13:
TurboGopher Save
Bookmark dialog
box.

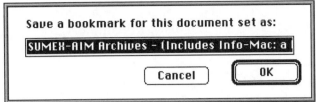

5. Enter a name for the Bookmark in the text box.

6. Click the OK button. The Bookmark will be added to the Bookmarks window, as shown in Figure 7-14.

Figure 7-14:
TurboGopher
Bookmarks
window with
several configured
Bookmarks.

Bookmarks
▼ Internet Gopher ©1991-1993 University of Minnesota.
📁 POPmail for Macintosh
📁 TurboGopher Distribution
📁 Info-Mac Archives (sumex-aim.stanford.edu)
📁 Weather Maps
📁 MRNet Gopher Server
📁 Univ. of Mich. Mac Archives
📁 EFF Gopher Server
📁 ACM SIGGRAPH
📁 O'Reilly & Associates
📁 West Georgia College
📁 Washington University Archive
📁 Boombox (Univ. of MN)
📁 Supreme Court Rulings (CWRU)

7. Select the Quit command from the File menu.

You can delete any Bookmark by clicking once on the item to select it and choosing the Delete Item command from the Gopher menu.

To use a Bookmark, just double-click on its icon in the Bookmarks window. TurboGopher will immediately log into that resource.

You can set Bookmarks for any resource within GopherSpace. For instance, if you're constantly downloading telecommunications software from the /info-mac/comm/ directory of the Info-Mac archive, you can set a Bookmark specifically for the comm folder. Double-clicking on the comm bookmark will cause TurboGopher to immediately log into Info-Mac's comm folder, rather than forcing you to navigate through the directory hierarchy. You don't even have to be logged into the Info-Mac Gopher server for this to work. Double-clicking on the comm bookmark will automatically log into the Info-Mac server and navigate instantly to the /info-mac/comm/ directory.

Sharing Bookmarks

TurboGopher's Bookmark feature is very useful for navigating GopherSpace efficiently. But the power of Bookmarks is increased by an order of magnitude when you realize you can *share* the Bookmarks you create with friends and associates. In effect, you can give someone else a cookie-crumb trail through enormous amounts of information to a single, specific spot on the Internet.

To export the Bookmarks you create,

1. Launch TurboGopher by double-clicking on its icon. It will automatically log into the home Gopher server you specified when you configured the program. The Home Gopher Server and Bookmarks windows will appear.

2. Click in the Bookmarks window to make it the active window.

3. From the File menu, select the Save as Bookmark File command. A standard Save File dialog box will appear.

4. Enter a name for the Bookmark file in the text box.

   ▪ The default name of Exported Bookmarks isn't very descriptive. Enter a name for the Bookmark file that is more representative of what it contains.

Locating e-mail addresses.

You can locate the e-mail address of anyone who has posted a network news article by sending the following message to mail-server@pit-manager.mit.edu (where *name* is the name of the person for whom you want an e-mail address):

    send usenet-addresses/*name*

5. Click the Save button. Your Bookmark file will be saved to your disk at the location you specified.

You can e-mail your Bookmark file to a friend or associate just as you would any other Macintosh file.

It's easy to use Bookmark files created by friends and colleagues. This is a handy way to find files and other resources on the Net that might otherwise take hours of hunting and searching. You launch TurboGopher and open a Bookmark file, which will open that file's Bookmarks only for that TurboGopher session, or you can import a Bookmark file, which will add that file's Bookmarks to your own resident Bookmark file.

To *open* a Bookmark file you have created yourself or received from someone else,

1. Launch TurboGopher by double-clicking on its icon. It will automatically log into the home Gopher server you specified when you configured the program. The Home Gopher Server and Bookmarks windows will appear.

2. From the File menu, select the Open Gopher Bookmark File command. A standard Open File dialog box will appear.

3. Double-click on the Bookmark file you want to open. The Bookmark file will be opened in a new TurboGopher window.

4. Double-click on any icon within the TurboGopher window to access its associated resource.

To *import* a Bookmark file you have created or received from someone else into your TurboGopher resident Bookmarks window,

1. Launch TurboGopher by double-clicking on its icon. It will automatically log into the home Gopher server you specified when you configured the program. The Home Gopher Server and Bookmarks windows will appear.

2. Select the Import Bookmarks command from the Gopher menu. A standard Open File dialog box will appear.

3. Double-click on the Bookmark file you want to import. The items contained in the external Bookmark file will be added to the items in your resident Bookmarks window.

4. Double-click on any icon within the Bookmarks window to access its associated resource.

Items from Bookmark files you import will remain part of your resident Bookmark file the next time you launch TurboGopher. Bookmark files you've opened will remain closed until you manually reopen them.

Remember, you can export and save your own Bookmark files for your own use. You might consider creating a main file that you use most often as your resident Bookmark file, which will be opened whenever you launch TurboGopher. But you can also create Bookmark files for specific areas of interest, like all your favorite Mac archives, or sites of social and political interest, or whatever tickles your fancy. That way, when you launch TurboGopher and you know you're only looking for Mac files, you can open your Mac sites Bookmark file and navigate directly from it, and so on.

Gopher Servers

There are a number of unique and information-rich sites throughout the Internet that support the Gopher protocol. The following table provides a listing of just a few of the more interesting Gopher servers available on the Internet.

Table 7-1: Some interesting Gopher servers.

Domain Address	Comments
boombox.micro.umn.edu	Gopher/TurboGopher distribution archive
sumex-aim.stanford.edu	Stanford University's Info-Mac archive
gopher.uis.itd.umich.edu	University of Michigan Macintosh archive
ashpool.micro.umn.edu	Washington University (St. Louis) archive
wx.atmos.uiuc.edu	Weather maps
gopher.eff.org	Electronic Frontier Foundation archive
ashpool.micro.umn.edu	Supreme Court rulings
gopher.well.sf.ca.us	Whole Earth 'Lectronic Link (WELL) archive
gopher.bu.edu	Boston metropolitan guide
sunsite.unc.edu	University of North Carolina archives
wiretap.spies.com	White House press release service
siggraph.org	Conference proceedings and materials from the graphics special interest group (SIGGRAPH) of the Association for Computing Machinery

Domain Address	Comments
ashpool.micro.umn.edu	Internet Resource Guide
hunter.cs.unr.edu	Search Gopherspace using Veronica
wcni.cis.umn.edu	Academic Position Network
gopher.cpsr.org	Computer Professionals for Social Responsibility archive
gopher.msen.com	Search for individuals on the Internet
akasha.tic.com	Sample issues of John Quarterman's *Matrix News Internet newsletter*
internic.net	Internet directory services
info.hed.apple.com	Apple's Internet Pilot program

TurboGopher Tips

TurboGopher is at the same time incredibly powerful and deceptively simple. Here are a few tips and tricks for using TurboGopher to its fullest potential:

- Eliminate screen clutter by holding down the Option key while double-clicking on a folder. This will re-use the current window instead of opening a new one.

- TurboGopher list views work the same way as the Mac's standard Open File dialog box: you can quickly type the first couple of letters of an item to automatically scroll to that item in the list.

- Download any file in its native state by holding down the Control key while double-clicking on the file icon. This is especially useful for downloading MS-DOS or UNIX files.

- Close all open TurboGopher windows by holding down the Option key while clicking any window's close box, just as in the Macintosh Finder.

- TurboGopher remembers the last question-mark icon you used to initiate a full text search. Holding down the Option key while double-clicking on a word within a document window results in a search for all documents containing the word on which you double-clicked.

- If you're a keyboard maven, you can speed your navigation through GopherSpace by using the Up and Down arrow keys to move up and down within lists. Pressing the Enter or Return key when an item is selected is equivalent to double-clicking on that item. The Right and Left arrow keys move to previous and next windows, respectively.

The Gopher of the future.

Although the original Gopher protocol is frozen, a forward-compatible protocol (called Gopher+) is currently in development by the Gopher team at the University of Minnesota.

Gopher is currently the tenth-most-used protocol in terms of number of connections and the ninth-most-used protocol in terms of the number of bytes transferred.

Gopher+ will support multiple views of a document, allowing information providers to include Microsoft Word, PostScript, RTF and ASCII text versions of a single document, for example.

Support for forms is also planned for inclusion in Gopher+. This will allow an interface to database back-ends as well as user information ranking, user-created items and directories, and conferencing systems.

Authentication support will be included in Gopher+. This will allow a finer control of information access on Gopher servers. Although it's not designed to replace public-key encryption or Kerberos, Gopher+ authentication will allow access to particular information to be granted on an individual basis. Interestingly, the password is never sent across the network, so security will also be enhanced.

Moving On

TurboGopher is one of the best ways to navigate parts of the Internet you aren't familiar with, because it sports a familiar interface of folders and icons. And because Gopher is a *stateless* software program, it makes the most efficient possible use of network resources.

In the next chapter we'll look at another great stateless program for navigating the Net: Ventana Mosaic. Mosaic is a powerful graphical "front end" used to browse the World Wide Web, an online hypertext system spanning most of the Internet. The Web is one of the most exciting developments in the evolution of the Net, so fasten your seat belts—our tour bus is about to drive straight into it.

CHAPTER 8

THE WORLD WIDE WEB
Browsing With Mosaic

"Surfing the Net" has become a cliché for describing many kinds of Internet activities. The World Wide Web (WWW) takes the analogy a step further. Using what are called *hypertext links,* you are able to jump from topic to topic, finding information, files, pictures, sounds and even movies, all with a single click of your mouse.

One of the best software tools for exploring the power of the World Wide Web is Ventana Mosaic, included on the companion disks at the back of this book. A little later in the chapter you'll get some hands-on experience using Mosaic, but first a little more background on the World Wide Web itself.

What Is the World Wide Web?

Created in 1989 by CERN, the European Center for Particle Physics in Switzerland, the World Wide Web is an online hypertext system spanning most of the Internet. The concept of *hypertext* (nonlinear textual presentation) was first promoted by computing theorist Ted Nelson in the early 1960s. Nelson's vision called for a global information structure that users could browse at will, freely investigating cross-referenced material. Typically, in a hypertext document the reader clicks a highlighted word or phrase (a *hotlink*) to access associated information that may be contained in the same file or in another file thousands of miles away.

The World Wide Web is a system of documents (called pages), linked together by a hypertext format. For instance, if you were reading a Web page on Rocky and Bullwinkle, and you noticed that a paragraph referred to the occasional appearance of Dudley Doright in the series, the words *Dudley Doright* might appear in a different color (usually blue) and underlined. Clicking anywhere on *Dudley Doright* would take you a related page giving the history of Dudley, and maybe a few pictures or a QuickTime movie of the hero.

These links also work to automate the FTP process. If you wanted to download a movie of Dudley in action from the Web, you would be able to do it easily. Instead of logging into ftp.hanna.barbera.com and navigating to the /pub/mounties/canadian/heroic/ directory, you would just click on a picture of Dudley or the words describing that particular movie file. The file is then automatically FTPed to your system.

If that were all (and it's not), WWW would be a wonderful thing. But the list of Amazing Stupendous Things That WWW Does goes on. You can use the Web to search for information via Gopher or WAIS. Most of the pages have embedded pictures that you can view while you read the page, and some even include QuickTime movies or sound.

The combination of text, still images, sound and motion pictures (or video) is commonly referred to as *multimedia*. This type of presentation has become popular in education and corporate training environments, as it presents information in a very interesting and entertaining format. Educators and trainers know the power of multimedia to speed learning and increase retention levels.

The combination of hypertext and multimedia, presented in a browsing context, is what is commonly defined as *hypermedia*. When we click on embedded graphics, video and sound objects in a compound-document Web page, we are fulfilling Ted Nelson's predictions for the future of global information systems. The current popularity of the World Wide Web attests to the lasting power of Nelson's concepts.

The Web analogy.

The reason the WWW is a Web, and not a cocoon, or knothole, or some other place an insect resides, is because the hypertext links form strands that connect the pages of the Web one to another. There may be hundreds of references to one document, and many other references from that page onward. The quickest route to a Web site is not necessarily a straight line, but the least number of links needed.

What Is Mosaic?

NCSA Mosaic, developed by the National Center for Supercomputing Applications at the University of Illinois, is a software "front end," or interface, used to access the World Wide Web. It was designed specifically to simplify navigation through the thousands (soon to be millions) of pages that constitute the Web. The software is free from NCSA, and can be downloaded via FTP at ftp.ncsa.uiuc.edu. The companion disks at the back of this book include a copy of Ventana Mosaic, a version of Mosaic enhanced for commercial use. The latest version of Ventana Mosaic is always available from Ventana Online (see Appendix A for more information about Ventana Online).

Browsing the Web With Mosaic

Mosaic will install from the companion disks with the other Internet applications. To start using it, just double-click the Mosaic icon when your Internet connection has been established. The first time you use Mosaic (and every time thereafter until you set up a new home page), the introductory page will appear, as shown in Figure 8-1.

Figure 8-1: The
introductory page.

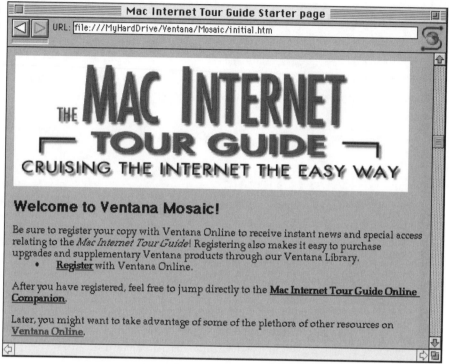

At this point, you really haven't connected to a location yet; the page shown in Figure 8-1 actually resides on your hard drive rather than on the Web. Go to the File menu, select Open URL, and enter the following into the text field: **http://www.ncsa.uiuc.edu/SDG/Software/Mosaic/NCSAMosaicHome.html**

Make sure you get the upper- and lowercase right, and don't insert any spaces. Click the OK button. After a few seconds, the NCSA Mosaic home page should appear (see Figure 8-2). Every Web server site has a *home page*, or main document. From this page you can jump to other resources by simply selecting the embedded hypertext links on the current page, indicated by colored, underlined text. If the home page doesn't appear, or you get a message saying that no connection could be made, make sure that you are properly hooked up to the Internet either by modem or direct connection, and that the connection is active.

Figure 8-2: The
NCSA Mosaic
home page.

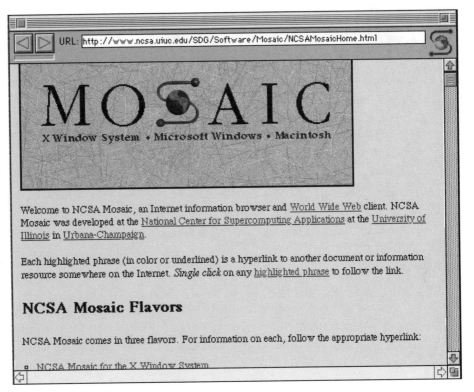

So that you don't have to type in that long URL again, select Add
current to hotlist from the Navigate menu. The next time you want to
access the Mosaic home page, all you will have to do is select Hotlist
from the Navigate menu (or just hit Command-H), choose NCSA
Mosaic Home Page from the list itself, and click the Go To button. The
hotlist is one of Mosaic's most powerful features, and you can add any
URL to it that you'd like.

What's a URL?

URL is short for Uniform Resource Locator. A URL is a notation system that lets you specify a document or other resource anywhere on the Internet. If you know a resource's URL, you can tell Mosaic to retrieve it.

A URL is divided into three parts. The first part specifies the resource type. For instance, the prefix http:// means that we are talking about a Web page, while the prefix gopher:// means that we're talking about a directory on a Gopher server. The second part of the URL specifies the network address of the machine on which the resource is located, as in www.ncsa.uiuc.edu. The last part of the URL specifies the exact path to the target resource. For instance, the Mosaic home page is located in the SDG/Software/Mosaic/ directory on the NCSA Web server.

Navigating in the Document Window

"Pages" in Mosaic can be any length. You can scroll through a page by clicking on the up or down arrow on the scroll bar at the right of the page window. If you resize your window, the text will automatically reflow. To customize the size of the window, drag the bottom right square around until the window is the new size.

To move quickly up and down through a document, use the navigational keys on your keyboard: Home, End, Page Up, and Page Down. Home will take you to the top of the page, End will take you to the bottom. Page Up will move you to the information above what you can currently see, while Page Down moves you down.

All About Links

As we have seen, links are the core of the WWW. A link is a word or phrase (sometimes a picture) that connects you to another page. Mosaic allows you to traverse these links simply by clicking on these words or phrases. Links appear as underlined text (pictures usually have informative captions describing the link). Links that you haven't clicked on yet appear as blue; links that you have taken already appear as green.

Mosaic remembers the links you have chosen from session to session, so you can follow previously explored links like a trail of bread crumbs to pages you'd like to revisit.

A Quick Tour Through the Web

This section contains a sample trip of exploration through the World Wide Web that you can follow along with. The top of each new Web page (and lower sections where applicable) is shown so that you can be sure you're in the right place.

We'll start at the home page shown above. One of the best places to begin exploring is at the Starting Points for Internet Exploration link, shown in Figure 8-3.

Figure 8-3: The Starting Points for Internet Exploration link.

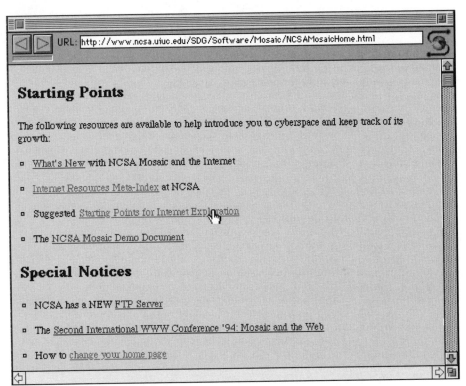

Click on the link. The bar or animated icon at the top of the window will indicate that the program is retrieving information. Shortly thereafter (the time it takes depends on your type of connection), the Starting Points page will appear, as shown in Figure 8-4.

Figure 8-4: The
Starting Points for
Internet
Exploration page.

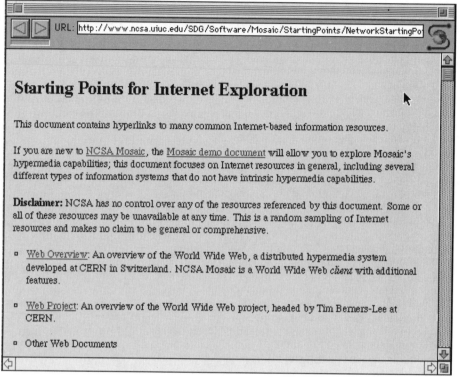

Scroll down this page just a little until you see the Information By Subject link, shown in Figure 8-5, and then click on that link.

Figure 8-5: Click on
the Information By
Subject link.

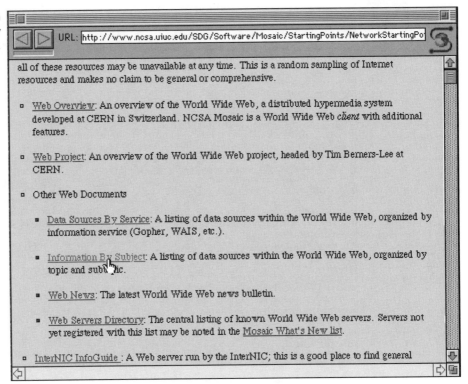

Once again, the bar or icon at the top will indicate that Mosaic is
looking for the next page. When it appears, it should look like this the
page shown in Figure 8-6.

Figure 8-6: The subject index of The WWW Virtual Library.

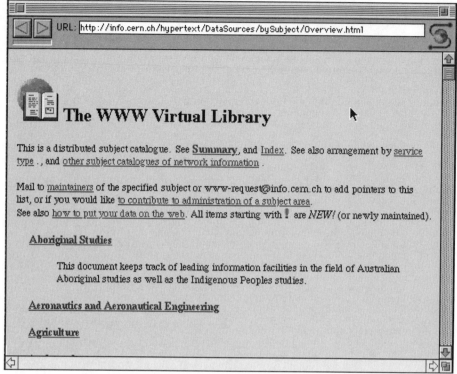

Once the page appears, take some time to scroll through the different subjects that are available. New categories are added all the time, so venture to this page as often as you can, looking for new entries. New entries are indicated by an exclamation point (!). In this particular case, let's scroll down to something fun: Games, shown in Figure 8-7.

Figure 8-7: The
Games link.

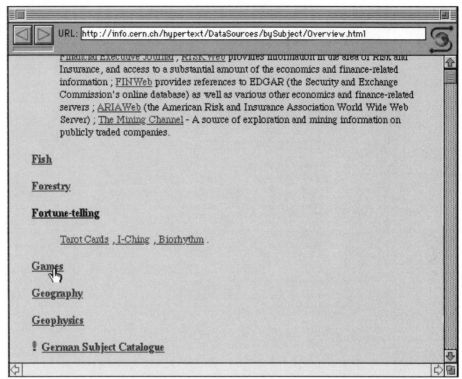

Click on the link, and after a few seconds the Games and Recreation page will appear, as shown in Figure 8-8.

Figure 8-8: The
Games and
Recreation page.

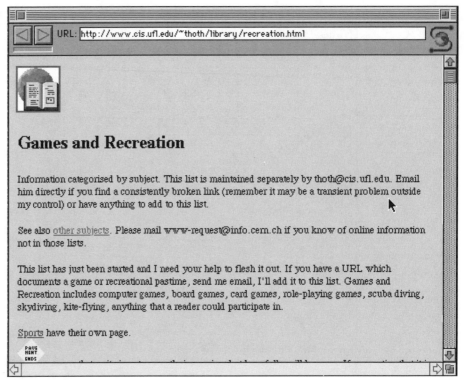

There are all sorts of categories and games, from computer games that can be played on the Internet to pages for card games, magic clubs and board games. Let's take a look at the Table Games section, and specifically the link for the Foosball archive, shown in Figure 8-9.

Figure 8-9: The
Foosball archive
link.

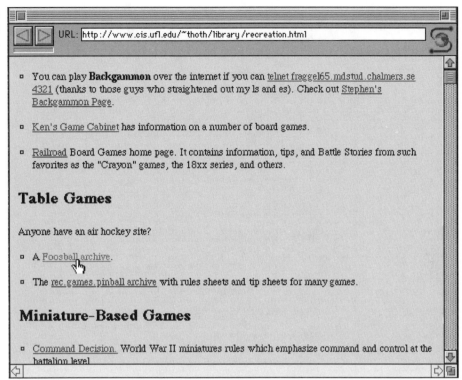

URL: http://www.cis.ufl.edu/~thoth/library/recreation.html

□ You can play **Backgammon** over the internet if you can telnet fraggel65.mdstud.chalmers.se
  4321 (thanks to those guys who straightened out my ls and es). Check out Stephen's
  Backgammon Page.

□ Ken's Game Cabinet has information on a number of board games.

□ Railroad Board Games home page. It contains information, tips, and Battle Stories from such
  favorites as the "Crayon" games, the 18xx series, and others.

Table Games

Anyone have an air hockey site?

□ A Foosball archive.

□ The rec.games.pinball archive with rules sheets and tip sheets for many games.

Miniature-Based Games

□ Command Decision. World War II miniatures rules which emphasize command and control at the
  battalion level.

Click on the Foosball archive link and the Foosball page will appear. This page contains a long list of files and subdirectories, as shown in Figure 8-10.

Figure 8-10: The
Foosball archive.

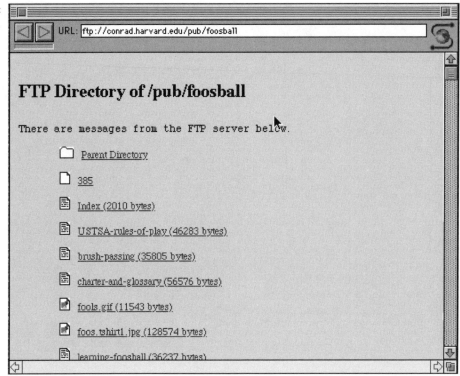

This page looks a bit different from the previous ones. That's because it is actually the directory listing from an FTP site. If you click on one of the files, it will be sent automatically to your computer using the FTP protocol that's built right into Mosaic.

But let's say you don't want to download one of these files. In fact, let's say you've just decided you're really not the slightest bit interested in foosball and would like to take a look at some of the other game options instead. To go back up a level, simply click the left arrow button near the top left corner of the window. You will be returned to the Games and Recreation page. You can keep backtracking through all the pages you've seen using this button and click on new links at any point. Similarly, the right arrow button will move you *forward* through the pages you've already visited.

There's another way to move back and forth through pages, too. Click on the Navigate menu at the top of the Mosaic window, select History, and then select The World Wide Web Virtual Library: Games and Recreation. Click the Go To button. You'll be taken back to the Games page, right where you clicked the Foosball link. (You can use that same menu to go back to any page you've visited during your current session. To get back to where you started, you can simply select Home from the Navigate menu.)

This time, let's take a look at one of the more colorful and interesting pages. Scroll down to Miscellaneous Hobbies and click on the Juggling Information Service link, shown in Figure 8-11.

Figure 8-11: The Juggling Information Service link.

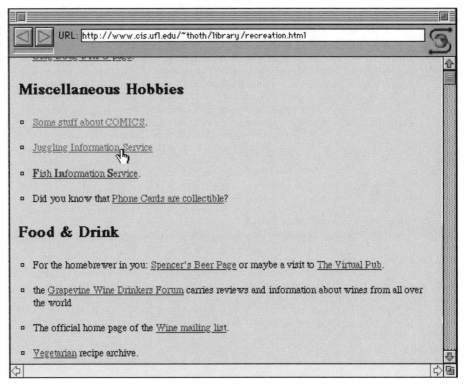

The Juggling Information Service page will appear next, as shown in Figure 8-12. As you scroll through the list of different options, you'll see that all sorts of things are available, like movies (in QuickTime or MPEG format), pictures, text files and even merchandise.

Figure 8-12: The
Juggling
Information
Service page.

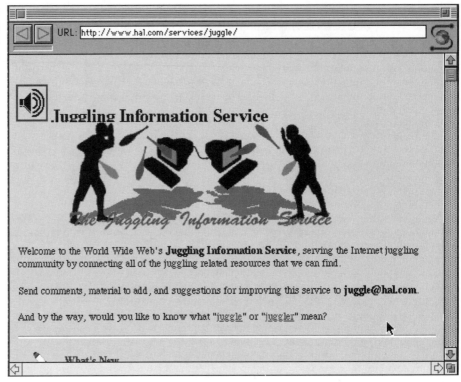

Retrieving Files

If you do decide to download a file, it couldn't be simpler. To demon-
strate the process, let's click on the Juggling Movie Theater link on the
Juggling page. The Juggling Movie Theater page is shown is shown in
Figure 8-13.

Figure 8-13: The
Juggling Movie
Theater page.

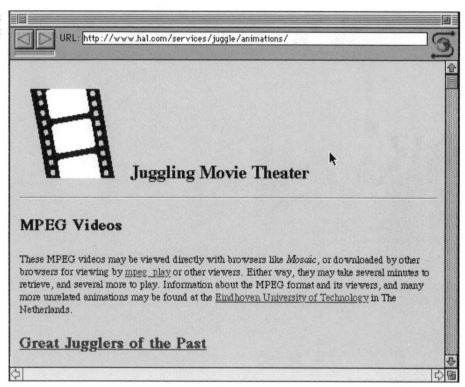

Scroll down to the Performances in the Modern Era link and click on it. The Performances in the Modern Era page will appear, as shown in Figure 8-14.

Figure 8-14: The
Performances in
the Modern Era
page.

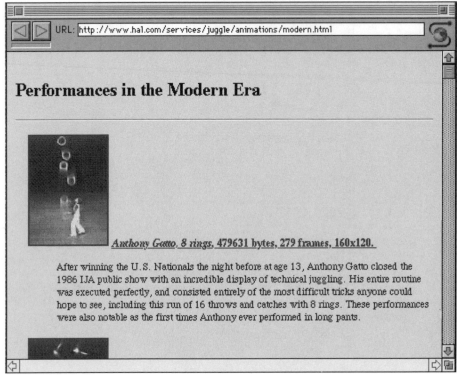

URL: http://www.hal.com/services/juggle/animations/modern.html

Performances in the Modern Era

Anthony Gatto, 8 rings, 479631 bytes, 279 frames, 160x120.

After winning the U.S. Nationals the night before at age 13, Anthony Gatto closed the 1986 IJA public show with an incredible display of technical juggling. His entire routine was executed perfectly, and consisted entirely of the most difficult tricks anyone could hope to see, including this run of 16 throws and catches with 8 rings. These performances were also notable as the first times Anthony ever performed in long pants.

To download any of the MPEG movies, just click on the picture next to the description. (**Note:** If you have a modem connection, one of these downloads could take several minutes.)

Unfortunately, the ease of retrieving files using Mosaic doesn't make up for the general difficulty of actually finding specific files. There is no search function within Mosaic to find a file, nor is there a guarantee that you will be allowed to download files (a few are password protected).

Ventana Online.

You can use Mosaic to access and download files from the Ventana Online Web server, where you'll find the latest versions of all the software included on *The Mac Internet Tour Guide Companion Disks*, as well as a variety of other interesting and valuable resources. See Appendix A for more information about Ventana Online (http://www.vmedia.com/) and *The Mac Internet Tour Guide Online Companion* (http://www.vmedia.com/mitg.html).

Going Directly to Another Page

If you know the URL of any WWW page, you can go there directly. For instance, to go directly to the Juggling page you can enter the URL for that page as follows:

1. In the File menu, select Open URL.

2. Enter **http://www.hal.com/services/juggle/** into the text field and click the OK button (or press Return).

Throughout the Internet, you'll see all sorts of WWW pages noted by various groups and individuals. Because these URLs are so long, the best thing to do is to highlight the URL and copy it, and then paste it into a document (I use the Stickies provided with System 7.5). This way you can't misspell or type incorrectly. Chapter 10, "Hot Spots on the Net," provides URL addresses for a variety of interesting Web pages.

Setting Up a New Home Page

Let's say you *always* use the subject index to explore the WWW. There's no need for you to have to click through two other pages to get there each time you use Mosaic. To remedy this situation, you can use the subject catalogue page as your home page. It's easy to make this change:

1. Go to the page you want to start as your new home page.

2. Highlight the URL that appears in the URL box at the top of the page, and copy it using the Edit menu or the Stickies.

3. Select Preferences from the Edit menu.

4. Place your cursor in the Home Page field and then paste in the URL you copied.

5. Click the OK button.

That's it. The next time you run Mosaic, you'll go directly to the subject catalogue page. If you ever want to use a different home page, just enter its URL in the Preferences dialog box.

Graphics & Modem Connections

If you're connected to the Internet via a SLIP or PPP modem connection, some of the pictures that are part of many WWW pages can take quite a while to reach your screen. In fact, some of them may not be worth the wait! It's easy to configure Mosaic so that it does not automatically download images: Select Preferences from the Edit menu, uncheck the Load Images Automatically check box, and click the OK button.

Accessing FTP Sites With Mosaic

Earlier we saw that Mosaic uses the FTP protocol to retrieve files with a single mouse click from whatever Web page you may be browsing. But you can also use Mosaic to download files directly from any of the literally thousands of servers that provide files to Internet users via the FTP protocol, even servers that may not have Web home pages. Typically you access FTP sites using a stand-alone FTP client program (such as Fetch, covered in Chapter 6, "Transferring Files"). But since Mosaic has FTP built right in, you may never need to use a stand-alone FTP program unless you want to upload files.

In the steps that follow we'll use Mosaic to get a file from the Ventana Online FTP server (see Appendix A for more information about Ventana Online).

1. When your Internet connection has been established, launch Mosaic by double-clicking its icon.

2. Select Open URL from the File menu.

3. Enter **ftp://ftp.vmedia.com/** in the URL field.

4. Hit the OK button to activate your URL selection. The directory listing for the Ventana Online FTP server will appear in the main Mosaic window after a few seconds.

5. Clicking on the name of a directory takes you to that directory, where other files will be listed. Clicking on a file name downloads that file. For now, click on the file welcome.msg. Since this is a text file, it will be displayed in the Mosaic window. If you select a file for downloading that is not a text file, the Transfer file to dialog box will appear, where you may specify a new name and location for the file. Click OK to proceed with the download.

Accessing Gopher Sites With Mosaic

What if you don't know exactly what you're looking for on the Net and want to refine your search carefully as you explore? What if you want to delve deeply into a particular area of interest? Typical Web sites may not help you, for often the links to other information are as arbitrary, whimsical and wild as the imagination of the page's author. Gopher servers, on the other hand, serve up information in tidy hierarchical menus and submenus, sticking to a subject and presenting it in top-down outline format. With HTML documents you leap rapidly from peak to peak; using Gopher, you follow logically related information trails. There is a time and place for both methods, and fortunately Mosaic supports them both.

Gopher servers are usually accessed with specialized Gopher client programs (such as TurboGopher, covered in Chapter 7, "Using Gopher"), but Mosaic makes extra software unnecessary. Mosaic can log onto a Gopher server and then present you with the information so that it looks very much like any Web page. Menu items are blue like other Web links, and clicking on them brings up the appropriate submenus. Let's give it a try using the WELL Gopher as an example. The WELL (Whole Earth 'Lectronic Link) is a large information service known for the variety of its online forums and the lively interactions of its users, but it also maintains a very interesting Gopher site. To begin exploring the WELL Gopher site,

1. With your Internet connection established, launch Mosaic by double-clicking its icon.

   ■ **Note:** For the purposes of this exercise, it doesn't matter what Web page is currently displayed.

2. Select Open URL from the File menu. The Open URL dialog box will appear.

3. Type **gopher://gopher.well.com/** in the URL field and click OK. In a few seconds the top level menu of the WELL Gopher appears.

   ■ Notice that when you connect to a Gopher server, virtually all the text in the Mosaic window consists of hotlinks.

4. Click the top menu item, About this gopherspace. A new submenu appears.

5. Click the top item, What is this place? (The basic story). This time a text file appears.

6. After reading the file, use Mosaic's Back button to return to the top-level WELL Gopher menu. From there you can begin to explore many different areas. Feel free to browse. The WELL Gopher is especially known for its information on media, communications and cyberpunk literature.

Although every Gopher site looks about the same in terms of structure, the content varies greatly. There are Gopher sites that specialize in just about any academic field you can think of, from art to astrophysics. In addition there are some Gopher sites that are just plain fun. Chapter 10 covers many Gopher sites of particular interest.

Building Your Own Web Pages

Now that you've traveled the Web and seen how simple it is, you may want to start creating your own Web pages. All Web pages are written in a language called HTML (HyperText Markup Language), a subset of SGML (Standard Generalized Markup Language, a system designed for typesetting and document page description). HTML is simply ASCII text with embedded codes representing instructions for the proper display of that text. The most basic HTML commands instruct the Web browser client program regarding the display of the information (what size and style of type, etc.).

More importantly, HTML commands can include display information and links to other data types (video, graphics and audio) and even other servers. This is the real power of the Web—its ability to let you access an amazingly wide variety of information types, across the entire Internet, with a click of the mouse.

A good starting point for HTML authoring is creating a local home page for yourself—a file on your hard drive that's loaded when you start Mosaic and that contains some of your favorite links. After you feel comfortable with your authoring skills, you may want to set up your own server, or at least your own home page area on one. If you have access to a server site, it's a relatively simple matter. Some SLIP/PPP service providers even let you set up Web pages on their system as part of a shell account.

Chapter 8: The World Wide Web

I have found that the best way to start learning the HTML techniques for creating Web pages is to study the content and structure of the pages you visit. You can look at the source code for the page you're on simply by selecting View Source from Mosaic's Edit menu. The dialog box that pops up even lets you save the source under a different file name on your own system. You can then use it as a template for your new HTML file. You can edit it in the Note Pad or any other text editor. There are even some special editors designed specifically for automating the process of applying HTML tags to text. Mosaic even lets you preview or test any HTML documents you create. To view a local HTML file in Mosaic, select Open Local from the File menu.

HTML files on most Web servers have the extension HTML. If you do not use the HTML extension, Mosaic and other browsers will not recognize your files as valid HTML pages.

There are several excellent HTML reference areas online, as shown in Table 8-1. These pages will teach you the basics of HTML authoring.

Table 8-1: Popular HTML references.

Site	URL
CERN HTML Reference	http://info.cern.ch:80/hypertext/WWW/MarkUp/MarkUp.html
Peter Flynn's How to Write HTML	http://kcgl1.eng.ohio-state.edu:80/www/doc/htmldoc.html
Dr. Ian Graham's Guide to HTML	http://www.utirc.utoronto.ca/HTMLdocs/NewHTML/html

If you want to start with more general information regarding the World Wide Web (straight from the horse's mouth), the best resource is the CERN Web server (http://info.cern.ch/). CERN engineers developed the Web, and this is a great clearinghouse for software information.

Moving On

This completes our brief introduction to the vast expanses of the World Wide Web, and to the Mosaic software used for navigating and browsing through it. You are now ready to set out on your own, leaping across cyberspace and blazing pathways not yet trod upon. On the Web there are as many ways to get from here to there as there are users, and you'll start to realize that the map you're following is really the map of the way you think.

While previous chapters of this book have focused on the most widely used programs and most frequently visited spots on the Internet, the next chapter will take a look at some of the smaller, yet still important, Internet resources. You'll learn about telnet, Finger, WAIS and Archie, as well as a couple of organizations—the Electronic Frontier Foundation and the Internet Society—whose actions have repercussions for every Internet user.

CHAPTER 9

OTHER INTERNET RESOURCES

Geez, What Is All This Stuff?

By this point in our tour, you're an old pro at cruising the Internet. You've learned the terrain of the network, the language and customs of its inhabitants and the quickest routes to the information you need. Yet there are still dozens of helpful but lesser-known resources that can make your time online more productive and enjoyable. For this last leg of our tour, we're loading up the bus for a final loop around the outer fringe of the Net. We'll be moving pretty fast, so climb aboard and hang on.

For those who use Macintosh computers on the Internet, electronic mail, network news, FTP, Gopher and Mosaic are some of the most widely used resources. For non-Macintosh users, telnet is likely the most commonly used Internet resource. Macintosh users enjoy task-specific software programs that make telnet less necessary on the Internet. But some specialized applications require the use of telnet. This chapter offers a look at telnet, as well as some of the many organizations and resources available via the Internet. We'll also cover some of the less commonly used Macintosh software tools available for use on the Internet.

What Is Telnet?

Using telnet, you can log into other computers on the Internet in an interactive, command-line mode. You use telnet to access experimental services, library card catalogs, weather reports and various other specialized databases. If you have a UNIX account on another computer on the Internet, you use telnet to log in remotely to your account on that computer.

In the early days of the Internet, telnet was one of the few tools available to the infonaut. Today, many of the services available by telnet also provide an alternative method of access, like WAIS (discussed later in this chapter), Gopher (covered in detail in Chapter 7, "Using Gopher") or WWW (covered in Chapter 8, "The World Wide Web"). Although more and more telnet services are becoming accessible via other methods, some Internet services still require a telnet connection.

Using NCSA Telnet

NCSA Telnet is a freeware application program for the Macintosh that lets you take full advantage of the telnet protocol. It is available by anonymous FTP from ftp.ncsa.uiuc.edu in the /Telnet/Mac/ directory. Extensive documentation is also available in the same directory.

Configuring NCSA Telnet

Before you can use NCSA Telnet to log in remotely to another computer on the Internet, you must configure the program for use with your domain. NCSA Telnet can be customized in many different ways, but this section provides only the configuration information necessary to establish a remote login connection.

To configure NCSA Telnet for basic use,

1. Launch NCSA Telnet by double-clicking its icon.

2. From the Edit menu, select Preferences, and then select FTP Users. Click the New button, and the dialog box shown in Figure 9-1 will appear.

Vendor e-mail addresses.
One site on the Internet offers a collection of e-mail addresses, BBS numbers and fax numbers for more than 250 Macintosh software and hardware vendors. The list is provided in Microsoft Word, Microsoft Excel and tab-delimited text formats. It's available by FTP from mac.archive.umich.edu in the /mac/misc/documentation/ directory.

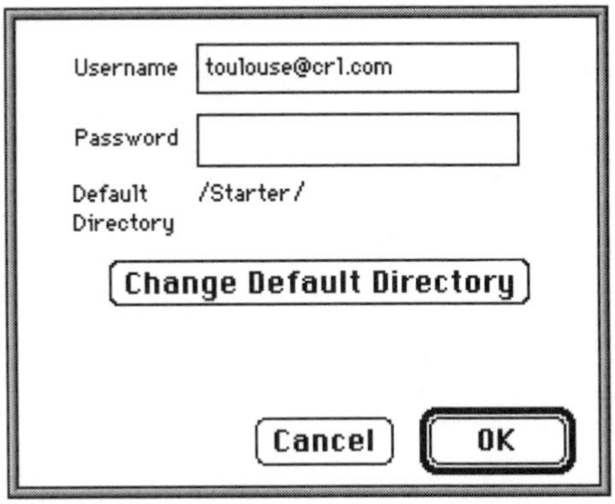

Figure 9-1:
NSCA Telnet
User Preferences
dialog box.

Username	toulouse@crl.com
Password	
Default Directory	/Starter/

Change Default Directory

Cancel   **OK**

3. In the Username box, enter your username and domain—in the username@domain.top-domain format—and click OK. NCSA Telnet is now configured for basic use.

For information on customizing the NCSA Telnet program, see the extensive NCSA Telnet User Guide (available by anonymous FTP from ftp.ncsa.uiuc.edu in the /mac/ directory).

Opening an NCSA Telnet Session

You can use telnet to access an Internet resource or archive in much the same way you might use Gopher or FTP. To initiate a remote login session with NCSA Telnet,

1. Double-click on the NCSA Telnet icon to launch the program.

2. Select the Open Connection command from the File menu. A Connection dialog box will be displayed, as shown in Figure 9-2.

Figure 9-2: NCSA Telnet Connection dialog box.

| Host/Session Name | nowhere.loopback.edu ▾ |
| Window Name | |

☐ **FTP session (⌘F)**
☐ Authenticate (⌘A)
☐ Encrypt (⌘E)

[Cancel] [**Connect**]

3. In the Host/Session Name box, enter the domain name—in the domain.top-domain format—for the host you want to log into.

   ▪ This exercise will use the weather information available from the University of Michigan's Weather Underground as an example, so if you're following along, enter **downwind.sprl.umich.edu 3000** in the Host/Session Name box. Alternatively, several other telnet resources—including online library card catalogs, Supreme Court rulings and major league baseball schedules—are mentioned in Chapter 10, "Hot Spots on the Net."

4. Optionally, enter a name for the telnet window to be opened in the Window Name box.

   ▪ Window names aren't of much use in a single connection, but they're very useful if you open more than one connection at a time.

5. Click the OK button. NCSA Telnet will establish a connection to the host you specified, and a Session window will be opened, as shown in Figure 9-3.

Figure 9-3: NCSA
Telnet Session
window.

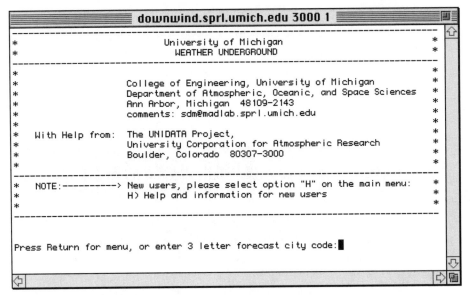

```
╔══════════════════ downwind.sprl.umich.edu 3000 1 ═════════════════╗
--------------------------------------------------------------------
*                          University of Michigan                  *
*                          WEATHER UNDERGROUND                      *
--------------------------------------------------------------------
*                                                                   *
*                College of Engineering, University of Michigan     *
*                Department of Atmospheric, Oceanic, and Space Sciences *
*                Ann Arbor, Michigan  48109-2143                    *
*                comments: sdm@madlab.sprl.umich.edu                *
*                                                                   *
*    With Help from:  The UNIDATA Project,                          *
*                     University Corporation for Atmospheric Research *
*                     Boulder, Colorado  80307-3000                 *
*                                                                   *
--------------------------------------------------------------------
*    NOTE:----------> New users, please select option "H" on the main menu: *
*                     H> Help and information for new users         *
*                                                                   *
--------------------------------------------------------------------


Press Return for menu, or enter 3 letter forecast city code:█
```

■ Note that some hosts may prompt you for a terminal type (the University of Michigan's Weather Underground service doesn't). Sometimes there is a menu selection available, but many times there is simply a TERMINAL prompt. NSCA Telnet emulates a VT102 terminal by default, so you can enter **VT100** (or **VT102**) at the prompt. Almost every host will support a VT102 terminal.

■ Note that if you are logging into a remote host on which you have an account, you may have to set the terminal type yourself. For a UNIX host, using the C shell, enter **set term=vt100;tset** at the command prompt. For a VAX/VMS host, enter **set term /inq** at the command prompt.

6. You can navigate through the choices and information on the host by entering commands and menu selections at the command prompt.

■ Menu selections are usually self-explanatory. The commands available to you vary from host to host; refer to each specific host's documentation for an explanation of the commands that may be available.

7. Enter **exit** or **logout** at the command prompt to log out, ending the remote session. Alternatively, select the Close Connection command from the File menu. The Session window will disappear when the connection is closed.

Using the TCP/Connect II Telnet Module

InterCon's popular commercial Mac Internet software, TCP/Connect II, includes a Telnet module that provides more terminal emulations than NCSA Telnet. Use TCP/Connect II's Telnet module to log into other computers on the Internet in an interactive, command-line mode.

Configuring the TCP/Connect II Telnet Module

Like NCSA Telnet, TCP/Connect II can be customized in many different ways. This section provides only the configuration information necessary to establish a basic remote login connection.

To configure TCP/Connect II's Telnet module for basic use,

1. Launch TCP/Connect II by double-clicking on its icon.

2. From the Edit menu, select the Configure command. The Configuration dialog box will appear.

3. Click on the Hosts icon in the scrolling list of configuration items at the left side of the window. The Hosts Configuration panel will be displayed, as shown in Figure 9-4.

Figure 9-4: TCP/Connect II Hosts Configuration panel.

	TCP/Connect II Configuration
General	— Default — Apple (A/UX Support) Apple (Cambridge) Baseball Schedules (Telnet) Bucknell (Telnet/Knowbot)	Appalachian State CWIS (Telnet) Apple (Bric-a-Brac) Apple (General Archive) Biosphere Newsletter CARL (Telnet)	New... Rename... Delete

IP Addresses:

Full Domain Name:

Operating System: CPU Type:

RWIN:

Paste Style: ○ Full Speed ● By Line ○ Blocked to
Paste Delay: 1   ticks (60ths of a second)

FTP Client:
☒ Automatically log in   ☒ Automatically show file list
☒ Use PORT commands   ☐ Transfer unknown file types as ASCII

Network

File Transfer

Hosts

4. Click the New button. A dialog box will appear, prompting you to enter the name of the host.

Note Pad II

Note Pad II is a replacement for Apple's standard Note Pad desk accessory. This desk accessory has up to 35 pages for notes, multiple notepad files, a Find command, a ruler and handles styled text. It's available by FTP from mac.archive.umich.edu in the /mac/system.extensions/da/ directory.

5. Enter a reference name for the host and click the OK button. A new entry will be created in the Hosts scrolling list.

■ This example in the next section will use a specific host to log in remotely to the Library of Congress card catalog. Again, you can choose another telnet site from the list of resources in Chapter 10.

6. Enter **dra.com** in the Full Domain Name box. Alternatively, enter **192.65.218.43** in the IP Addresses box. The entry to log in remotely to the Library of Congress card catalog should look like the example in Figure 9-5.

Figure 9-5: TCP/Connect II host entry for Library of Congress card catalog.

TCP/Connect II Configuration
Grateful Dead Archive II   Internet Mail Guide   **New...**
Internet Services   InterNIC (Directory)   **Rename...**
Law Library (Telnet)   Libraries (Telnet)   **Delete**
Library of Congress (Telnet)   Lyrics Archive
Macintosh (Info-Mac)   Macintosh (Sounds/Rochester)

General

IP Addresses: 192.65.218.43

Full Domain Name: dra.com

Operating System: CPU Type:

RWIN:

Network

Paste Style: ○ Full Speed ● By Line ○ Blocked to

Paste Delay: 1   ticks (60ths of a second)

File Transfer

FTP Client:

☒ Automatically log in   ☒ Automatically show file list

☒ Use PORT commands   ☐ Transfer unknown file types as ASCII

Hosts

7. Click on the Sessions icon in the scrolling list of configuration items. The Sessions Configuration panel will appear, as shown in Figure 9-6.

Figure 9-6:
TCP/Connect II
Sessions Config-
uration panel.

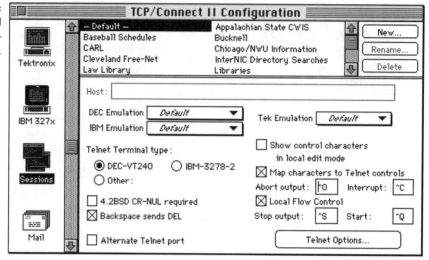

8. Click the New button. A dialog box will appear, prompting you to enter the name of the host.

9. Enter a reference name for the host (something that describes the contents of that resource, for instance) and click the OK button. A new entry will be created in the Hosts scrolling list.

   ■ The example in the next section will use a specific host to log in remotely to the Library of Congress card catalog.

10. From the Host pop-up menu, select the host you defined in step 6.

11. Close the Configuration dialog box by clicking the close box.

Opening a TCP/Connect II Telnet Session

Once you've configured TCP/Connect II, you can use it to access telnet sites via remote login just as you do with NCSA Telnet. To initiate a remote login session with TCP/Connect II,

1. Launch TCP/Connect II by double-clicking on its icon.

2. From the Terminal menu, select the Connect command. The Terminal Connect dialog box will appear, as shown in Figure 9-7.

Figure 9-7:
TCP/Connect II
Terminal Connect
dialog box.

```
┌─────────────────────────────────────────────┐
│              Terminal Connect                 │
├─────────────────────────────────────────────┤
│  Session Name   entropy.farces.com      ▼    │
│                                               │
│  Window Name    ┌─────────────────────────┐  │
│                 └─────────────────────────┘  │
│  ( Cancel )                    ┌───────────┐  │
│                                │    OK     │  │
│                                └───────────┘  │
└─────────────────────────────────────────────┘
```

3. Select the Library of Congress session you created in the "Configuring the TCP/Connect II Telnet Module" section from the Session Name pop-up menu.

4. Optionally, enter a name for the telnet window to be opened in
   the Window Name box.

   ▪ Window names aren't of much use in a single connection, but
     they're very useful if you open more than one connection at a
     time.

5. Click the OK button. TCP/Connect II will establish a connection
   to the host and a new Telnet Session window will be opened, as
   shown in Figure 9-8.

Figure 9-8:
TCP/Connect II
Telnet Session
window.

```
┌────────────────────────────────────────────────────────────┐
│ ▣□            Library of Congress                       □▣ │
├────────────────────────────────────────────────────────────┤
│ Data Research Associates, Inc.              Guest Access  ▲ │
│                                                            │
│ Select a command option from the following list.  Enter   │
│ the code between the <> characters and press the <RETURN>  │
│ key after entering the command.                            │
│                                                            │
│     <A>uthor         To find authors, composers,           │
│                      performers, illustrators,             │
│                      conferences, and corporate authors.   │
│                                                            │
│     <T>itle          To find a work by title, or generic   │
│                      title.                                │
│                                                            │
│     <EX>it           To logoff                             │
│     <N>ext page      To do other types of searches         │
│     <NEW>            Read what's NEW in this catalog        │
│                                                            │
│     Records in this database orginating with the Library   │
│     of Congress are copyrighted by the Library of Congress │
│     except within the U.S.A.                               │
│                                                            │
│     This service is not affiliated with the Library of     │
│     Congress.                                              │
│                                                            │
│     Mail comments, or suggestions to CATALOG@DRA.COM       │
│                                                            │
│ Enter your command or search below and press the <RETURN>  │
│ key.                                                     ▼ │
│ >> █                                                       │
│ ◁                                                      ◁▷▣ │
└────────────────────────────────────────────────────────────┘
```

■ Note that some hosts may prompt you for a terminal type (the Library of Congress card catalog doesn't). Sometimes there is a menu selection available, but many times there is simply a TERMINAL prompt. TCP/Connect II emulates a VT102 terminal by default, so you can enter **VT100** (or **VT102**) at the prompt. Almost every host will support a VT102 terminal.

■ Note that if you are logging into a remote host on which you have an account, you may have to set the terminal type yourself. For a UNIX host, using the C shell, enter **set term=vt100;tset** at the command prompt. For a VAX/VMS host, enter **set term /inq** at the command prompt.

6. You can navigate through the choices and information by entering commands and menu selections at the command prompt.

■ Menu selections are usually self-explanatory. The commands available to you vary from host to host; refer to each specific host's documentation for an explanation of the commands that may be available.

7. Enter **exit** or **logout** at the command prompt to logout, ending the remote session. Alternatively, click the Telnet Session window's close box to end the remote session. The Telnet Session window will disappear when the connection is closed.

Knowbots

Knowbots are knowledge robots—or at least that's the theory behind them. Think of them as electronic librarians that can help you find what you're looking for when you don't know where to look. Currently, Knowbots are used mostly for looking up Internet addresses, but the potential for using Knowbots for other purposes is very exciting. In theory, you should be able to send a Knowbot into the Internet with a set of search criteria. When it finds sources for the information you're looking for, the Knowbot would return with the information it finds.

CTerm.

CTerm is an IBM 3270 terminal emulator—Macintosh software that mimics the functions and commands of a particular piece of hardware. Some Internet services require IBM 3270 terminal emulation. CTerm requires System 7 (or higher) or the Communications Toolbox with System 6. The program is available by FTP from mac.archive.umich.edu in the /mac/util/comm/ directory.

Unfortunately, I've never been able to log into a site where the Knowbots live, and the general consensus of those on the Net is that Knowbots aren't quite ready for prime time.

Netfind

Netfind is a program that searches certain databases to help you find an e-mail address. It's not very easy to use, and requires that you log in remotely using telnet, but Netfind can be useful when other options prove fruitless.

To use Netfind to locate someone's e-mail address,

1. Use NCSA Telnet or TCP/Connect II to log into bruno.cs.colorado.edu.

2. At the login prompt, enter **netfind** and press Return.

3. Select the Search item from the menu.

4. At the prompt, enter the name and general location (called *keys*) for the person you're looking for.

   ■ For example, let's say you're trying to find the e-mail address of your pal, Wanda Caldwell, at the University of Georgia. You think she might have "wanda" as part of her address, but it's a pretty good bet that she'll have "caldwell" in her address, so you would enter **caldwell uga edu** at the prompt. A list of people named Caldwell at the University of Georgia will be displayed, and you can select the entry that matches the person you're looking for.

5. Select the Exit item from the menu.

The key to working with Netfind is to learn how to conduct searches that are neither too vague nor too specific. If you enter a search that is too vague—like **Caldwell Georgia**—the search will return too many possible choices. Conversely, if you enter a search that is too specific—like **W_Caldwell peachnet uga edu**—the search will yield no results.

Finger

Finger is a useful program for searching the user log on a computer connected to the Internet. This allows you to find someone's e-mail address, provided you know the name of the computer he or she uses.

Peter Lewis has written a shareware Finger program for the Macintosh. You can download it by FTP from the Info-Mac archive at Stanford University (sumex-aim.stanford.edu) in the /info-mac/comm/ directory. The file name is finger1.35.sit.hqx.

The word "Finger"—like many of the other Internet terms including "FTP" and "telnet"—is used as both a noun and a verb. You use the word "Finger" to refer to the program you use to "finger" (the process of obtaining information with the Finger program) a person or resource on the Net.

To locate someone using Finger,

1. Double-click on the Mac Finger application's icon to launch the program. The Finger dialog box will appear, as shown in Figure 9-9.

Figure 9-9: Finger dialog box.

```
┌──────────────────────── Finger ────────────────────────┐
│                                                          │
│  User     ┌──────────────────────────────────────────┐  │
│           └──────────────────────────────────────────┘  │
│  Machine  ┌──────────────────────────────────────────┐  │
│           └──────────────────────────────────────────┘  │
│  ☐ Whois Server ⌘S                                       │
│  ┌────────┐        ┌─────────────┐    ┌────────┐         │
│  │ Cancel │        │ Set Default │    │ Finger │         │
│  └────────┘        └─────────────┘    └────────┘         │
└──────────────────────────────────────────────────────────┘
```

2. In the User box, enter the name of the person you're looking for and the name of the host computer—in the username@domain.top-domain format.

3. Click the Finger button. The results will be displayed in a new window, as shown in Figure 9-10.

Figure 9-10: Finger
search results.

```
┌────────────────────────────────────────────────────────────────┐
│ ▢  ▤              mfraase@mr.net (137.192.2.5)              ▣    │
├────────────────────────────────────────────────────────────────┤
│ finger: /usr/adm/lastlog open error                       ⇧    │
│ Login name: mfraase      In real life: Michael Fraase           │
│ Directory: /home/mfraase         Shell: /bin/csh                │
│ Never logged in.                                                │
│ New mail received Fri Apr 16 15:38:11 1993;                     │
│   unread since Fri Apr 16 15:24:33 1993                         │
│ No Plan.                                                  ⇩     │
│ ⇦                                                         ⇨ ▣   │
└────────────────────────────────────────────────────────────────┘
```

4. Select the Quit command from the File menu.

You can also use Finger to get a list of everyone currently logged into a computer on the Internet. The basic steps are the same as those you use for searching for an individual, except you enter the name of the computer—using the @domain.top-domain format—in the Machine box (note the "@" symbol). The results will be displayed in a new window, as shown in Figure 9-11.

Figure 9-11: Finger
machine search
results.

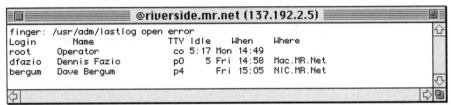

```
┌────────────────────────────────────────────────────────────────┐
│ ▢  ▤             @riverside.mr.net (137.192.2.5)           ▣    │
├────────────────────────────────────────────────────────────────┤
│ finger: /usr/adm/lastlog open error                       ⇧    │
│ Login      Name          TTY Idle    When     Where            │
│ root       Operator      co 5:17 Mon 14:49                     │
│ dfazio     Dennis Fazio  p0    5 Fri 14:58   Mac.MR.Net         │
│ bergum     Dave Bergum   p4      Fri 15:05   NIC.MR.Net    ⇩    │
│ ⇦                                                         ⇨ ▣   │
└────────────────────────────────────────────────────────────────┘
```

You can also use Finger as a sort of general information server. Finger has the ability to display a text file (named .plan, if you're curious) to any Finger query. You can find all sorts of interesting information on the Internet by using Finger. For example, if you finger jtchern@ocf.berkeley.edu, a list of today's baseball scores will be displayed.

Making the world a smaller place.

Sheldon Smith forwarded news of a project undertaken by his wife's fith and sixth grade class in San Luis Obispo, CA.

"This is an example of how the Internet brings the world into the classroom. We, as educators, cannot take the kids out into the world, but the Internet can bring the world to the kids.

"Last October, about the time Ross Perot re-announced his candidacy, an American ship accidentally shot a Turkish ship during a NATO exercise, killing the Captain and three crew members. Because of the Presidential election, there was not much about it in the news.

"My wife's students heard about the accident and felt the U.S. should apologize. The kids wrote notes of apology, which were compiled into a class letter.

"I sent their letter to the Turkish newsgroup, and I forwarded it to my sister, who moderates a Middle Eastern conference on PeaceNet. She works for AWAIR, which is a non-profit group that produces curriculum materials on the Middle East. In any case, after posting their letter, my wife and I received about 30 replies over a two week period."

Here are excerpts from two students' letters:

"Hi my name is Jesse Cutburth. I do not understand why we shot your ship. I think we should apologize, and this is what I am doing. I don't understand how we shot your ship on accident. I think we should replace your ship with one of ours, but we can't replace four people."

"Hi, my name is Brianne Reimer. As an American, I am very sorry about what we did. I don't know what we were doing there. But I am only a child. Someday, I hope I will go to Turkey. And if I do go, I will surely apologize to you face to face. Sorry."

Perhaps the strangest Finger resources are the cold-drink vending machines that some universities have connected to the Internet. When fingered, these machines report which bins in the vending machine are empty and which bins hold the coldest drinks, as shown in Figure 9-12.

Figure 9-12: Finger
cold-drink vending
machine.

```
drink@csh.rit.edu (129.21.60.4)
Login: drink              Name: Drink (Coke Machine)
Directory: /u0/drink                Shell: /u0/drink/shell/shell
Office: NRH Hallway
Last login Wed Mar 31 18:08 (EST) on ttypb from nick.csh.rit.edu
Plan:
    Balance:  $  0.00

    1) Lipton Iced Tea $ 0.50  Empty   (4/44)
    2) Mountain Dew    $ 0.50  Full   (24/44)
    3) Hawaiian Punch  $ 0.50  Full   (36/44)
    4) Dr Pepper       $ 0.50  Full   (25/44)
    5) Coke Classic    $ 0.50  Full   (20/44)

        Drink    3+ hrs   1-3 hrs   0-1 hrs     Total
        :::::    :::::::   :::::::   :::::::     :::::
Lipton Iced Tea        4         0         0         4
   Mountain Dew       24         0         0        24
 Hawaiian Punch       36         0         0        36
      Dr Pepper       25         0         0        25
   Coke Classic       20         0         0        20
```

Since I'm sure you're going to ask, here are a couple of vending machines attached to the Internet:

coke@cs.wisc.edu (account fee required)

drink@csh.rit.edu

WAIS

WAIS (Wide-Area Information Server) is useful for searching through material on the Internet that has been indexed based on content. WAIS is somewhat analogous to Gopher. Both tools allow you to search for information without worrying about where the information is physically stored, but WAIS doesn't provide much in the way of browsing.

For example, WAIS indexes consist of every word in a document, and each word carries the same importance; there's no way to tell WAIS that "Macintosh" is more important than "and" in a search. This differentiation between the importance of words is called weighting, and WAIS doesn't support it.

Also, there is no context sensitivity within the WAIS environment. Searching for FrameMaker, for example, would return information about FrameMaker running on every computer platform; there's no way to limit the search to the just Macintosh version of FrameMaker, for instance.

You can download a copy of the current version of the Macintosh WAIS client (wais-for-mac-1.2.sea.hqx) by FTP from think.com in the /wais/ directory. Documentation is available in the same directory.

To initiate a WAIS search,

1. Launch the WAIS for the Macintosh program by double-clicking on its icon. The Sources and Questions window will appear.

2. From the Source menu, select the Open Source command. A standard Open File dialog box will be displayed.

3. Open the directory-of-servers file (located in the Sources folder inside the WAIS folder).

4. From the File menu, select the Save command. The directory-of-servers icon will be saved within the Sources window.

5. From the Question menu, select the New Question command. The Question dialog box will appear, as shown in Figure 9-13.

Figure 9-13: WAIS Question dialog box.

Question-1

Look for documents about

⬜ Run

Which are similar to   **In these sources**

Results   **0 documents**

6. Enter your question using natural English structure in the Look for documents about box.

7. Drag the icons representing the Internet resources you want to search from the Sources window into the In these sources box.

8. Click the Run button. The results of the search will appear in the Results scrolling list. An example of the results of a search for "what is the chief export of Argentina" within the World Factbook is shown in Figure 9-14.

Figure 9-14: WAIS search results.

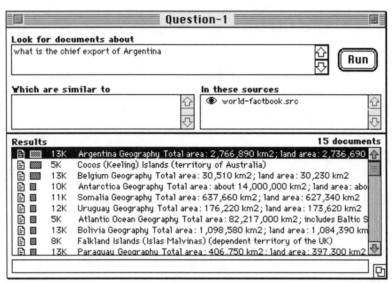

9. Double-click on any of the result icons to display their contents. If the icon is a source reference, select the Save command from the File menu to save the reference in your Sources folder. The source will also be added to the Sources window. The highlighted selection identifies meat, wheat, corn, oilseed, hides and wool as Argentina's chief exports (as shown in Figure 9-15).

Figure 9-15:
Contents of WAIS
search result.

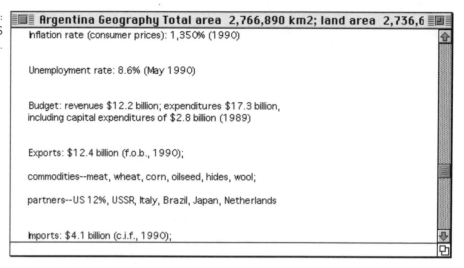

10. Repeat steps 6–9 to refine your search as necessary, adding or removing icons in the In these sources box.

Compact Pro.

Compact Pro and StuffIt continually vie for the top honors in Macintosh file compression. Compact Pro can decode archived files in BinHex and StuffIt formats, as well as its own format. With Compact Pro, you can create self-extracting files and segment files that are too large to fit on a single floppy disk. It's available by FTP from mac.archive.umich.edu in the /mac/util/compression/ directory.

Archie

Archie is an Internet service, originally developed at McGill University, that allows you to search indexes of available files on publicly accessible FTP servers. In other words, you can ask Archie if a certain file exists on the Internet, and if so, where it is. Archie can be helpful in a number of circumstances. You can use it to search for files when you know their names. You can enter just part of a file's name—like "Eudora," to search for the popular e-mail program.

You search Archie's indexes by specifying a string of characters. Archie returns a list of file names that match your search criteria, and the name of the FTP servers where they're located.

As a Macintosh user, you have three options for using Archie:

- You can telnet to an Archie server and muddle through a command-line interface.

- You can use the Macintosh-specific Archie client. Chris McNeil's Archie client for the Macintosh (called, simply, Archie) is available by FTP from sumex-aim.stanford.edu in the /info-mac/comm/ directory.

- You can use TurboGopher to search the Archie database.

Table 9-1 shows a list of Archie servers across the Net.

Table 9-1: Archie Servers.

Archie Server	Geographic Area
archie.ans.net	ANS Network sites
archie.au	Australia and Pacific Basin
archie.doc.ic.ac.uk	United Kingdom and Ireland
archie.funet.fi	Europe
archie.mcgill.ca	Canada
archie.rutgers.edu	Northeastern United States
archie.sura.net	Southeastern United States
archie.unl.edu	Western United States

Try to use the Archie server that is geographically closest to you. This will help balance network traffic.

Using the Macintosh Archie Client

Chris McNeil's Archie for the Macintosh is extremely easy to use.

1. Launch Archie by double-clicking on its icon. The Archie Query window will appear, as shown in Figure 9-16.

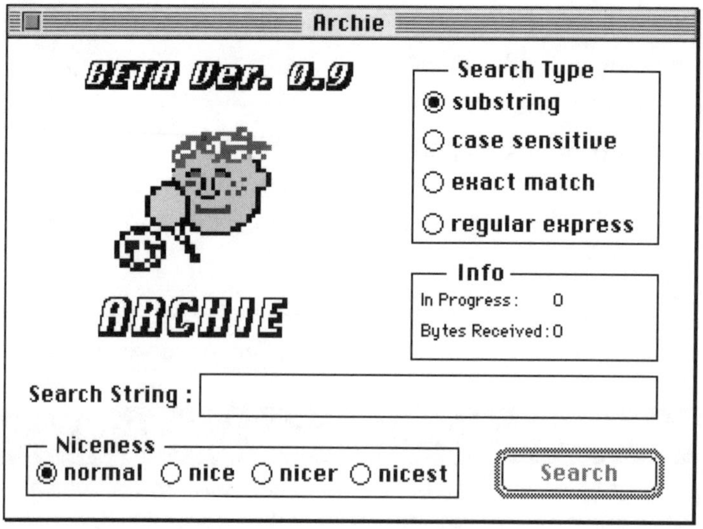

Figure 9-16: Archie
Query window.

Archie

BETA Ver. 0.9

ARCHIE

┌─ Search Type ─┐
◉ **substring**
○ **case sensitive**
○ **exact match**
○ **regular express**

┌─ Info ─┐
In Progress :   0
Bytes Received : 0

Search String : [   ]

┌─ Niceness ─┐
◉ **normal** ○ **nice** ○ **nicer** ○ **nicest**

[**Search**]

2. From the Prefs menu, select the Archie Server command. The Archie Server dialog box will appear, as shown in Figure 9-17.

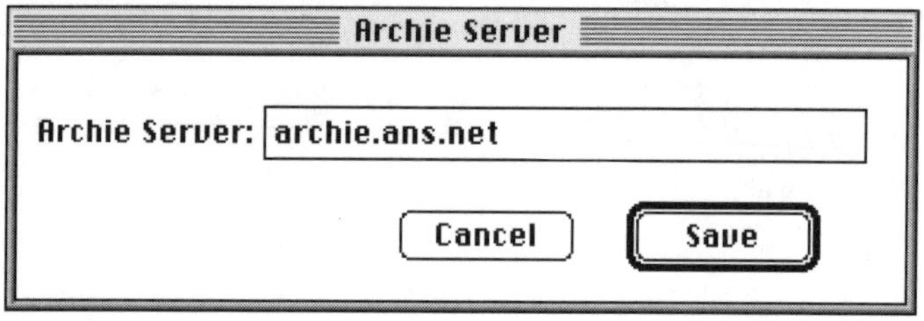

Figure 9-17: Archie
Server dialog box.

Archie Server

Archie Server: [archie.ans.net   ]

[Cancel]   [**Save**]

3. In the Archie Server box, enter the domain address—in the domain.top-domain format—of the closest Archie server.

4. Click the Save button to dismiss the Archie Server dialog box. Your server configuration will be saved to disk.

5. In the Archie Query window's Search String box, enter the character string for which you want to search.

6. Click the Search button. The search will be initiated on the Archie server you specified, and the results will be returned in a new window.

Using TurboGopher for Archie Searches

Although Chris McNeil's Macintosh Archie client is easy to use, I find that using TurboGopher to search within the Archie database is just as easy and yields results somewhat more quickly.

1. Launch TurboGopher by double-clicking on its icon. (For more about using TurboGopher, see Chapter 7, "Using Gopher.") TurboGopher comes preconfigured for use with the University of Minnesota's Gopher server, and the program will automatically log into the "mother" Gopher and display a Bookmarks window and a Home Gopher Server window, as shown in Figure 9-18.

Figure 9-18:
TurboGopher
initial display.

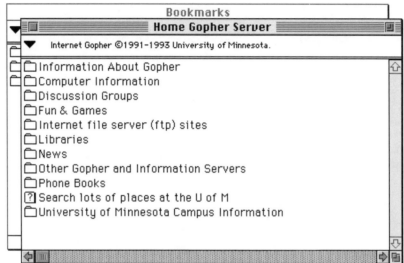

 - If you've already configured TurboGopher for use with another home Gopher server, your screen will reflect the items available on that server.

2. Navigate to the Search FTP sites (Archie) folder.

 - If you're using the University of Minnesota's "mother" Gopher as your home Gopher server, it's located inside the Internet file server (ftp) sites folder, as shown in Figure 9-19.

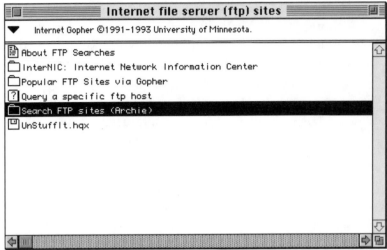

Figure 9-19:
TurboGopher
Archie Internet file
server (ftp) sites
folder.

3. Double-click on the Search FTP sites (Archie) folder. A new TurboGopher window will be opened displaying search icons, as shown in Figure 9-20.

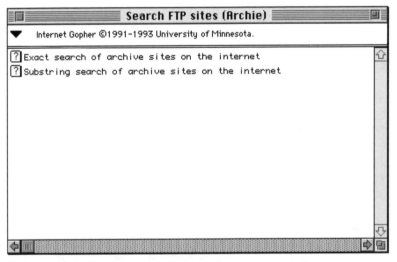

Figure 9-20:
TurboGopher
Archie search
folder.

4. Double-click on the Exact search of archive sites on the Internet icon. The Search dialog box will appear, as shown in Figure 9-21.

Figure 9-21:
TurboGopher
Search dialog box.

Find documents containing these words:

┌─────────────────────────────────────┐
└─────────────────────────────────────┘

[Cancel]　　[**OK**]

5. Enter a word or series of words contained in the document or file name you wish to download.

6. Click the OK button. TurboGopher will search within the Archie database for documents and file names matching the search words you specified. A new TurboGopher window will appear showing a list of the documents and files matching your search words, like the example of a search for "eudora" shown in Figure 9-22.

Figure 9-22:
TurboGopher
window with
search results.

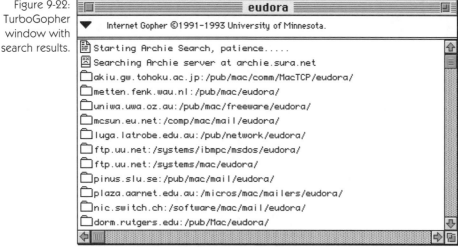

An advantage of using TurboGopher for Archie searches is that the search results window contains "live" Internet resources. You can simply double-click on any item in the search results window to automatically log into an anonymous FTP archive or download a file.

RFCs

An RFC (Request for Comments) is a document that defines a specific part of the Internet itself. Because of the anarchic nature of the Internet, anyone can write an RFC. Most are highly technical, and relate to topics that are of little interest to the average user. Some RFCs, however, are veritable goldmines of useful information for real people. RFCs are always referred to by their number, and may be available in either text or PostScript formats (text versions have a .txt suffix; PostScript versions have a .ps suffix).

RFCs are available from many FTP archives, including the "official" depositories shown in Table 9-2.

Table 9-2: Official RFC depositories.

FTP Site	Directory
nic.ddn.mil	/rfc/
nis.jvnc.net	/rfc/
wuarchive.wustl.edu	/doc/rfc/
nnsc.nsf.net	/rfc/
src.doc.ic.ac.uk	/rfc/

Because all RFCs are available only by RFC number, it's a good idea to first download the index of RFC files (rfc-index.txt). This file contains a complete index of all currently available RFCs.

You can also obtain RFCs by e-mail with these steps:

1. Launch your e-mail program.

2. Create a new message to the address mail-server@nisc.sri.com.

3. Enter the one-line message "send rfc*xxx*.txt" (leave out the quotes), where *xxx* is the number of the RFC you want to receive.

   ■ To receive the index, enter the one-line message "send rfc-index.txt."

4. Send your e-mail message.

A list of some of the RFCs that are useful for average users is provided in Table 9-3.

Table 9-3: Some useful RFCs.

RFC	Title
1432	Recent Internet books
1402	There's Gold in them thar Networks! or Searching for Treasure in all the Wrong Places
1392	Internet Users' Glossary
1359	Connecting to the Internet: What connecting institutions should anticipate
1325	FYI on questions and answers: Answers to commonly asked "new Internet user" questions
1296	Internet Growth (1981-1991)
1259	Building the open road: The NREN as test-bed for the national public network
1244	Site Security Handbook
1208	Glossary of networking terms
1207	FYI on Questions and Answers: Answers to commonly asked "experienced Internet user" questions
1192	Commercialization of the Internet summary report
1180	TCP/IP tutorial
1178	Choosing a name for your computer
1175	FYI on where to start: A bibliography of internetworking information
1167	Thoughts on the National Research and Education Network
1118	Hitchhikers guide to the Internet

FAQs

A FAQ (Frequently Asked Question) is a collection of questions (and their answers) most often asked by new Internet users. FAQs exist for all network news newsgroups and most mailing lists. Until you get your Internet legs, read the FAQs for the newsgroups you frequent. You can save yourself a lot of embarrassment by skimming FAQ files.

Most FAQs are posted to their related newsgroups on a monthly basis. In addition, FAQs for all the newsgroups are consolidated and posted to the news.answers newsgroup. You can also obtain FAQs by FTP from pit-manager.mit.edu in the /pub/usenet/ directory.

Internet Organizations

As the Internet has evolved from a project researching ways to ensure communications in the event of a nuclear attack into a research and business tool used by millions of individuals, a number of diverse and vital organizations have sprung up. The actions of two of these organizations—the Internet Society and the Electronic Frontier Foundation— have repercussions for every Internet user.

Electronic Frontier Foundation

On July 10, 1990, two unlikely cohorts announced they were forming a foundation to "address social and legal issues arising from the impact on society of the increasing pervasive use of computers as a means of communication and information distribution." Mitch Kapor is best known as the founder of Lotus Development Corporation, the publisher of the Lotus 1-2-3 spreadsheet program. John Perry Barlow is a sometime lyricist for the Grateful Dead, one-time Congressional candidate and a Wyoming rancher.

A number of factions are battling for control and influence over cyberspace, and the Electronic Frontier Foundation (EFF) is entrenched in the front lines of the battlefield. On one side of the battle lines are a number of government agencies, corporations and other entities that want to limit access to information and dictate what people can do in cyberspace. On the other side, there are those—like the members of the EFF—who want to widen (and deepen) everyone's access to information, and extend to cyberspace the rights most Americans enjoy in physical reality.

Kapor and Barlow came together when both were questioned by the FBI following an incident at Apple Computer where a group calling itself the NuPrometheus League had distributed the Color QuickDraw source code to members of the computer press and luminaries in the computer industry.

John Perry Barlow was amazed at the level of computer ignorance exhibited by the FBI agent who visited him in May 1990. Barlow had been a longtime member of the Internet-connected Whole Earth 'Lectronic Link (WELL), and describes himself as a "techno-crank." From the agent, Barlow learned that computer hackers—all computer hackers—were under suspicion as Evil Criminals. He also learned that the FBI was tracing anyone who had visited the Hackers Conference, an invitation-only affair begun in 1984 that drew attendees from the top levels of the computer industry, including executives, consultants, pundits and journalists.

It's important to draw the distinction between hackers (those who like to explore systems for the sake of learning something about those systems) and crackers (those who are out to wreak havoc by breaking into systems, deleting files and reaping financial gain illegally).

Barlow, alarmed at the implications of computer ignorance within the FBI (and the possibility of a high-tech witch hunt), sounded the alarm on the WELL. One of the many WELL inhabitants who took note of Barlow's outcry was Mitch Kapor, who had already endured being fingerprinted by the FBI.

Kapor flew to Barlow's Wyoming ranch in June 1990 to lay the groundwork for the EFF, and Barlow wrote "Crime and Puzzlement," an article announcing the pair's intention of forming a political organization intent on extending Constitutional rights to cyberspace.

The response from the computing community was astounding. Original funding for EFF was provided by Kapor and Apple co-founder Steve Wozniak. John Gilmore (one of the founders of Sun Microsystems) contributed, and others quickly followed.

The Electronic Frontier Foundation continues to fight for a careful balance of freedom, access and privacy throughout the networks, and they've even won a few battles.

You can download a wealth of information from the EFF's FTP or Gopher server at ftp.eff.org and gopher.eff.org respectively. Here's a sampling of what's available:

- Back issues of EFFector Online, the electronic newsletter of the EFF.

- Testimony of EFF staff and board members.

- Papers and articles by EFF staff and board members.

- EFF Newsnotes and informational postings.

- Papers and articles about cyberspace from such online luminaries as Bruce Sterling, John Perry Barlow and Dorothy Denning.

- Information about various legal issues affecting the Internet.

- Text of various laws and proposed laws relevant to the electronic frontier.

Electronic Frontier Foundation
666 Pennsylvania Avenue, SE
Suite 303
Washington, DC 20003
202/544-9237
202/547-5481 (Fax)
617/576-4510 (Legal hotline)
eff@eff.org

Internet Society

The Internet Society exists to encourage cooperation among the various networks that make up the Internet, fostering a global communications infrastructure. The organization focuses on the future of the Internet and the emerging and established technologies that impact the Net. The Internet Society appoints a small group of members to the Internet Architecture Board—the closest thing the Internet has to a board of governors, although it's perhaps more accurate to think of the body as a group of tribal elders.

The Internet Architecture Board (IAB) is responsible for the technical management of the Internet. It adopts proposed standards and allocates addresses. The Internet Architecture Board also oversees two groups:

- The Internet Engineering Task Force (IETF) is responsible for the technical operation of the Internet.
- The Internet Research Task Force (IRTF) is responsible for research and development issues surrounding the Internet.

The Internet Society sponsors an annual conference, publishes a quarterly newsletter, and supports an electronic mail distribution list.

Internet Society
1895 Preston White Drive
Suite 100
Reston, VA 22091
703/620-8990
isoc@nri.reston.va.us

Moving On

This concludes our side-trip into some of the lesser-known, but still important, resources on the Internet. The next chapter, "Hot Spots on the Net," is just what it sounds like: an extensive listing of useful and interesting Internet sites that you can explore using the software we've discussed in this book. There's a lot to see and do, so now would be a good time to stock up on provisions and get a little rest, because the final leg of our tour promises to be the most exciting one yet.

CHAPTER 10

HOT SPOTS ON THE NET
Notable Sites & Servers

New information resources are added to the Internet every minute. It's impossible to keep up with everything on the Net—about the best you can do is seek out those things that specifically interest you. Keep in close touch with your friends and associates, tipping them off to new files, sites and resources that they might be interested in—and ask them to do the same for you. When you find something worth sharing, e-mail pointers (a "trail" through the Net) to each other. Exchange Gopher bookmarks and Mosaic hotlists.

The Ventana Online Visitor's Center is another great way to keep up with what's new and worthwhile on the Internet. For more details, see Appendix A, "The Companion Disks & Ventana Online."

Naturally, many of you will wonder why your favorite site or resource isn't listed with those that follow. The most likely answer is space limitations. As your tour guide, it's impossible for me to show you all of the Internet. (That's like trying to ride every ride at Disney World in just one day!) Because the Net is constantly changing, any collection of Internet resources is only a snapshot of what's interesting right now (fall 1994). Of course, what's interesting to me may not be interesting to you at all, so I'm providing pointers of general interest in addition to the more specialized resources.

The resources in the chapter are organized by category of interest, such as Art, Fun & Games, Science, etc. The individual resource entries are broken down as follows:

- The Type field tells you what software tool or protocol you need to use to access the resource.
- The Address field tells you the domain-name address for the resource.
- The Path field tells you the pathname for the directory or file of the resource.
- The Summary field provides a brief description of the resource and any necessary login information.
- The Contact field gives any additional contact information associated with the site.

Art

The Andy Warhol Museum
Type: WWW
Address: http://www.warhol.org/warhol/
Summary: Tour the Andy Warhol Museum in Pittsburgh, PA.

Arts Online
Type: FTP
Address: nic.funet.fi
Path: /pub/doc/library/artbase.txt.Z
Summary: A list of arts-related resources on the Net.

Australian National University Art History Server
Type: WWW
Address: http://rubens.anu.edu.au/
Summary: Michael Greenhalgh, professor of Art History at Australian National University, compiled this collection of over 2,800 print images from the 15th to 19th centuries and another 6,000 images of classical and European architec-

ture and architectural sculpture. Some highlights: a tutorial on the Palace of Diocletian at Split, a survey of the architecture of Islam and a tour of classical sites in Turkey.

Fractals

Type: FTP
Address: csus.edu
Path: /pub/alt.fractals.pictures/*
Summary: Tons of fractal images in GIF format. They're arranged in directories by date; as of this writing, the latest is 1991, but there's a lot of cool stuff.

Gallery of Interactive On-Line Geometry

Type: WWW
Address: http://www.geom.umn.edu/apps/gallery.html
Summary: Use Kali to learn about the 17 crystallographic symmetry groups of the plane. This work is similar to that seen in some of M.C. Escher's woodcuts. Play a pinball-style game to explore the effects of negatively curved space. Much more involving symmetry groups and angle geometries. This page is maintained by The Geometry Center at the University of Minnesota. Figure 10-1 gives you a glimpse of the riches available here.

Figure 10-1: Gallery of Interactive On-Line Geometry.

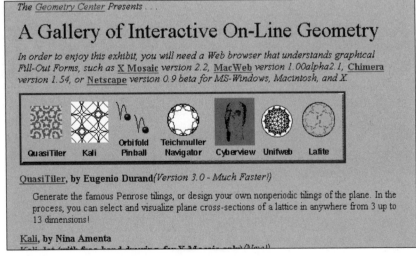

Images, Icons and Flags

Type: WWW

Address: http://white.nosc.mil/images.html

Summary: Links to lots of image sites and servers including NASA, space, travel and medical images. Comprehensive icon and flag archives.

Institute of Egyptian Art and Archaeology

Type: WWW

Address: http://www.memst.edu/egypt/main.html

Summary: Take a color tour of Egypt or view the exhibit of Egyptian artifacts at the University of Memphis. The Institute of Egyptian Art and Archaeology is part of the Department of Art at the University of Memphis. Figure 10-2 shows the very cool home page for this site.

Figure 10-2: The Institute of Egyptian Art and Archaeology home page.

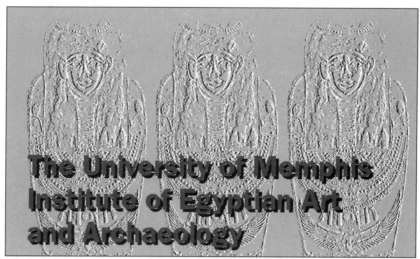

Kaleidospace

Type: WWW

Address: http://kspace.com

Summary: A commercial site, but well worth looking at. Independent artists gather here to display and sell their work.

Origami

      Type: FTP

   Address: nstn.ns.ca

      Path: /listserv/origami-l/*

 Summary: Learn new folding techniques, get display ideas, tips and bibliographies. Subscribe to mailing list by sending e-mail to origami-l-request@ntsn.ns.ca.

PC's and Macintoshes

      Type: Gopher

   Address: wiretap.spies.com

 Summary: Choose Wiretap Online Libarary/Technical Information/PC's and Macintoshes. Lots of articles and tips and tricks for both PC and Mac users.

Strange Interactions

      Type: WWW

   Address: http://amanda.physics.wisc.edu/show.html

 Summary: An online art exhibit by John Jacobsen. From his artist's statement, "My work is an attempt to give a concrete aspect to the subconscious." Definitely worth checking out! I really like the welcome page, so here it is (see Figure 10-3).

Figure 10-3: Strange Interactions welcome page.

STRANGE INTERACTIONS

An online art exhibit

Work by John Jacobsen

Welcome to *Strange Interactions!*

Some Art Newsgroups

alt.artcom
alt.postmodern
clari.news.arts
rec.arts.fine
rec.arts.misc
sci.fractals

Books, Literature & 'Zines

Basement Full of Books

Type: FTP
Address: rtfm.mit.edu
Path: /pub/usenet-by-group/news.answers/books/base-ment-full-of-books
Summary: Get autographed books (with personal inscriptions) directly from their authors. Lots of science fiction authors like Ursula Le Guin, Harlan Ellison, David Brin and Joe Haldeman. The list is updated every month. You get a short synopsis of each book, along with ordering information.

You can also get this list by sending an e-mail message to mail-server@rtfm.mit.edu. Put "send usenet/news.answers/books/basement-full-of-books" (without the quotes) in the body of the message.

Book FAQs and Info

Type: FTP
Address: quartz.rutgers.edu
Path: /pub/books/
Summary: Bookstore lists, book reviews, reading lists and other literary resources. You can also Gopher to this site: quartz.rutgers.edu. Choose Book FAQs and Info.

Bookstore (University of California, San Diego)

Type: telnet

Address: ucsdbkst.ucsd.edu (132.239.83.66)

Summary: Log in as ult. Provides information about titles in stock as well as titles on order and the *New York Times* bestseller lists. An example of the menu system is shown in Figure 10-4.

Figure 10-4: Telnet example of UCSD Bookstore menu system.

```
[1.00]                       UCSD Bookstore  BiblioFile                    [BK]

    1 - Browse Book Database

    2 - Special Request

    3 - Best Seller Lists

    4 - Special Events




                          OFF - Logoff

        Please enter Menu Selection and press <return>.
        ENTER MENU SELECTION:
```

Dartmouth College Library

Type: telnet

Address: lib.dartmouth.edu

Summary: Search by author, title or subject. One highlight: the entire text of the Petrocchi version of *Divine Comedy*, complete with line-by-line commentary, courtesy of the Dartmouth University Dante Project.

Electronic Publications

Type: Gopher
Address: gopher.cic.net
Summary: The ETEXT Archives on CICnet is probably the biggest archive available for electronic publications. Publications are organized by both alphabetical order and subject matter.
Contact: Paul Southworth
CICnet Archivist
pauls@cic.net

Electronic Serials List

Type: e-mail
Address: listserv@uottawa.bitnet
Summary: An automated distribution server of a comprehensive list of electronic serials on various topics including computers, science, politics, literature, etc.
Send the following two lines in an e-mail message: "GET EJOURNL1 DIRECTORY" and "GET EJOURNL2 DIRECTORY" (don't include the quotes).

HyperMedia Zines on the Net

Type: WWW
Address: http://www.acns.nwu.edu/ezines/
Summary: Reviews and links, lists of electronically available 'zines.

John Labovitz's e-zine list

Type: WWW
Address: http://www.ora.com:8080/johnl/e-zine-list/
Summary: A directory of over 175 'zines available on the Net.
Contact: John Labovitz
johnl@oralcom

Project Gutenberg

Type: FTP
Address: mrcnext.cso.uiuc.edu
Path: pub/etext/
Summary: Project Gutenberg was formed to encourage the creation and distribution of electronic text, hoping to have one trillion volumes available by the end of 2001. Texts currently available include *Alice in Wonderland*, *Peter Pan*, Shakespeare's complete works, and Milton's *Paradise Lost*.

Some Book & 'Zine Newsgroups

alt.books.reviews
alt.books.prose
alt.books.technical
alt.etext
alt.mythology
alt.usage.english
alt.zines
bit.listserv.literary
misc.writing
rec.arts.poems
rec.arts.prose
rec.mag

Business

Doing Business with Hong Kong

Type: WWW
Address: http://www.hk.super.net/~rlowe/bizhk/bhhome.html
Summary: Basic trade information, a trade contacts service and a list of companies by trade. Figure 10-5 shows the home page.

Figure 10-5: Doing Business with Hong Kong home page.

BizHK Doing Business with Hong Kong

Find your <u>trading partners</u> here!

Hong Kong: A major trading centre and gateway to China

Hong Kong's success as a manufacturing complex and top financial centre can be attributed to its economic policy of free enterprise, free trade, location, sophisticated communications and financial systems, and absence of strict government controls. China has pledged to keep Hong Kong's capitalist economy, currency and free-market policies unchanged for 50 years after 1997, with the

Downtown Anywhere

Type: WWW

Address: http://www.awa.com/

Summary: Businesses can establish a Net presence in this virtual community. But it's not all business. Lots of Net and general reference info. Check out the library and newsstand, museums, the financial district, the sports arena and, of course, Main Street.

Marshall Space Flight Center Procurement Home Page

Type: WWW

Address: http://procure.msfc.nasa.gov

Summary: Advance procurement information and small business assistance documents, Learn about federal streamlining initiatives. Pointers to other federal procurement sites such as the Johnson Space Center and Kennedy Space Center home pages.

Contact: Jim Bradford
GP01/Procurement Office
NASA/Marshall Space Flight Center
Huntsville, AL 35812
205/544-0306
jim.bradford@msfc.nasa.gov

Multilevel Marketing

Type: FTP
Address: rtfm.mit.edu
Path: /pub/usenet-by-group/alt.answers/mlm-faq
Summary: A FAQ that discusses different aspects of multilevel marketing.

STO's Internet Patent Search System

Type: WWW
Address: http://sunsite.unc.edu/patents/intropat.html
Summary: Do a title search through all U.S. patents issued since 1970.

StrategyWeb

Type: WWW
Address: http://www.onramp.net/~atw_dhw/home.htm
Summary: Question and answer hyperbook interactions with experts in business strategy. Check out the 60-second CyberCircuit for a brief "brain-training" session. Check out the quotes in Figure 10-6.

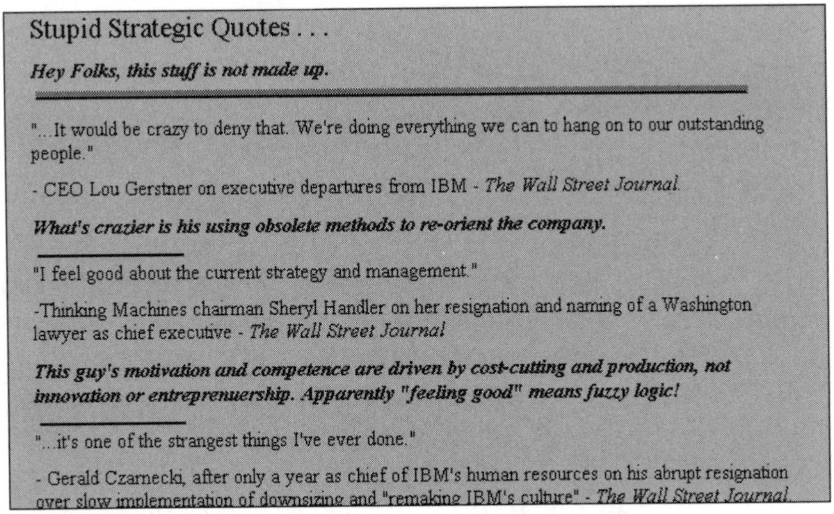

Figure 10-6:
StrategyWeb
Stupid Strategic
Quotes.

Stupid Strategic Quotes . . .

Hey Folks, this stuff is not made up.

"...It would be crazy to deny that. We're doing everything we can to hang on to our outstanding people."

- CEO Lou Gerstner on executive departures from IBM - *The Wall Street Journal.*

What's crazier is his using obsolete methods to re-orient the company.

"I feel good about the current strategy and management."

-Thinking Machines chairman Sheryl Handler on her resignation and naming of a Washington lawyer as chief executive - *The Wall Street Journal*

This guy's motivation and competence are driven by cost-cutting and production, not innovation or entreprenuership. Apparently "feeling good" means fuzzy logic!

"...it's one of the strangest things I've ever done."

- Gerald Czarnecki, after only a year as chief of IBM's human resources on his abrupt resignation over slow implementation of downsizing and "remaking IBM's culture" - *The Wall Street Journal.*

Some Business Newsgroups

alt.business.misc
alt.business.multi-level
clari.biz.labor
misc.entrepreneurs

Computing

Computer Professionals for Social Responsibility (CPSR) Mailing List

Type: mailing list
Address: listserv@gwuvm.gwu.edu
Summary: Computer Professionals for Social Responsibility is a professional organization that concerns itself with the social and political aspects of computing. Mailing list subscribers will receive updates on CPSR's current Freedom of Information Act (FOIA) requests, position statements and news releases on topics including privacy and cryptography.

Send a one-line message in e-mail: "subscribe CPSR *your name*" (don't include the quotes), where *your name* is your full name (not your e-mail address).

Free On-Line Dictionary of Computing

Type: WWW
Address: http://wombat.doc.ic.ac.uk/
Summary: Searchable dictionary that includes terms related to general computing, programming languages, networks, domain theory, acronyms, computing history and just about anything else that has to do with computers.

Global Monitor

Type: WWW
Address: http://www.globalx.net/monitor/
Summary: A cool electronic mag loaded with computer-related info.

Toll-Free Numbers

Type: FTP

Address: oak.oakland.edu

Path: /pub/misc/telephone/tollfree.num

Summary: Toll-free numbers for a bunch of computer companies.

UNB Graphic Services Desktop Publishing Resource Base

Type: WWW

Address: http://degaulle.hil.unb.ca/UNB_G_Services/ GSHomePage.html

Summary: Plenty of plugs for UNB's services, but enough pointers to clip-art collections, font banks and other desktop publishing resources to make it a valuable site.

The Virtual Contractor

Address: http://www.iquest.net/cw/VC/VC.html

Summary: A free service connecting people who need custom computer services with people who can provide services. Take a look at the disclaimer in Figure 10-7.

Figure 10-7: The Virtual Contractor home page.

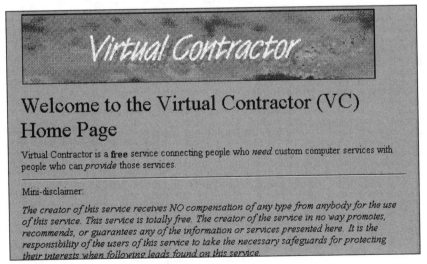

Welcome to the Virtual Contractor (VC) Home Page

Virtual Contractor is a **free** service connecting people who *need* custom computer services with people who can *provide* those services.

Mini-disclaimer:

The creator of this service receives NO compensation of any type from anybody for the use of this service. This service is totally free. The creator of the service in no way promotes, recommends, or guarantees any of the information or services presented here. It is the responsibility of the users of this service to take the necessary safeguards for protecting their interests when following leads found on this service.

Virus Information

Type: FTP
Address: oak.oakland.edu
Path: /pub/misc/virus
Summary: Technical information about most known viruses. Includes DOS and Mac data.

Some Related Newsgroups

alt.cad.autocad
alt.cyberpunk.tech
alt.privacy
clari.nb.general
comp.misc
comp.theory
comp.virus
comp.sys.misc

Culture & Diversity

American Memory from the Library of Congress

Type: WWW
Address: http://rs6.loc.gov/amhome.html
Summary: Lots of material on American culture and history, most of it from special collections of the Library of Congress.

Native American Net Server

Type: Gopher
Address: alpha1.csd.uwm.edu
Summary: Choose UWM Information, Native American Net Server. Articles and cases on Indian law, book reviews, job openings, education, Native newsletters, even Native American fonts.
Contact: Michael Wilson
University of Wisconsin at Milwaukee
mwilson@convex.csd.uwm.edu

Resources for Diversity

Type: WWW

Address: http://alpha.acast.nova.edu/diversity.html

Summary: This page has links to the African Studies Web, Chicano-LatinoNet, Disability Information, Diversity at the University of Michigan, the Inter-Tribal Network for Native Americans, the Latin American Network Information Center, Minority Online Service (MOLIS), Omni-Cultural Academic Resource, Gay/Lesbian Resources, and Women's Studies at the University of Maryland.

Women's Resources Project

Type: WWW

Address: http://sunsite.unc.edu/cheryb/women/wshome.html

Summary: Women's Studies: Pointers to women's studies programs at several colleges and universities. Women and Literature: Bios of female authors from Harriet Beecher Stowe to Marge Piercy, from Jane Austen to Maya Angelou. A guide to women's resources on the Net. Check out Figure 10-8.

Figure 10-8: The Women's Resources home page.

Welcome to The Women's Resources Project!

Our focus is to provide information about the resources about and for women. We have concentrated on resources available in the Triangle area, but we have also provided access to many women's resources that are available on the Internet.

Some Related Newsgroups

alt.discrimination
soc.culture.african.american
soc.women

Education

AskERIC

Type: Gopher
Address: ericir.syr.edu
Summary: Electronic library access for querying education-related resources. (Also available via telnet. Log in as gopher.)

Higher Education Resources and Opportunities

Type: WWW
Address: http:/web.fie.com
Summary: The Minority On-Line Information Service is an online database service with all sorts of information about scholarships, grants, fellowships, conferences, research opportunities and other opportunities for minorities and women.

Hillside Elementary School

Type: WWW
Address: http://hillside.coled.umn.edu/
Summary: Every student in Mrs. Collins' sixth grade class has created his or her own home page. Lots more plans for this site, a joint project of Hillside Elementary School in Cottage Grove, Minnesota, and the University of Minnesota College of Education.

National Council of University Research Administrators (NCURA)

Type: telnet

Address: fedix.fie.com

Summary: Log in as new. Choose NCURA. To quote from the summary, the NCURA is "an organization of individuals with professional interests in the administration of sponsored programs (research, education and training), primarily at colleges and universities...." Figure 10-9 shows a sample session.

   You can get more information by sending e-mail to info@ncura.edu. The phone number is 202/466-3894.

Figure 10-9: A sample Fedix session.

```
>>  U.S. Department of Energy Office of Reconfiguration, DP-25 is located <<
>>  under menu option # 8.  (New System Interface, Lynx).  Please select  <<
>>  option # 8 to access this information.                                <<

    *** If you leave a comment, please include your E-mail address. ***

    Item   Description
    ----   ------------------------------------------------------
     1     Federal Opportunities (FEDIX)
     2     Minority College & University Capability Information (MOLIS)
     3     Higher Education Opportunities for Minorities & Women (HERO)
     4     NCURA BBS
     5     What is NCURA?
     6     SRA BBS
     8     New System Interface (Lynx http://web.fie.com/) *** PLEASE USE ***
           (From Mosaic, Cello or Lynx; URL:http://web.fie.com/)
           (also US DOE Office of Reconfiguration, DP-25)

     9     Download FEDIX/MOLIS Files

     0     Exit
What is your choice  - >  █
```

Reading Disabilities

Type: FTP

Address: ftp.spies.com

Path: /Library/Article/Misc/disable.rd

Summary: Extremely clear and well-written paper, "Neuropsychological Bases of Educational Disabilities," by Robert Zenhausern, Ph.D., professor of psychology at St. Johns University. It's a scholarly paper, but its style makes it accessible to the lay public.

Schoolnet Resource Manual

Type: FTP
Address: schoolnet.carleton.ca
Path: /pub/schoolnet/manuals/Resource.txt
Summary: This is a huge file with about a kazillion pointers to science, technology and educational resources on the net. The manuals directory is full of net information. Check out Big Dummy's Guide to Internet, Electric Mystic Guide to Internet, FTP Introduction, E-Mail Intro, Gopher.FAQ, Internet Basics and Guidelines - Netiquette.

U.S. Department of Education

Type: WWW
Address: http://inet.ed.gov/
Summary: Get press releases and information about funding opportunities, speeches prepared for the U.S. Secretary of Education, Teachers' and Researchers' Guides to the U.S. Department of Education, and links to other educational resources.

Environment

Earthquake Information

Type: Finger
Address: quake@geophys.washington.edu
Summary: Reports recent earthquake information including location, magnitude and time of occurrence. This site is geared to Washington and Oregon, but there are instructions for getting info about other areas.

Environmental Groups

Type: Gopher
Address: ecosys.drdr.virginia.edu
Summary: Choose Environmental Groups and Programs.

Institute for Global Communications (IGC)

Type: Gopher

Address: gopher.igc.apc.org

Summary: From the welcome message: "IGC runs four computer networks known as PeaceNet(TM), EcoNet(TM), ConflictNet and LaborNet. IGC is the U.S. member of the Association for Progressive Communications, a 16-country association of computer networks working for peace, human rights, environmental protection, social justice, and sustainability."

Editorial comment: TIOTS! (This is one terrific site!)

Contact: Institute for Global Communications
18 De Boom St.
San Francisco, CA 94107
415/442-0220
igc-info@igc.apc.org

Linkages Home Page

Type: WWW

Address: http://www.mbnet.mb.ca:80/linkage/

Summary: Provided by the International Institute for Sustainable Development, publishers of the Earth Negotiations Bulletin. Links to information about international environment and development meetings such as the World Summit for Social Development, the International Conference on Population & Development, and the Earth Negotiations Bulletin. Figure 10-10 shows the home page.

Figure 10-10: The
Linkages home
page.

Ozone Depletion

Type: FTP

Address: rtfm.mit.edu

Path: /pub/usenet/news.answers/ozone-depletion

Summary: FAQ files about the depletion of the ozone layer are posted monthly. There's a special section for the Antarctic ozone hole.

U.S. Geological Survey Cascades Volcano Observatory Home Page

Type: WWW

Address: http://vulcan.wr.usgs.gov/home.html

Summary: Arm yourself with information about volcanoes and other natural hazards. Get hazard assessments and warnings during volcano crises. Find out about the International Volcano Disaster Assistance Program. Links to Alaska and and Hawaii volcano observatories. Figure 10-11 shows the home page.

Figure 10-11: The Cascades Volcano Observatory home page.

Some Related Newsgroups

bit.listserv.biosphere-l
sci.environment

Finance

Credit Info

Type: FTP
Address: rtfm.mit.edu
Path: /pub/usenet/news.answers/consumer-credit.faq
Summary: Is Mastercard better than Visa? What is a secured card? Do I want a fixed-rate or floating-rate card? Why is a discount better than a rebate? The answers to these and many other burning consumer questions can be found in the consumer-credit.faq, which was compiled from questions asked on the misc.consumers newsgroup.

Credit Info II

Type: Gopher

Address: gopher.fsl.orst.edu

Summary: Choose Other Sources of Information/Hugo's Lore-House/Where the Sun Doesn't Shine & Other Bottom-less Pits/All you should ever need to know about credit.

Currency Converter

Type: WWW

Address: http://www.ora.com/cgi-bin/ora/currency

Summary: This page is updated weekly. By default, the page shows the currency rates of over 50 countries relative to U.S. currency (e.g., one U.S. dollar is worth 1.3605 dollars in Australia). To get currency rates relative to another country, just click the country you want. (See Figure 10-48 later in this chapter.)

Economics

Type: Gopher

Address: nysernet.org

Summary: Choose Special Collections: Business and Economic Development. If the world of business is your world, have a blast exploring these resources. Among them are a FAQ on advertising on the Internet, the Basic Guide to Exporting, Commerce Business Daily and a U.S. Patent database.

Foreign Exchange Rates

Type: Gopher

Address: una.hh.lib.umich.edu

Summary: Choose ebb/monetary statistics/FRB foreign exchange rates. These figures from the Federal Reserve Bank of New York are updated weekly.

Nasdaq Financial Executive Journal

Type: WWW
Address: http://fatty.law.cornell.edu:80/usr2/wwwtext/ nasdaq/nasdtoc.html
Summary: The Nasdaq Stock Market and the Legal Information Institute at Cornell Law School have made available a hypermedia version of the *Nasdaq Financial Executive Journal* (NFEJ). The NFEJ is accessible via the World Wide Web in HTML format.

Some Related Newsgroups

clari.biz.commodity
clari.biz.finance
clari.biz.finance.services

Food & Drink

Big Drink List

Type: FTP
Address: ocf.berkeley.edu
Path: /pub/Library/Recreation/big-drink-list
Summary: Recipes for just about any mixed drink you can think of.

Food Recipes Database

Type: Gopher
Address: gopher.aecom.yu.edu
Summary: Choose Internet Resources/Miscellaneous/Search the Food Recipes Database. Huge searchable recipe list.

Over The Coffee

Type: WWW
Address: http://www.infonet.net/showcase/coffee/
Summary: If you're a coffee lover, it's all here. Coffee trivia and factoids, a travelers' guide to coffee houses, a list of coffee-related USENET groups, a coffee recipe collection, lists of coffee (and tea) books, a glossary of coffee terminology, and resources for coffee professionals.

Figure 10-12 gives you a sample of what's available—
check out the Read Me! file first.

Figure 10-12: Over
The Coffee
welcome page.

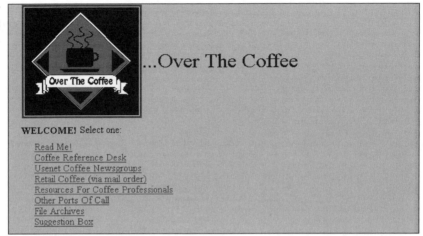

Recipes

Type: FTP
Address: gatekeeper.dec.com
Path: /pub/recipes
Summary: A collection of over 500 recipes.

The Recipes Folder

Type: WWW
Address: http://english-server.hss.cmu.edu/Recipes.html
Summary: If you're a vegetarian, you'll feel right at home here. If
you're a flesh eater, you'll have to put up with the
following subject headings: "Vegetarian Stuff," "Dead
Animals" and "Things Possibly Involving Dead Animals and Possibly Not." Whatever your culinary
predelictions, this is a terrific list of recipe sources.

Veggies Unite!

Type: WWW

Address: http://www-sc.ucssc.indiana.edu/cgi-bin/recipes/

Summary: A searchable index of over 900 vegetarian recipes. Links to other nutrition and health sites. A few of the links are shown in Figure 10-13.

Figure 10-13:
Veggies Unite!

Veggies Unite!

Welcome! This is a searchable index of over 1000 vegetarian recipes. You can enter your query with any single word, a phrase, or two words separated by an "and" or an "or".

- Recipe Index (by category)
- Master Recipe Index (alphabetically)
- Info on Veggies Unite
- Informative Papers and Miscellaneous
- Nutrition and Health WWW/Gopher Sites
- Other Food and Drink Recipe WWW/Gopher Sites
- Send in a recipe (via form)

Vegetarianism

Type: FTP

Address: flubber.cs.umd.edu

Path: /other/tms/veg

Summary: All kinds of info for vegetarians and would-be vegetarians—FAQs, recipes, etc. Another vegetarian resource to check out is the rec.food.veg newsgroup.

Some Food & Nutrition Newsgroups

alt.college.food
alt.folklore.herbs
alt.food.fat-free
alt.support.diet
rec.crafts.winemaking
rec.food.cooking
rec.food.historic
rec.food.recipes
rec.food.restaurants
rec.food.sourdough
rec.food.veg
sci.med.nutrition

Fun & Games

Crosswords

Type: FTP
Address: rtfm.mit.edu
Path: /pub/usenet/news.answers/crossword-faq/
Summary: Crossword aficionado heaven. Guides, dictionaries, solution tips, software info, etc. Also try /pub/usenet/ news.answers/puzzles/faq for a collection of mindbenders.

Games Domain

Type: WWW
Address: http://wcl-rs.bham.ac.uk/GamesDomain
Summary: If you have any interest in games, check out this page. It has links to USENET groups and games FAQs, a Walkthroughs link that can get you unstuck from several popular games, and over 100 links to games-related Web pages and FTP sites. Figure 10-14 gives you a small taste of the stuff you can get here.

Figure 10-14:
Games Related
Home Pages from
the Games
Domain.

Games Related Home Pages

- Battleships on the Web - maintained by Richard Clegg
- Chess pages - maintained by Rudolf Steinkellner
- WWW Chess archives - maintained by
- A Darts home page - maintained by Chris Patterson
- Empire Users Guide and info on currently running games
- Empire FAQ and editions of EMPIRE NEWS - maintained by Karl S. Hagen
- Electronic football (soccer) league - maintained by Doug Ingram
- The Last Homely House - maintained by Aaron Fuegi
- GWU Gamers Society - maintained by Steve Morrow
- Line Wars II - maintained by Patrick Aalto
- Collection of MUD home pages - maintained by Lydia Leong
- The Automated MUSH list - maintained by Lydia Leong
- Myst home page - maintained by Roger Carasso
- OKbridge (Bridge on the Internet) - maintained by Dave DeMers

Killer List of Video Games

Type: Gopher

Address: wiretap.spies.com

Summary: Choose Wiretap Online Library/Mass Media/Games and Video Games/The Killer List of Video Games. Get the inside scoop on your favorite games through files like Definitive Arcade Video Cheats, SEGA Genesis Secrets, Killer List of Video Games, Home Video Games History and (yes, this is for real) The Rules of Tiddlywinks.

Roller Coasters

Type: FTP

Address: gboro.rowan.edu

Path: /pub/Coasters/*

Summary: FAQs, reviews of parks and coasters, animations, JPG and GIF images. Also available via WWW (http://sunsite.unc.edu.darlene/coaster/coaster.html).

Health, Medicine & Recovery

AIDS

Type: Gopher

Address: selway.umt.edu 700

Summary: Choose Sexuality/Acquired Immune Deficiency Syndrome (AIDS). Lots of statistics and resources, as well as the full text of *Aids Treatment News.*

Americans with Disabilities Act

Type: Gopher

Address: scilibx.ucsc.edu

Summary: Choose The Library/Electronic Books and other Texts/ Americans with Disabilities Act. Get the full text of the 1990 Americans with Disabilities Act.

Cornucopia of Disability Information (CODI)

Type: Gopher

Address: val-dor.cc.buffalo.edu

Summary: A great resource for those with disabilities and health professionals. Lots of digests, info on legal issues and assistance, college guides, independent living centers and employment resources.

Forensic Medicine

Type: Gopher

Address: gopher.vifp.monash.edu.au

Summary: Choose Medical/Forensic Medicine. Lots of articles concerning how medicine and the law interact.

Health Newsletters

Type: FTP

Address: nigel.msen.com

Path: /pub/newsletters/Health

Summary: A bunch of newsletters about medicine, therapy and medical research.

Insomnia (Healthline Information Database)

Type: Gopher

Address: wilcox.umt.edu700/1

Summary: Choose General Health Information/Antidepressants and Sleep Disorders. Or choose General Health Information/Do's and Don'ts for Poor Sleepers

Institute for Molecular Virology

Type: WWW

Address: http://www.bocklabs.wisc.edu/

Summary: Info about the AIDs virus, 3D images and animations of virus structures, 2D electron micrographs of viruses, online virology course material, phone book of virologists on the Net, and virology-related journal articles. A sample of what's available is shown in Figure 10-15.

Figure 10-15: Institute for Molecular Virology.

What's new

- Link added to Veterinary Sciences at The Queen's University of Belfast
- Ebola Recommended Reading List
- Hantaviruses, with emphasis on Four Corners Hantavirus
- Biology of AIDS course material
- Guidelines for contributors
- Animations-
  - simulation of a virus binding to a host cell receptor
  - flying inside a Rhinovirus 16 capsid
  - Spin animation of reovirus virion, ISVP, and core particles.
- A paper which will be presented at the Second International World Wide Web Conference: Communicating Information about Virus Structure and Biology Via the World Wide Web
- Visualizations of Individual Viral Proteins
- solved structure of HIV p17 protein
- Render your own virus images locally
  - Complete particles
  - Individual viral proteins
- "Intro to Molecular Virology" tutorial

Migraine Headaches

Type: telnet

Address: selway.umt.edu

Summary: Log in as health. Learn how to cope with (and avoid) migraines.

National Toxicology Program (NTP) Home Page

Type: WWW

Address: http://www.niehs.nih.gov/ntp/ntp.html

Summary: Established by the Secretary of Health and Human Services "to coordinate toxicology research and testing activities within the Department, to provide information about potentially toxic chemicals to regulatory and research agencies and the public, and to strengthen the science base in toxicology. In its 16 years, the NTP has become the world's leader in designing, conducting, and interpreting animal assays for toxicity." The annual plan describes current work being done in carcinogenesis, toxicology, genetic toxicology and chemical disposition.

New York State Breast Cancer Information Clearinghouse

Type: Gopher

Address: nysernet.org/

Summary: Choose Special Collections: Breast Cancer Information Clearinghouse. A great resource for breast cancer patients, family members and health professionals. Lots of info on treatment and rehabilitation, a list of names and phone numbers of support groups throughout the U.S., and pointers to other cancer resources.

Psycoloquy

Type: WWW

Address: http://info.cern.ch/hypertext/DataSources/bySubject/Psychology/Psycoloquy.html

Summary: An electronic journal sponsored by the American Psychological Association. Contains reports on new ideas and findings in all areas of psychology. Contributors solicit peer feedback, and contributions are referreed by members of Psycoloquy's Editorial Board.

USENET newsgroup: sci.psychology.digest. Or, to get articles automatically, send e-mail to listserv@pucc.bitnet or listserv@pucc.princeton.edu.

Leave the Subject line blank and put the following in the body of the message: "sub psyc *Firstname Lastname*" (leave out the quotes), where *Firstname* and *Lastname* are your own name, not your Internet address.

Sexual Assault Recovery Service

Type: Gopher

Address: wilcox.umt.edu

Summary: Choose University of Montana Info/HEALTHLINE/ Sexual Assualt Recovery Service. Documents and discussions on dealing with sexual assault experiences and prevention.

You can also telnet to selway.umt.edu and log in as health. Figure 10-16 shows a sample session.

Figure 10-16: Sexual Assault Recovery Service.

```
              University of Montana Student Health Services

                  Sexual Assault Recovery Service (SARS)
-->█ 1.  About the Sexual Assault Recovery Service
     2.  A Note to Those Closest to Rape Survivors
     3.  ACQUAINTANCE RAPE PREVENTION: What Men and Women Need To Know
     4.  How to Handle Sexual Pressure
     5.  If Your Lover Gets Raped
     6.  Morning After Angst: How to Handle the Most Common Post-Sex Disaste..
     7.  SAFE: Helping Sexual Assault Survivors at the University of Montana
     8.  SARS Referral Phone List
     9.  The Intimacy Report




Press █ for Help, █ to Quit, █ to go up a menu              Page: 1/1
```

12-Step

Type: e-mail

Address: muller@camp.rutgers.edu

Summary: The purpose of this group is to share experiences about 12-step programs.

University of Montana Student Health Services (Healthline)

Type: telnet

Address: selway.umt.edu

Summary: Log in as health. Lots of general health information, much of it of particular interest to students.

Check out the Health & Human Performance Department. You'll find articles on plyometrics, how air pollutants affect exercise, exercise during pregnancy, and the history of the marathon.

The Sexuality section contains a broad range of articles on topics such as breast exams, AIDS and other sexually transmitted diseases, and birth control/disease prevention (take a look at "Everything You Need to Know about Condoms").

An example session is shown in Figure 10-17.

Figure 10-17: A Healthline telnet session.

```
                 University of Montana Student Health Services
                            HEALTHLINE Gopher Server
    --> 1.  About the Student Health Services HEALTHLINE Gopher/
         2.  Student Health Service Information/
         3.  What's (New) on HEALTHLINE/
         4.  Calendar/Events/Presentations/
         5.  Insurance Information/
         6.  General Health Information/
         7.  Drug & Alcohol Information/
         8.  Sexuality/
         9.  Sexual Assault Recovery Service (SARS)/
        10.  Health & Human Performance Dept at U. of Montana/
        11.  Health Care Reform in Montana (NEW)/
        12.  Internet Health-related Resources/
        13.  Search HEALTHLINE Files and Menus/




    Press ? for Help, q to Quit                          Page: 1/1
```

The Wellness List

Type: mailing list

Address: majordomo@wellnessmart.com

Summary: This list includes discussions of health, nutrition, wellness and life expectancy. Lots of healthy recipes, nutrition- and fitness-related product announcements, book reviews, and nutrition-related position papers.

To subscribe, send a one-line message in e-mail: "subscribe wellnesslist *your name*" (leave out the quotes), where *your name* is your full name (not your e-mail address).

Some Related Newsgroups

alt.folklore.herbs
alt.health.ayurveda
alt.med.cfs
alt.support.diet
bit.listserv.c+health
clari.tw.health
clari.tw.health.aids
misc.fitness
misc.health.diabetes
talk.politics.medicine
sci.med.aids
sci.med.pharmacy

History

Dead Sea Scrolls

Type: WWW

Address: http://sunsite.unc.edu.expo/deadsea.scrolls.exhibit/intro.html

Summary: Exhibit exploring the Dead Sea Scrolls.

History Sources

Type: FTP

Address: byrd.mu.wvnet.edu

Path: /pub/history

Summary: The directories are broken down by topic: diplomatic, general, maritime, military, etc. The files include everything from Roosevelt's Inaugural Addresses to a paper on psych operations in the Gulf War to a Civil War bibliography. Sponsored by Marshall University Department of History.

Contact: Michael J. McCarthy
mmccarth@muvm6.wvnet.edu

MEDEIV-L

Type: mailing list

Address: listserv@ukanvm.cc.ukans.edu

Summary: Send message with the word SUBSCRIBE in body. This mailing list is for discussing all aspects of the middle ages.

Contact: Jeff Gardner
jgardner@ukanvm.ukans.edu

Some History Newsgroups

alt.history.what-if
alt.revisionism
alt.war
alt.war.civil.usa
bit.listserv.history
soc.history

Humor

Calvin and Hobbes Archive

Type: WWW

Address: http://www.eng.hawaii.edu/Contribs/justin/Archive/Index.html

Summary: An archive of Calvin and Hobbes cartoons, updated daily.

Cartoons

Type: USENET

Address: alt.binaries.pictures.cartoons

Summary: Download pictures of your favorite cartoon characters. Also check out the alt.binaries.sounds.cartoons for cartoon sounds.

The Comic Book and Comic-Strip Page

Type: WWW

Address: http://dragon.acadiau.ca:1667/~860099w/comics/comics.html

Summary: Links to lots of comic book and comic strip pages, comics conventions, reviews, lots of mailing lists you can subscribe to. A few related newsgroups: rec.arts.comics.misc, rec.arts.comics.strips and alt.comics.alternative.

The Doctor Fun Page

Type: WWW

Address: http://sunsite.unc.edu/Dave/drfun.html

Summary: A new cartoon every day. Also available via FTP (sunsite.unc.edu in the /pub/electronic-publications/Dr-Fun directory) and USENET (alt.binaries.pictures.misc).

Funny Guys

Type: FTP

Address: cathouse.org

Path: /pub/cathouse/humor/

Summary: In the quotes and standup directories you'll find quotes and funnies from such notable laugh inducers (depending on your taste) as Woody Allen, Oscar Wilde, W.C. Fields, Andrew Dice Clay, Lenny Bruce, Rodney Dangerfield, Groucho Marx and Mark Twain. One of my favorites is the british.humor directory. That's where Monty Python and Peter Cook reside. And check out the sports directory for Yogi Berra quotes and a selection of golf, racquetball and bowling humor.

Hacker Test

Type: Gopher
Address: pfsparc02.phil15.uni-sb.de
Summary: Choose INFO-SYSTEM BENUTZEN/Fun/Hacker. Are you a computer illiterate, nerd, hacker, guru or wizard? Better find out soon!

The Joke File

Type: Gopher
Address: uts.mcc.ac.uk
Summary: Choose Gopher Services/The Joke File. Huge joke database. Find just the right joke for any occasion.

Mini-Annals of Improbable Research (mini-AIR)

Type: Gopher
Address: saturn.soils.umn.edu:70
Summary: ChooseSelected Archives of Email Lists/Mini-Journal of Irreproducible Results. AIR is a new science humor magazine, edited by Marc Abrahams, the father of the annual Ig Nobel Prize Ceremony, which "honors people whose achievements cannot or should not be reproduced." I must forewarn you, however. The following is a direct quote from the mini-AIR FAQ. Question: "Do you promise that there will be a minimum of puns involving the nickname 'AIR'?" Answer: "No."

Netwit

Type: mailing list
Address: help@netwit.cmhnet.org
Summary: If stupid Internet humor is your thing, send a message with your Internet address in the body of the message.

Tests

Type: FTP
Address: quartz.rutgers.edu
Path: /pub/humor/Tests/
Summary: Take the feminist quiz. Find out if you're a nerd. Check out the multitude of quizzes that test the strength of your funnybone.

The Unofficial Tank Girl WWW Site

Type: WWW

Address: http://www.dcs.qmw.ac.uk/~bob/stuff/tg/index.html

Summary: Tank Girl is a creation of Jamie Hewlett and Alan Martin. On this page, you'll find a gallery of Tank Girl pictures, a Tank Girl FAQ and everything else you need to be Tank-Girl-literate.

Some Related Newsgroups

alt.comedy.british

alt.comics.superman

alt.fan.firesign-theatre

alt.fan.wodehouse

alt.fan.tank-girl

alt.folklore.college

alt.humor.best-of-usenet

clari.feature.dave_barry

rec.arts.comics.marketplace

rec.arts.comics.strips

rec.humor.d

rec.humor.funny

Internet Stuff

Acceptable Use Policies

Type: FTP

Address: nic.merit.edu

Path: /acceptable.use.policies/*.txt

Summary: Acceptable Use Policies for several networks that are part of the Internet. Policies are available for CICnet, CREN, JVNCnet, MICHnet, NorthWestNet, NSFnet, OARnet and SURAnet.

Alex

Type: FTP
Address: alex.sp.cs.cmu.edu
Path: /doc/README
Summary: Alex provides a way to transparently read remote files at anonymous FTP sites, just as though they were on your local drive.

A Beginner's Guide to HTML

Type: WWW
Address: http://www.ncsa.uiuc.edu/demoweb/html-primer.html
Summary: Learn to create HTML documents that can be placed on the Web.

Community Computer Networks: Building Electronic Greenbelts

Type: FTP
Address: ftp.apple.com
Path: /alug/commanet/
Summary: Steve Cisler's excellent overview of community networks examining what kinds of information and services can be found on these systems, what groups are running community networks, and cost aspects. The essay discusses current models for community networks and the impact these networks have on their local (physical) environments.
Contact: Steve Cisler
Apple Library
4 Infinite Loop
MS 304-2A
Cupertino, CA 95014
408/974-3258
sac@apple.com

E-Mail Address Locator

Type: e-mail

Address: mail-server@pit-manager.mit.edu

Summary: In body of letter enter "send usenet-addresses/*name*" (leave out the quotes), where *name* is the name of the person you want to locate. The service will return the e-mail address of the person in the username@domain.top-domain format. This service works only if the person you are looking for has posted an article to one of the USENET newsgroups.

Economic Case for Public Subsidy of the Internet

Type: FTP

Address: ssugopher.sonoma.edu

Path: /pub/schickele.txt (or schickele.ps for PostScript version)

Summary: Sandra Schickele's economic analysis of a publicly funded Internet.

Electronic Frontier Foundation (EFF) Mailing List

Type: mailing list

Address: eff-request@eff.org

Summary: Send a brief e-mail message requesting to be added to the mailing list. The Electronic Frontier Foundation is a professional organization concerned with the legal, social and political aspects of civilizing cyberspace. If you subscribe to the EFF mailing list, you'll receive copies of the *EFFector Online* electronic newsletter and news releases.

Electronic Journal on Virtual Culture

Type: FTP
Address: byrd.mu.wvnet.edu
Path: /pub/ejvc/
Summary: Very interesting and well-written journal of virtual community and the Internet. Each issue contains three or four feature articles, non-refereed opinion columns and essays, and the Cyberspace Monitor (a listing of important happenings, publications, products and services related to cyberspace and the Net).

FEDLINE

Type: FTP
Address: ftp.nwnet.net
Path: /user-docs/government/fedline.*
Summary: Not just politicians are interested in the electronic distribution of government information. "FEDLINE: A Feasibility Study of Establishment and Operation of FedWorld, A Government-Wide Information Locator System at NTIS," is a document that outlines a governmental study on electronic distribution of information our tax dollars have already paid for. ASCII text, WordPerfect 5.1 and PostScript versions of the study are available.

Good Internet Books

Type: Gopher
Address: nysernet.org
Summary: Choose Special Collections: Internet Help/Good Books about the Internet. A great list of books about the Net. There's a short summary, the ISBN number and the price.

Internet Maps

Type: FTP

Address: ftp.merit.edu

Path: /maps/

Summary: A collection of PostScript-format maps of the Internet. You must have a PostScript-capable printer to be able to print and view these maps.

Internet Monthly Report

Type: FTP

Address: nis.nsf.net

Path: /internet/newsletters/internet.monthly.report/

Summary: Monthly Internet usage reports. The reports contain information from the Internet Research Group concerning the accomplishments and problems of the participating organizations. Each report usually contains an article from the Internet Architecture Board and a few Internet Engineering reports. Brief articles are also submitted by the various regional networks, and a calendar of upcoming events is included.

Internet Society

Type: WWW

Address: http://info.isoc.org/home.html

Summary: The Internet Society was created in 1991 to be the international organization that promotes global cooperation and coordination for the Internet and its technologies. Individuals and organizations can join. There's a great general info Internet FAQ. Figure 10-18 shows some of the documents related to Internet ethics and standards.

Contact: Internet Society
org-membership@isoc.org
800/468-9507 (U.S. only)
703/648-9888

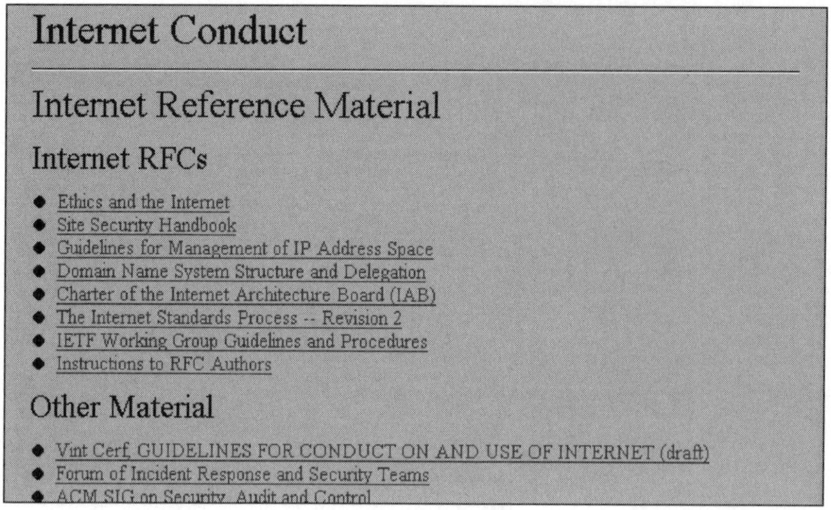

Figure 10-18:
Internet Conduct,
from the Internet
Society.

Internet Conduct

Internet Reference Material

Internet RFCs

- Ethics and the Internet
- Site Security Handbook
- Guidelines for Management of IP Address Space
- Domain Name System Structure and Delegation
- Charter of the Internet Architecture Board (IAB)
- The Internet Standards Process -- Revision 2
- IETF Working Group Guidelines and Procedures
- Instructions to RFC Authors

Other Material

- Vint Cerf, GUIDELINES FOR CONDUCT ON AND USE OF INTERNET (draft)
- Forum of Incident Response and Security Teams
- ACM SIG on Security, Audit and Control

Internet Web Text

Type: WWW

Address: http://www.rpi.edu/Internet/Guides/decemj/
text.html

Summary: Created in spring of 1994 (but updated since) by John December for a course in Computer-Mediated Communication at Rensselaer Polytechnic Institute. His goal: to create an interface students could use to familiarize themselves with the Internet—how to use it, how to find information, how to connect with people. He makes use of icons to create memory aids to remembering sources. This page also has links to lots of online Internet guides and resources, such as *Zen and the Art of the Internet*. Take a look at Figure 10-19.

Contact: John December
decemj@rpi.edu

Figure 10-19: Internet Web Text.

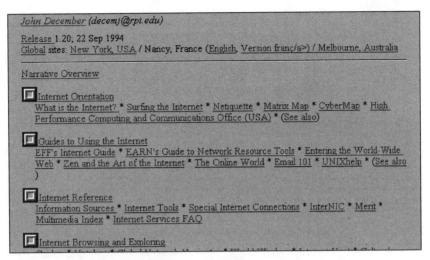

IRC Thesis

Type: FTP

Address: ftp.spies.com

Path: /Library/Cyber/electrop.txt

Summary: This honors thesis by E.M. Reid, "Electropolis: Communication and Community on IRC," explores the culture of Internet Relay Chat.

List of New Mailing Lists

Type: Mailing List

Address: request-NEW-LIST@VM1.NoDak.EDU

Summary: Subscribe to this list and you'll always be on top of the latest mailing list info. Whenever a new mailing list is formed or an old one is updated, you'll receive a message describing the additions or changes.

To subscribe, send a one-line message in e-mail: "subscribe New-list *your name*" (leave out the quotes), where *your name* is your full name (not your e-mail address).

NCSA Mosaic

Type: WWW

Address: http://www.ncsa.uiuc.edu/SDG/Software/Mosaic/
NCSAMosaicHome.html

Summary: Download the latest release of NCSA Mosaic, get installation and configuration instructions, info about bugs
and bug fixes, FAQs and an online users' manual. Also
get graphics viewers, HTML editors, PKunzip and
winsocks. Figure 10-20 shows the NCSA Mosaic home
page.

Figure 10-20:
NCSA Mosaic
home page.

MUD FAQ

Type: FTP

Address: ftp.math.okstate.edu

Path: /pub/muds/misc/mud-faq/part*

Summary: MUD is an acronym for Multi-User Dimensions (or
Dungeons). A MUD is a real-time interaction that is
usually based upon some sort of social role-playing.

Net Savvy

Type: FTP
Address: ftp.gsfc.nasa.gov
Path: /pub/internet/general.info
Summary: An Archie manual, basic TCP/IP commands, a guide to finding stuff on the Internet, LAN and ethernet FAQs, an FTP site list and much more.

Netnews Filtering Service

Type: e-mail
Address: netnews@db.stanford.edu
Summary: Sign up with this Stanford service to help you zero in on the Internet stuff you want. You send a profile to the service, and they send you relevant news articles. Send an e-mail message with the command HELP in the body of the message to get more information.

The Online World

Type: FTP
Address: oak.oakland.edu
Path: /pub/msdos/info/online17.zip
Summary: Norwegian author Odd de Presno has released his book *The Online World* as shareware. *The Online World* was previously published in Norwegian as a 275-page hardcover (ISBN: 82-90628-67-6) and is still available in bookstores. The work covers the practical side of using global networks and provides examples ranging from databases to entertainment. The FTP-accessible file is in ASCII text format and can be read with any text editor or word processing program.
Contact: opresno@extern.uio.no

Why are Internet Resources Free?

Type: Gopher
Address: wiretap.spies.com
Summary: Choose Wiretap Online Library/Cyberspace/Why are Internet Resources Free? Ever wondered why you can get to most of the stuff on the Net without having to pay? This article explains it all for you.

Some Related Newsgroups

alt.answers
alt.culture.internet
alt.culture.usenet
alt.newbie
alt.online-service
alt.security.pgp
bit.listserv.new-list
misc.answers
misc.legal.computing
news.software.readers

Jobs

Federal Jobs

Type: Gopher
Address: dartcms1.dartmouth.edu
Summary: Choose Job Openings in the Federal Government. Lists of federal job opportunities and information that'll help you apply for a federal job.

Online Career Center

Type: Gopher
Address: msen.com
Summary: Select The Online Career Center. You can post your resume and search job lists at no charge, get career counseling, and connect with recruiting agencies. Be sure to read the Online Career Center Liability Policy.
Contact: occ@mail.msen.com

Some Job-Related Newsgroups

bionet.jobs
bionet.women-in-bio
biz.jobs.offered
misc.jobs.misc
misc.jobs.contract

misc.jobs.offered
misc.jobs.offered.entry
misc.jobs.resumes

Languages

Esperanto-English Dictionary

Type: Gopher
Address: wiretap.spies.com
Summary: Choose Wiretap Online Library/Articles/Language/
Esperanto English Dictionary.

The Human-Languages Page

Type: WWW
Address: http://www.willamette.edu/~tjones/Language-
Page.html
Summary: This page currently contains more than 100 links to over
40 different languages. Tutorials, dictionaries, sofware
and literature. Check out Figure 10-21 for a glimpse of
the riches to be found.

Figure 10-21: The
Human-Languages
Page home page.

This page is devoted to bringing together information about the languages of the world. The
language resources listed here come from all around the world, and range from dictionaries to
language tutorials to spoken samples of languages. Many languages are represented here, but many
more are missing. If you have something you would like to contribute, please send mail to Tyler
Jones, *tjones@willamette.edu*.

- Klik hier om deze inleiding in het Nederlands te lezen.
- Deutsche Einführung.
- Cette page en Français.
- Clique aqui para ler a introdução em português.
- Tämä sivu suomeksi.
- Trykk her for å lese denne siden på norsk (bokmål)

At the moment, this page is geared towards English-speakers only (because these introductions, and
the explanations of the links below, are all in English). Volunteers are needed to translate this page

Japanese/English Dictionary Gateway

Type: WWW

Address: http://www.cs.cmu.edu:8001/cgi-bin/j-e

Summary: This page is also available in Japanese. The dictionary entries can be viewed with text-based browsers or with Japanese text sent as images.

Web Italian Lessons by Lucio Chiappetti

Type: WWW

Address: http://www.willamette.edu/~tjones/languages/Italian/Italian-lesson.html

Summary: Lessons are available as PostScript files, as well as in HTML format.

Welsh Lessons

Type: WWW

Address: http://www.cs.brown.edu/fun/welsh/home.html

Summary: A complete course in Welsh, featuring audio clips and an index of key words and terms.

Some Related Newsgroups

alt.chinese.text

alt.japanese.text

k12.lang.francais

k12.lang.russian

sci.lang

soc.culture.esperanto

soc.culture.french

Law

Advertising Law Internet Site

Type: WWW

Address: http://www.webcom.com/~lewrose/home.html

Summary: Legal aspects of marketing. Stuff about infomercials, home shopping and 900-number regulations. You can also get FTC guides and consumer advisories.

American Civil Liberties Union (ACLU)

Type: Gopher

Address: aclu.org:6601/1

Summary: As of this writing, a lot of stuff in this Gopher is still under construction. Right now you can join the ACLU and check out the ACLU free reading room. Coming soon: legislative alerts and Congressional testimony, info about Supreme Court cases in which the ACLU is involved, and much more.

Criminal Justice Country Profiles

Type: Gopher

Address: uacsc2.albany.edu

Summary: Choose United Nations Justice Network/U.N. Criminal Justice Country Profiles. Find out how the criminal justice system works in different countries.

LawNet

Type: telnet

Address: lawnet.law.columbia.edu

Summary: Log in as lawnet. Offers legal information and card catalog access. Columbia University's Law School library card catalog, information server, academic services and career services are all accessible. An example session screen is shown in Figure 10-22.

Figure 10-22: A
sample LawNet
session.

```
                        CU-LawNet Info System
---------------------------------------------------------------
1 - Law Library Catalog PEGASUS
2 - University Catalog  CLIO
3 - Project JANUS experimental textual search interface
4 - Law School Academic Services
5 - Law School Career Services
6 - ColumbiaNet
7 - Advanced World wide library access (HytelNet)
h - Help message


---------------------------------------------------------------

Please make a selection or enter Q to quit.
■
```

Legal Information Institute

Type: WWW

Address: http://www.law.cornell.edu/

Summary: Get information about recent Supreme Court decisions, search an e-mail address directory of faculty and staff at U.S. law schools. Lots of links to other law-related stuff.

West's Legal Directory (WLD)

Type: Gopher

Address: wld.westlaw.com

Summary: Select West's Legal Directory via WAIS. Search for attorneys or law firms by specialty in any area in the U.S. or Canada. Profiles include information on such things as years of practice and offices held. You can also search for former students of law schools. E-mail questions to wldhelp@research.westlaw.com. Phone 800/777-7089.

Some Related Newsgroups

bit.listserv.lawsch-l
clari.biz.courts
clari.news.law.civil
clari.news.law.profession
misc.int-property
misc.legal
misc.legal.computing

Miscellany

Acronyms by E-Mail

Type: e-mail
Address: freetext@iruccvax.ucc.ie
Summary: The Irish have always had a way with the language, and the University of Cork offers an e-mail based Acronym Server. Send an e-mail message with the word "help" (without the quotes) in the body of the message to get instructions on using the server.

Almanac

Type: Finger
Address: copi@oddjob.uchicago.edu
Summary: Provides a list of notable birthdays, events in history and planetary occurrences for each day, as shown in the example in Figure 10-23.

Figure 10-23: Finger
Almanac results.

```
              Day 303 and Week 44 of current year
          26,171,853 seconds elapsed in current year
                 56 shopping days until Christmas

                Day 25 of Marcheshvan, 5755
                    Year 17 of Machzor 302
                29 shopping days until Chanukah

                     For Chicago (CST)
          Sun rise: 6:21 AM, set: 4:48 PM (today)
          Sun rise: 6:22 AM, set: 4:47 PM (tomorrow)

                Phase of moon: waning crescent
            Age of moon: 4 days (to next new moon)

                   The year of the Dog

*********************** Special Events for 10/30 *************************
************** Birth: Christopher Columbus (543 years ago) **************
***************** Birth: John Adams (259 years ago) *****************
***************** Birth: U.S. Navy (219 years ago) *******************
******* Birth: Feodor Mikhailovich Dostoyevsky (173 years ago) ********
************** Birth: Ezra Loomis Pound (109 years ago) **************
************** Birth: Homi Jehangir Bhabha (85 years ago) **************
***************** Birth: Henry Winkler (49 years ago) *****************
********* Death: Willebrod van Roijen Snell (368 years ago) *********
** Death: Prime Minister Indira Gandhi (assassinated) (10 years ago) **
```

Animals

Type: FTP

Address: rtfm.mit.edu

Path: /pub/usenet/news.answers

Summary: You'll find all sorts of animal stuff here. A few of the subdirectories to check out: cats-faq, pets-birds-faq, fleas-ticks and dogs-faq.

Multimedia

Index to Multimedia Information Sources

Type: WWW

Address: http://cui_www.unige.ch/OSG/MultimediaInfo/

Summary: Links to film and video resources, media archives, MPC specs, cable regulations, desktop publishing, art, music, 'zines, publishers, MIDI, MPEG, satellite TV, Nielsen ratings, the Billboard chart, hypertext and hypermedia, multimedia software, newsgroups and about a zillion other multimedia-related resources. Multimedia FAQ heaven and lots of conference announcements. A (very small) portion of the table of contents is shown in Figure 10-24.

Figure 10-24: Index
to Multimedia
Information
Services.

Table of Contents
Current Events
Ratings and Guides
FAQs
Software
Media Delivery Services
Companies
Media Archives
Research
Conference Announcements
Bibliographies
Newsgroup Archives
Standards
The CD Family
Digital Galleries
Educational
Commercial Services
Magazines, Books and Journals
Publishers
Hypertext and Hypermedia
Miscellaneous Information

Music

Captain Beefheart
Type: WWW
Address: http://129.21.21.53/hpr.html
Summary: Lots of pictures, unreleased recordings, concert materials, artwork (done under his real identity as Donald Van Vliet), sound bites, and info on Gerry Pratt's Beefheart fanzine.

Classical Music
Type: USENET
Address: rec.music.classical.performing
Summary: Lots of interesting and serious discussions (low garbage ratio).

The Death of Rock 'n' Roll

Type: WWW

Address: http://alfred1.u.washington.edu:8080/~jlks/pike/
DeathRR.html

Summary: *The Death of Rock 'n' Roll: Untimely Demises, Morbid
Preoccupations and Premature Forecasts of Doom in Pop
Music* by Jeff Pike was published by Faber & Faber in
1993. This site contains lots of samples from the book.
They're meant to entice you to buy the book, but you'll
find plenty of info about your favorite dead rock stars
even if you don't plan to make a purchase.

Contact: Faber & Faber
800/666-2211

Digital Tradition Folk Song Database

Type: WWW

Address: http://pubweb.parc.xerox.com/digitrad

Summary: A searchable database containing words and music to
thousands of folk songs collected by Dick Greenhaus
and friends. Figure 10-25 shows you some of the options
available.

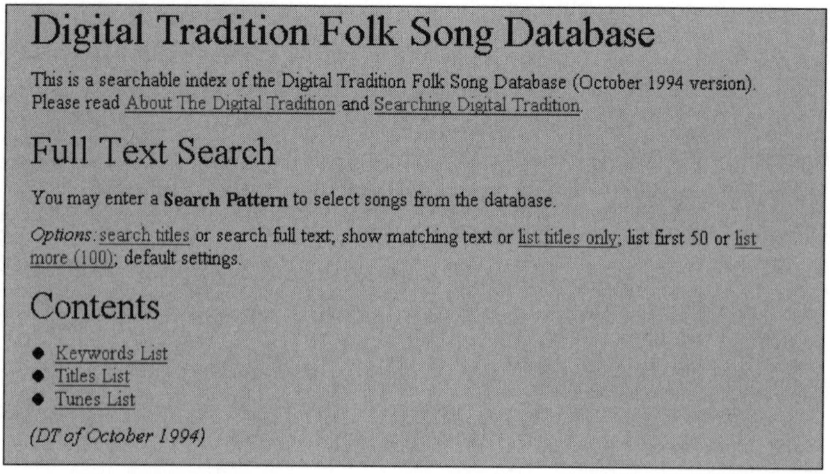

Figure 10-25:
Digital Tradition
Folk Song
Database.

Digital Tradition Folk Song Database

This is a searchable index of the Digital Tradition Folk Song Database (October 1994 version).
Please read <u>About The Digital Tradition</u> and <u>Searching Digital Tradition</u>.

Full Text Search

You may enter a **Search Pattern** to select songs from the database.

Options: <u>search titles</u> or search full text; show matching text or <u>list titles only</u>; list first 50 or <u>list
more (100)</u>; default settings.

Contents

- <u>Keywords List</u>
- <u>Titles List</u>
- <u>Tunes List</u>

(DT of October 1994)

Gregorian Chants

Type: Gopher

Address: vmsgopher.cua.edu

Summary: You can get lyrics to Gregorian chants through this Catholic University site. This site keeps a database of hundreds of chants, along with related technical information.

Hyperreal - the Techno/Ambient/Rave Archive

Type: WWW

Address: http://hyperreal.com/

Summary: The Rave Archive will take you to the alt.rave FAQ, The List of Rave Lists, and pointers to tons of rave home pages. Check out Figure 10-26.

Contact: Brian Behlendorf, founder of the SFRaves mailing list brian@hyperreal.com

Figure 10-26: Welcome to Hyperreal.

Welcome to HYPERREAL

Internet Underground Music Archive (IUMA)

Type: WWW
Address: http://sunsite.unc.edu/IUMA/index_text.html
Summary: IUMA was founded by Rob Lord and Jeff Patterson to showcase unsigned musicians. Listen to clips from over 140 independent rock bands. Also available via FTP (ftp.iuma.com).

Kitaro: The Man and His Music

Type: WWW
Address: http://mindspring.com/users/shadow/kitaro.html
Summary: A page devoted to Japanese new age artist Kitaro. As of this writing, there are plans to add sounds, images and digitized film sequences.

List of Coordinators

Type: WWW
Address: http://www.update.uu.se/~vick/Coordinator.html
Summary: Reviews and tech info about coordinators (a piece of equipment that can be used to control and/or program the performance of either an internal or an external sound source). Some coordinators: drum machines, sequencers, bass machines, MIDI arpeggiators. A major site for electronic music aficionados. Specifications, performance notes, and personal reflections concerning the categorized equipment. Regularly updated.

Lyrics

Type: FTP
Address: cathouse.org
Path: /lyrics
Summary: Forgotten the words to "Poisoning Pigeons in the Park" or "The Vatican Rag"? Can't remember the refrain to "Honky Tonk Woman"? Your kid insists on hearing "It's Not Easy Being Green" with the *correct* words? Never fear. This site has lyrics for all of Tom Lehrer's, the Stones' and the Muppets' songs, as well as over 50 other musical groups and artists.

On-Line Music Database

Type: WWW
Address: http://www.cecer.army.mil/~burnett/MDB/
Summary: Search Andy Burnett's database of over 1300 artists.

Rolling Stones Web Site

Type: WWW
Address: http://www.stones.com/
Summary: Be the first on your block with a "black polar fleece ear warmer with embroidered tongue." Yes, folks, this is where you'll find the official Stones merchandise catalogue. Also tour schedules, music clips, picture collections and interviews. As of this writing, a live Internet Stones concert was being touted.

The Vangelis WWW Page

Type: WWW
Address: http://www.nets.com/vangelis
Summary: Pictures, sounds and digitized film sequences. Biographical information, as well as info about his solo and collaborative works, including motion picture scores.

Violin and Bow Makers

Type: WWW
Address: http://www.eskimo.com/~dvz/violin-makers.html
Summary: Get a regularly updated list of e-mail addresses for bowed stringed instrument makers throughout the U.S. There's a short bio for each person. This site also includes info about The American Federation of Vioin and Bow Makers.

WNUR-FM Jazz Information Server (The Jazz Web)

Type: WWW
Address: http://www.acns.nwu.edu/jazz/
Summary: Discographies, jazz media info (radio stations, etc.). History of jazz, live performance schedules, biographical info on artists, FAQ, lots of info on other jazz resources. Figure 10-27 gives you a taste of what's here.

The Jazz Web

Cool New Stuff To Check Out

● Jazz Album Charts -- WNUR's Top Ten (will appear under the "media" section of the Jazz Web)
● KLON Jazz Radio (Cal State Long Beach) *added 10/10/94* (will appear under the "media" section of the Jazz Web)
● Charts of Original Jazz Compositions by members of the net community. Maintained by Sam Hokin. (added 6/1/94)
● Search a database of Cadence Music Listings*added 3/23/94; updated 5/18/94* (will soon move to the "media" section of the Jazz Web)

The Usual Stuff

● Search the contents or titles of the JazzWeb. *Note: Please refrain from performing a full-contents search during peak hours (0900 - 1700, Central Daylight Time, UTC - 5 hrs)*
● A hyper-map of the history of Jazz
● Our collection of discographies.
● Live Performance Schedules and Reviews
● Jazz Media Info (Radio Stations, etc.)

Woodstock '94 Internet Multimedia Center

Type: WWW
Address: http://www.well.com/woodstock/
Summary: Woodstock '94 is immortalized in this site. Everything in here was created during Woodstock by on-site partici-pants and the Internet community. Over 300 pages of pictures, sounds and text. Figure 10-28 shows the home page. Peace, dude.

The Woodstock '94 Internet Multimedia Center

Click here or in the image above for the Speed Browser (all of the links with none of the wait!

From August 12-14, 1994, the WELL had a tent available on-site at Woodstock '94 from which

Some Related Newsgroups

alt.emusic
alt.guitar.tab
alt.music.a-cappella
alt.music.filk
alt.music.misc
alt.music.rush
alt.music.yes
alt.rock-n-roll.hard
alt.rock-n-roll.metal
rec.music.afro-latin
rec.music.bluenote
rec.music.celtic
rec.music.christian
rec.music.classical
rec.music.country.western
rec.music.funky
rec.music.indian.misc
rec.music.marketplace

New Age

New Age Cosmic Newsletter

Type: FTP
Address: etext.archive.umich.edu
Path: pub/Politics/Conspiracy/Cosmic.Awareness/
Summary: Introduce yourself to cosmic awareness.

News

Commercial News Services on the World Wide Web

Type: WWW
Address: http://www.jou.ufl.edu/commres/webjou.htm
Summary: Links to all the newspapers on the Net, campus as well as commercial, and to other newspaper and journalism-related resources. Figure 10-29 shows some of the links.

Figure 10-29:
Commercial News
Services on the
World Wide Web.

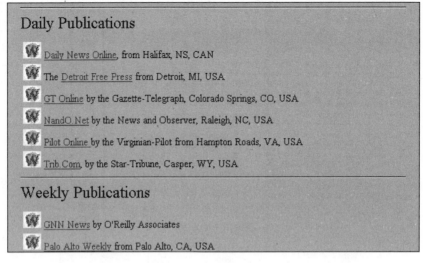

Internet Talk Radio

Type: WWW

Address: http://juggler.lanl.gov:80/itr.html

Summary: Internet Talk Radio is modeled on National Public Radio. Its goal is to provide in-depth technical information to the Internet community through a series of audio files. "Geek of the Week" features interviews with key Net personalities. As of this writing, "The Incidental Tourist, "The Internet Hall of Flame" and coverage of industry functions were in the works.

Occult

Dark Side of the Net

Type: Mailing List

Address: carriec@eskimo.com

Summary: Subscribe to this list if you want to find out about all sorts of occult-related resources, including stuff about vampires.

To subscribe, send a one-line message in e-mail: "subscribe dark side of the net *your name*" (leave out the quotes), where *your name* is your full name (not your e-mail address).

Freud's Studies of the Occult

Type: FTP
Address: ftp.spies.com
Path: /Library/Fringe/Occult/freud.occ
Summary: Freud actually dug into paranormal studies, and this paper gives all the spooky details.

Occult

Type: FTP
Address: ftp.funet.fi
Path: /pub/doc/occult/
Summary: Lots of pictures and documents—everything from astrology to wicca to magic.

Philosophy

The American Philosophical Association

Type: Gopher
Address: apa.oxy.edu *or* kasey.umkc.edu
Summary: Lots of philosophy stuff. Check out the International Philosophical Preprint Exchange, a collegial gathering of philosophers circulating prepublication drafts of their work and commenting on the work of others.

Ayn Rand

Type: USENET
Address: alt.philosophy.objectivism
Summary: Discussion of Ayn Rand's philosophy.

Politics, Government & Social Issues

Amnesty International

Type: WWW

Address: http://cyberzine.org/html/Amnesty/aihomepage.html

Summary: Contains the full text of the Universal Declaration of Human Rights, which was adopted by the General Assembly of the United Nations on December 10, 1948.

Contact: Hilary Naylor
AIUSA PeaceNet Coordinator
hnaylor@igc.apc.org
Amnesty International USA
500 Sansome St. #615
San Francisco, CA 94111
415/291-9233

Figure 10-30: Amnesty International home page.

Amnesty International

`Better to light a candle than to curse the darkness'

Universal Declaration Of Human Rights

Amnesty International Contact Information By E-mail

For information about Amnesty International you can contact Hilary Naylor, AIUSA PeaceNet

Anarchist Electronic Contact List

Type: WWW

Address: http://www.cwi.nl/cwi/people/Jack.Jansen/spunk/
Spunk_Resources.html

Summary: Spunk Press maintains this collection of anarchist and alternative resources. Newsgroups such as alt.society.anarchy, alt.society.revolution and misc.activism.progressive. A Marx and Engels Gopher hole. Alternative literature and mailing lists. The Spunk Press home page is shown in Figure 10-31.

Figure 10-31:
Spunk Press home
page.

Spunk Press

Easter Egg

Welcome to the Spunk Press index. Spunk Press collects and distributes literature in electronic format, with an emphasis on anarchism and related issues. For a more complete description of what Spunk is about you can view the Spunk Press Manifesto. In case you are only wondering where the name comes from, look here.

We also have flyers in different languages, which you can take and distribute, copy in magazines, etc. and a Call for Contributions (in English) that fits nicely on an A4 (or folio for you americans), also for distribution.

There is a catalog, listing all documents sorted by subject. There is also a numerical catalog, which is quicker if you know the 'spunk number' of a document. Eventually there will also be an Abstract Document, allowing you to locate documents by browsing through abstracts.

Bibliography of Senate Hearings

Type: FTP

Address: ftp.ncsu.edu

Path: /pub/ncsu/senate/

Summary: Monthly bibliographies of Senate hearings.

Censorship

Type: FTP

Address: ftp.spies.com

Path: /Library/Article/Rights/censored.bk

Summary: A list of books that have been banned, burned or otherwise challenged in the last fifteen years.

Center for Civic Networking

Type: FTP
Address: ftp.std.com
Path: /associations/civicnet
Summary: Resources and services related to civic networking.

Diana: An International Human Rights Database

Type: WWW
Address: http://www.law.uc.edu:80/Diana/
Summary: This site is dedicated to "completing the pioneering work in human rights information of Diana Vincent-Daviss." It's a searchable database of human rights and law-related resources. As of this writing, there were over 10,000 pages available, with the volume increasing daily.

Government Documents

Type: Gopher
Address: wiretap.spies.com
Summary: Choose Government Docs (US and World). Full text files of government acts such as the Americans with Disabilities Act, the Brady bill and the Fair Credit Reporting Act. This area also has world constitutions, as well as NATO and White House press releases.

Mother Jones Interactive

Type: WWW
Address: http://www.mojones.com/mojo_interactive/mojo_interactive.html
Summary: The Mother Jones Interactive page is organized into ten "campaign" areas such as Making Our Democracy Work, Waging Peace, Curbing Violence in America, Fostering Diversity and Community, Improving Our Nation's Education, and Keeping the Media Honest. You'll find articles from *Mother Jones Magazine*, resource guide listings and "chat" rooms.

National Child Rights Alliance

Type: WWW

Address: http://www.ai.mit.edu/people/ellens/NCRA/ncra.html

Summary: A collection of documents about the NCRA and issues pertaining to child abuse.

Contact: Jim Senter
JIMSENTER@delphi.com

North American Free Trade Agreement (NAFTA)

Type: Gopher

Address: gopher.lib.umich.edu

Summary: Choose Social Sciences Resources/Government and Politics/U.S. Government Resources: Legislative Branch/Legi-Slate Gopher. Get the full text of this act, which was signed into law in 1993.

United Nations

Type: Gopher

Address: nywork1.undp.org:70

Summary: Info about UN conferences, sessions highlights and press releases, UN System directories, UN Development Programme documents, links to other UN and related Gophers.

United States Department of Justice Home Page

Type: WWW

Address: http://www.usdoj.gov

Summary: Legal issues of the U.S, also organizations within the Department of Justice, and information servers.

U.S. Bureau of the Census

Type: WWW

Address: http://www.census.gov/

Summary: Census Bureau news releases, population information and projections, tips on genealogy, financial data for state and local governments and schools, and summarized demographic data.

Figure 10-32: The U.S. Bureau of the Census home page.

U.S. Department of Health and Human Services

Type: WWW

Address: http://www.os.dhhs.gov/

Summary: A starting point for accessing DHHS organizations. Cancer- and AIDS-related information, NIH grants and contracts, molecular biology databases, poverty guidelines, and links to other federal government resources.

U.S. Government Today

Type: Gopher

Address: wiretap.spies.com

Summary: Choose Government Docs (US & World)/US Government Today. Current membership lists for the House and Senate, phone and FAX numbers for members of Congress.

Voice of America (VOA)

Type: Gopher

Address: gopher.voa.gov

Summary: Check out the International News and English Broadcasts radio newswire reports. You'll get daily reports, features and documentaries on worldwide news events.

Contact: Chris Kern
202/619-2020
ck@voa.gov

Welcome to the White House

Type: WWW

Address: http://www.whitehouse.gov

Summary: Tour the White House, check out Al Gore's favorite political cartoons, download a picture of Socks, read the electronic citizens' handbook, get detailed info about Cabinet-level and independent agencies, daily press releases, briefings on economic and environmental policy, information on government funded childcare and disaster assistance, and lots more. This page just opened, so expect to see a lot more documents and links by the time you get this book. Figure 10-33 shows the home page.

Figure 10-33: Welcome to the White House.

Some Related Newsgroups

alt.activism
alt.censorship
alt.politics.greens
alt.politics.libertarian
alt.politics.media
alt.save.the.earth
alt.society.conservatism
alt.society.revolution
bit.listserv.politics
bit.org.peace-corps
talk.politics.soviet
talk.politics.theory

Reference

loQtus

Type: WWW
Address: http://pubweb.ucdavis.edu/Documents/Quotations/homepage.html
Summary: Jason Newquist at the University of California at Davis has put together a comprehensive quotations resource. It includes his own quotations list and pointers to a whole bunch of other quotations sources.
Contact: Jason Newquist
jmnewquist@ucdavis.edu

Online Reference Works

Type: WWW
Address: http://www.cs.cmu.edu:8001/Web/references.html
Summary: A great collection of links to dictionaries, geographical information, legal and governmental references, phone books and other reference resources.

Religion & Spirituality

The Bhagvad Gita

Type: WWW

Address: http://www.cc.gatech.edu/gvu/people/Phd/ Rakesh.Mullick/gita/gita.html

Summary: The Hindu scripture in the original Sanskrit. Each chapter is a separate PostScript document. An English translation and a summary are also available from this page.

Buddhist Studies

Type: WWW

Address: http://coombs.anu.edu.au/WWWVL-Buddhism.html

Summary: Buddhist organizations, several Buddhist studies databases, links to Gopher and Web resources. A good place to start. From here, you should be able to find out whatever you want about Buddhism. This page also contains links to other religion resources.

Catholic Resources on the Net

Type: WWW

Address: http://www.cs.cmu.edu:8001/Web/People/spok/ catholic.html

Summary: Some of the sections: Liturgy and Worship, Scripture, Writings from the early Church, Vatican II documents (1962-1965), selected papal encyclicals and pronouncements, History and Culture, and related resources. Full text of several books such as *Confessions of St. Augustine*, *The Imititation of Christ* and *The Practice of the Presence of God*.

Confession Booth

Type: WWW

Address: http://anther.learning.cs.cmu.edu/priest.html

Summary: Choose a sin (murder, gluttony, didn't put printouts in bin), enter the number of days since your last confession, and your Digital Priest will give you your penance (to music). Take a look at Figure 10-34.

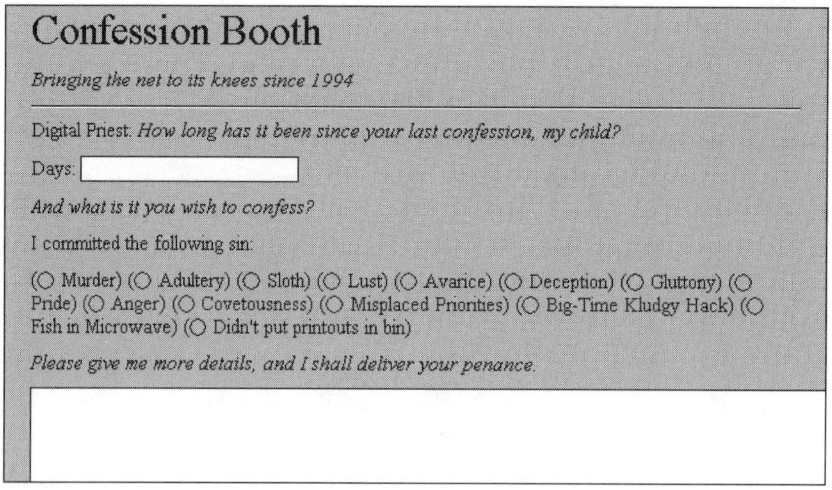

Figure 10-34:
Confession Booth
page.

Confession Booth

Bringing the net to its knees since 1994

Digital Priest: How long has it been since your last confession, my child?

Days: [   ]

And what is it you wish to confess?

I committed the following sin:

(○ Murder) (○ Adultery) (○ Sloth) (○ Lust) (○ Avarice) (○ Deception) (○ Gluttony) (○ Pride) (○ Anger) (○ Covetousness) (○ Misplaced Priorities) (○ Big-Time Kludgy Hack) (○ Fish in Microwave) (○ Didn't put printouts in bin)

Please give me more details, and I shall deliver your penance.

[   ]

Electric Mystics

Type: FTP
Address: panda1.uottawa.ca
Path: /pub/religion/electric-mystics-guide
Summary: Complete bibliography of online religious studies resources. Electronic documents, conferences, serials, software and archives.

Hindu Names

Type: FTP
Address: ftp.spies.com
Path: /Library/Article/Language/hindu.nam

Israel Project

Type: FTP
Address: israel.nysernet.org
Path: /israel
Summary: Information about all aspects of Judaism and the state of Israel. Never forget. Change to the /israel/holocaust directory for a wealth of information, including data on the neo-Nazi movement.

Lubavitch

Type: Gopher

Address: lubavitch.chabad.org

Summary: The Chabad-Lubavitch Movement offers courses on Judaism, discussion groups, translations of the Jewish prayer book and other theological works. If you subscribe to the Lubavitch mailing list, you can get daily lessons on Chasidic philosophy, a Chasidic thought for the day and weekly Torah readings. To subscribe, send e-mail to yyk@lubavitch.chabad.org, with the subject line SUBSCRIBE ME and the text SUBSCRIBE ALL.

Spirituality & Consciousness

Type: WWW

Address: http://err.ethz.ch/~kiwi/Spirituality.html

Summary: Pointers to info about channeling, meditation, yoga, Veda, Theosophy, astrology, Bhakti-Yoga, Free Daism, paranormal phenomena, and lots more having to do with metaphysical and alternative views. Figure 10-35 show a small sample of what's available.

Figure 10-35: Spirituality & Consciousness.

Spirituality & Consciousness

Last update Oct 25, 1994

Spirituality & Consciousness:

Spirit-WWW*(René K. Müller)*
　　Channelings, Lightwork, Healing (Alternative Methods), UFO-Phenomena, Light-Technology, Out Of Body Experience, Meditation, Yoga-Paths, Veda & Dharma, Theosophy, Astrology, etc.

Bhakti-Yoga-WWW*(Anand Ravipati)*
Free Daism*(Chris Tong)*
Zen/Sufi Info-Service*(Wes Miller)*
Dharma Electronic Files Archive (DEFA)*(Barry Kapke)*
WWW-VL: Religions*(Armin Müller)*
Society & Culture: Religion*(Yahoo)*

Metaphysical and Alternative Views:

Romance

Find Romance
Type: USENET
Address: alt.romance
soc.personals.fsm
soc.personals.msf
soc.motss
Summary: Personals posted only sporadically. Mostly discussion.

Weddings
Type: USENET
Address: alt.wedding
Summary: Discussions about weddings.

Science

Alfred Wegener Institute for Polar and Marine Research
Type: WWW
Address: http://www.awi-bremerhaven.de/
Summary: The Alfred Wegener Institute has laboratories in Bremerhaven and Potsdam, bases in the Arctic and Antarctic, and research ships and aircraft. Lots of gifs, maps, and charts of the polar region. Includes a detailed hydrographic atlas of the Southern Ocean. There's a database of polar- and marine-related documents on the Web, pointers to other WWW servers related to polar, marine and global change research.

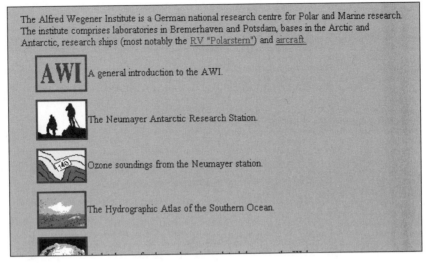

Figure 10-36:
Alfred Wegener
Institute Welcome
Page.

The Alfred Wegener Institute is a German national research centre for Polar and Marine research. The institute comprises laboratories in Bremerhaven and Potsdam, bases in the Arctic and Antarctic, research ships (most notably the RV "Polarstern") and aircraft.

A general introduction to the AWI.

The Neumayer Antarctic Research Station.

Ozone soundings from the Neumayer station.

The Hydrographic Atlas of the Southern Ocean.

Avion Online

Type: WWW

Address: http://avion.db.erau.edu/avion/avionhome.html

Summary: The first online aviation/aerospace newspaper. The Space Technology section routinely covers activity at Kennedy Space Center, including shuttle launches and landings. The Aeronautica section routinely covers activity in the aviation and aeronautics industry, including aviation trade news and special flying events.

Biological Sciences Resources

Type: FTP

Address: ksuvxa.kent.edu

Path: /library/acadlist.file5

Summary: This is a list of a whole bunch of mailing lists that have to do with the biological sciences.

Biology Newsletter

Type: FTP
Address: nigel.msen.com
Path: /pub/newsletters/Bio
Summary: Newsletters about agriculture, botany, ecosystems, genetics and general biology.

Center for Coastal Studies

Type: WWW
Address: http://www-ccs.ucsd/edu/
Summary: The Center for Coastal Studies is a research unit of UC San Diego's Scripps Institution of Oceanography. You'll find all sorts of studies on subjects like global warming, long-term climate change, earthquake prediction, coastal protection and sediment management. Also available via Gopher (gopher-ccs.ucsd.edu).

Comet Shoemaker-Levy

Type: WWW
Address: http://newproducts.jpl.nasa.gov/sl9/sl9.html
Summary: When Comet Shoemaker-Levy 9 collided with Jupiter in July 1994, it was the first time the collision of two major solar system bodies was observed and recorded. This page contains lots of background information and animations, and takes you to photo files from NASA and worldwide observatories. There's a whole section full of links to other Comet Shoemaker-Levy home pages (currently there are seven). Figure 10-37 shows one of the images available from this site.

Figure 10-37: Jupiter image from Comet Shoemaker-Levy site.

Jupiter as Seen by Galileo

Jesuits and the Sciences

Type: WWW
Address: http://www.luc.edu/~scilib/jessci.html
Summary: Works from the Society of Jesus from 1580–1800.

Lunar Institute of Technology

Type: WWW
Address: http://lunar.org/LIT/
Summary: The Lunar Institute of Technology was established in 2032, and its School of Starship Design is renowned throughout the Solar System. If you are one of the lucky few to attend this prestigious institution, you will participate in the design of a manned interstellar vehicle. Pick a specialty—Mission/Operations, Structure/Shielding or Payload/Sciences—and become part of the design team.

My description may be somewhat tongue-in-cheek, but you'll find some serious science here. Figure 10-38 shows some of the choices on the home page.

Figure 10-38:
Starship Design
home page.

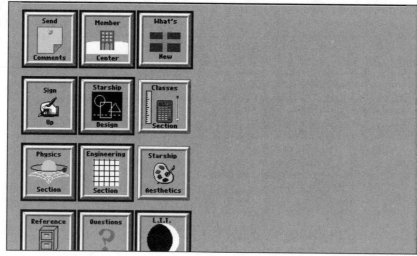

Mercury Project

Type: WWW

Address: http://www.usc.edu/dept/raiders/

Summary: A team at the University of Southern California created this site to allow users to take part in an archaeological dig by controlling a robot arm. You select a viewpoint and use the robot arm to blow compressed air. A video camera mounted on the robot arm shows you the results of your "dig."

The NASA Newsroom

Type: WWW

Address: http://www.gsfc.nasa.gov/hqpao/newsroom.html

Summary: All sorts of NASA press releases, press kits, status reports, fact sheets and official statements. Take a look at Figure 10-39.

Figure 10-39: The
NASA Newsroom.

Periodic Table

Type: FTP
Address: freebsd.cdrom.com
Path: /.12/games/msdos/educate/periodic.zip
Summary: Graphical DOS program that shows periodic table of the
elements. Get detailed information about any element
by moving to it and pressing Enter.

Planet Earth Images and Movies

Type: WWW
Address: http://white.nosc.mil/earth_images.html
Summary: Collection of images of earth, organized by continent.
Movies and still pictures. Figure 10-40 shows one of the
images you can get from this site.

Figure 10-40: An image from the Planet Earth Images and Movies site.

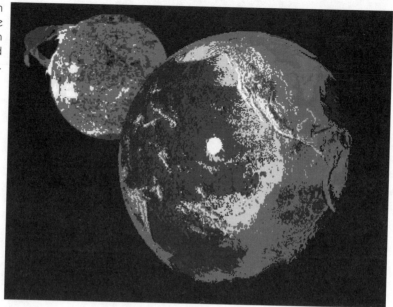

Primate Info Net

Type: Gopher

Address: saimiri.primate.wisc.edu

Summary: This entire Gopher site is devoted to primate biology. You'll find stuff about animal welfare legislation and behavioral patterns. Lots of newsletters and discussions.

Smithsonian Institution's Natural History Gopher

Type: Gopher

Address: nmnhgoph.si.edu

Summary: This Gopher contains newsletters, projects and lots of pointers to other natural history resources. If you're interested in botany, vertebrate zoology, biodiversity, biological conservation, global volcanism or anything else involving natural history, check out this cool site.

Space Movie Archive

Type: WWW

Address: http://www.univ-rennes1.fr/ASTRO/anim-e.html

Summary: We're not talking science fiction here. We're talking solar eclipses, meteorology and space exploration (with some science fiction thrown into the mix for good measure). Tons of animations and instructions for getting animation viewers if you don't already have one. Figure 10-41 shows the home page. Also available via FTP (ftp.univ-rennes1.fr in the /pub/Images/ASTRO/ anim directory).

Figure 10-41: Space Movie Archive home page.

Stephen Hawking's Black Hole Theory

Type: Gopher

Address: wx.atmos.uiuc.edu

Summary: Choose Documents/fun/hawking.black.holes. The full text of Hawking's 1988 presentation "Baby Universes, Children of Black Holes."

United States Geological Survey

Type: WWW

Address: http://info.er.usgs.gov/

Summary: Geologic map of the United States and information about public issues, education and environmental research.

Visual Interface for Space and Terrestrial Analysis (VISTA)

Type: WWW

Address: http://bradbury.nrl.navy.mil/vista/

Summary: A GUI system developed at the Backgrounds Data Center in Washington D.C. to "bring visualization to its databases of multiple remote sensing platforms." Users can query, visualize and analyze geophysical and celestial data and metadata.

Some Related Newsgroups

alt.sci.planetary
bionet.genome.arabidopsis
bionet.genome.chromosomes
bionet.molbio.ageing
bionet.plants
bionet.photosynthesis
bionet.population-bio
bionet.women-in-bio
sci.astro
sci.astro.hubble
sci.astro.planetarium
sci.bio.ecology
sci.bio.technology
sci.engr.chem

Science Fiction

FAQ for alt.books.isaac-asimov

Type: WWW

Address: http://www.lightside.com/SpecialInterest/asimov/asimov-faq.html

Summary: This FAQ is full of fascinating stuff about the master and his works.

J.R.R. Tolkien Information Page

Type: WWW

Address: http://csclub.uwaterloo.ca/u/relipper/tolkien/rootpage.html

Summary: This page, put together by Eric Lippert, is an amazingly complete Tolkien resource. In addition to FAQs, book lists, newsgroups, language resources, info about the Tolkien Society, a Middle-Earth map, Noldor and Great Houses family trees, there are several query tools.

Contact: Eric Lippert
relippert@descartes.uwaterloo.ca

Red Dwarf Home Page

Type: WWW

Address: http://www.hal.com/~markg/docs/RedDwarf/rd-home_page.html

Summary: An episode guide, FAQs, favorite quotes, sounds and images.

Science Fiction Resource Guide

Type: WWW

Address: http://gandalf.rutgers.edu/pub/sfl/sf-resource.guide.html

Summary: From the SF-Lovers Archives at Rutgers University. The ultimate SF link. It's all here: authors, awards, bookstores, fandom, fiction, movies, 'zines, conventions and more.

Speculative Fiction Clearing House

Type: WWW

Address: http://thule.mt.cs.cmu.edu:8001/sf-clearing-house/

Summary: Science fiction, fantasy and horror archives, authors, awards, conventions, 'zines and newsletters. Also resources for SF writers.

Unofficial Xanth Page

Type: WWW

Address: http://www.cs.indiana.edu/hyplan/awooldri/Xanth.html

Summary: For fans of Piers Anthony's Xanth world novels. Some highlights: a cheat list for Companions of Xanth, a Qbasic program that allows you to generate Xanth-like talents, the Piers Anthony FAQ, a Xanth family tree, the Xanth calendar, and a color image of Piers and his dog. Newsgroup: alt.fan.piers-anthony.

Related Newsgroup

rec.arts.sf.reviews

Security

Privacy Forum Digest

Type: WWW

Address: http://www.vortex.com/privacy.htm

Summary: Discussions of privacy in the information age. This directory includes all issues of the Privacy Forum Digest, as well as lots of related reports and materials. The home page gives complete instruction for subscribing to the Privacy Forum. Also available via FTP (ftp.vortex.com in the /privacy/ directory) and Gopher (cv.vortex.com—choose Privacy Forum).

Showbiz

Elvis Lives!

Type: WWW
Address: http://128.194.15.32/~ahb2188/elvishom.html
Summary: Created by superfan Andrea Berman to "honor his cultural and musical legacy." Take a tour of Graceland, inspect Elvis' shopping list, and check out the results of an online seance conducted in January 1994. Feast your eyes on Figure 10-42.

Figure 10-42: The Elvis Aaron Presley home page.

The Elvis Aron Presley Home Page

(where The King lives on in cyberspace)

Updated October 11, 1994!

Gossip

Type: USENET
Address: alt.showbiz.gossip
Summary: Don't get bogged down with the facts—this is pure unadulterated gossip.

Software

Sandra's Clip Art Server

Type: WWW

Address: http://www.cs.yale.edu/HTML/YALE/CS/HyPlans/loosemore-sandra/clipart.html

Summary: Tons of clip art from her own collection and other archive sites. Can also FTP to this site (www.cs.yale.edu in the /WWW/HTML/YALE/CS/HyPlans/loosemore-sandra/clipart/ directory).

Sports

Aquanaut

Type: WWW

Address: http://www.opal.com/aquanaut

Summary: Everything scuba—a database of diveable shipwrecks, reviews of dive gear and equipment, reviews of popular dive destinations and underwater pictures. Newsgroup: rec.scuba.

The Art of Fencing

Type: WWW

Address: http://www.ii.uib.no/~arild/fencing.html

Summary: Articles, fencing clubs and associations, events lists and the Internet Fencing Encyclopedia (a collection of links to pages about fencing).

Footbag WorldWide

Type: WWW

Address: http://www.cup.hp.com:80/~footbag/

Summary: Footbag is a new sport, similar to the game of Hacky Sack. Get tournament results, equiment information, images and video clips of footbag action. To join the mailing list and chat with other players at all levels, send e-mail to ba-footbag-request@cup.hp.com. Include your first and last name somewhere in the message.

George Ferguson's Ultimate Page

Type: WWW

Address: http://www.cs.rochester.edu/u/ferguson/ultimate/

Summary: Ultimate frisbee is a non-contact team sport. Get the official rules and tournament handbook here. Part of the home page is shown in Figure 10-43.

Figure 10-43: George Ferguson's Ultimate Page.

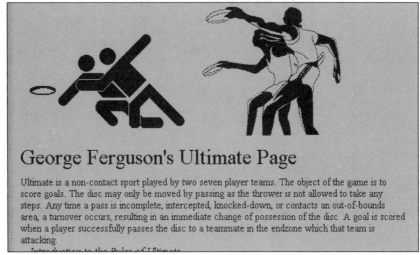

Hawaii's NHL Home Page

Type: WWW

Address: http://maxwell.uhh.hawaii.edu/hockey/hockey.html

Summary: Welcome to the world of hockey. From here, you can get to all of the NHL team home pages, the NHL Statserver, game schedules and Stanley Cup info. Currently, there are plans to provide daily statistical updates on teams and players.

Korfball

Type: WWW

Address: http://www.earth.ox.ac.uk:80/~geoff/

Summary: Korfball is a mixed team sport that's kind of like basketball, but without backboards or dribbling. Get the latest information about this rapidly growing sport.

Figure 10-44:
Korfball in action.

Mountain Biking

Type: WWW

Address: http://xenon.stanford.edu/~rsf/mtn-bike.html

Summary: Info about biking trails in various parts of the U.S., as well as a link to a mountain bike page in the U.K.

The Nando X Baseball Server

Type: WWW

Address: http://www.nando.net/baseball/bbmain.html

Summary: National and American League stats, standings and other info.

The 19th Hole

Type: WWW

Address: http://dallas.nmhu.edu/golf/golf.htm

Summary: The rules of golf, equipment sources, a scorecard archive, golf art, golf associations and pointers to other golf pages.

Orienteering and Rogaining Home Page

Type: WWW

Address: http://www2.aos.Princeton.EDU:80/rdslater/ orienteering/

Summary: Get out your old Scout compass and hit the road. Announcements about these two popular sports, federation and club information, and links to related pages.

The Running Page

Type: WWW

Address: http://sunsite.unc.edu/drears/running/running.html

Summary: Info about upcoming races, race results, places to run, running related products and running publications. Check out the Exercise Trails Network. Members of the American Running and Fitness Association have been contributing maps of their favorite running and exercise trails. You can get a free map by contributing one of your own, even if you're not a member. Otherwise, maps cost one dollar.

Speleology Information Server

Type: WWW

Address: http://speleology.cs.yale.edu/

Summary: For the uninitiated, *speleology* means hanging around in caves in a serious way. Newsletters, cave studies, caving clip art and cartoons, and speleological societies around the word.

Sports World BBS

Type: WWW

Address: http://debussy.media.mit.edu/dbecker/docs/ swbbs.html

Summary: Stats for NHL, NFL, NBA and major league baseball pools.

Unicycling Home Page

Type: WWW
Address: http://nimitz.mcs.kent.edu/~bkonarsk
Summary: If you're a unicyclist, an aspiring unicyclist, or just curious, check out this page. Join the Unicycling Mailing List by sending a request to unicycling-request@mcs.kent.edu.

Volleyball Information Service

Type: WWW
Address: http://www.cup.hp.com:80/~vball/
Summary: This page was created by Tom Jack, a software design engineer who coaches volleyball in his spare time, as a way of centralizing information about the sport. You'll find FAQs, info about the volleyball USENET newsgroup, equipment, TV coverage, and coverage of Olympic and professional teams. Because Tom lives in Cupertino, CA, there's lots of info about classes, clubs, tournaments and such in the San Jose/San Francisco area. Links to volleyball sites throughout the U.S.
Contact: Tom Jack
taj@cup.hp.com
408/447-4239

WWW Sports Information Service

Type: WWW
Address: http://www.mit.edu:8001/services/sis/sports.html
Summary: This won Best Entertainment Site in the Best of the Web '94 contest. As of this writing, it consists mainly of links to the Professional Basketball Server and Professional Football Server, but there are plans to add more sports. Get information about any NBA or NFL team or player. Scores, schedules, stats and other stuff.

Figure 10-45:
WWW Sports
Information
Service.

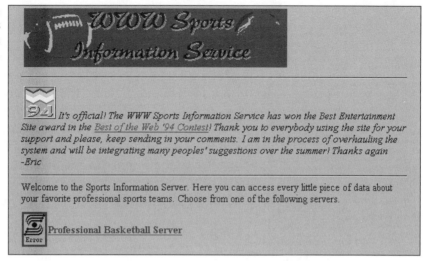

Related Newsgroup
alt.sport.korfball

Star Trek

British Starfleet Confederacy
Type: WWW
Address: http://deeptht.armory.com/~bsc/
Summary: If you join the British Starfleet Confederacy, you'll get a certificate of commission, officers' manual, identity card, stardate calendar and six bimonthly newsletters and chapter bulletins. Even if you don't want to join the fleet, this page contains comprehensive links to all things Trek.
Contact: starfleet@subspace.demon.co.uk

Klingon Language Institute

Type: WWW

Address: http://www.kli.org/

Summary: The Klingon Language Institute was founded in 1992 "to promote, foster, and develop the Klingon language, and to bring together Klingon language enthusiasts from around the world." You'll find sound files, information about their postal course and how to subscribe to the mailing list, and a fascinating background on the development of the language (it's one of the few artificial alien languages developed by a trained linguist).

Star Trek

Type: FTP

Address: ftp.spies.com

Path: /Library/Media/Trek

Summary: Tons of Trek-related files, including a Klingon vocabulary and a Deep Space Nine bibliography.

Star Trek II

Type: FTP

Address: scam.berkeley.edu

Path: /misc/trek-info

Summary: Get your fill of press releases, episode credits, synopses and articles.

Strange USENET Newsgroups

alt.angst
alt.barney.die.die.die
alt.buddha.short.fat.guy
alt.flame.roommate
alt.food.sugar-cereals
alt.geek
alt.happy.birthday.to.me
alt.pantyhose
alt.religion.santaism
alt.rumors

alt.spam
alt.tasteless
alt.wesley.crusher.die.die.die
talk.bizarre

Technology

Telecom Information Resources on the Internet

Type: WWW

Address: http://www.ipps.lsa.umich.edu/telecom-info.html

Summary: A plenitude of pointers to telecommunications resources. It's all here—voice, data, video, wired, wireless, cable TV, satellite. You can find info about aspects of telecom issues, from technical to public policy, from economic to social impacts.

Contact: Jeff MacKie-Mason
jmm@umich.edu

Theater & Film

Andrew Lloyd Webber

Type: Mailing List

Address: majordomo@world.std.com

Summary: To subscribe to this list for Andrew Lloyd Webber fans, send a one-line message in e-mail: "subscribe alw" (leave out the quotes).

Cardiff's Movie Database Browser

Type: WWW

Address: http://www.cm.cf.ac.uk/Movies/moviequery.html

Summary: This is the hypertext front end to the rec.arts.movies database. Figure 10-46 shows the home page.

Figure 10-46: The
Cardiff's Movie
Database Browser
home page.

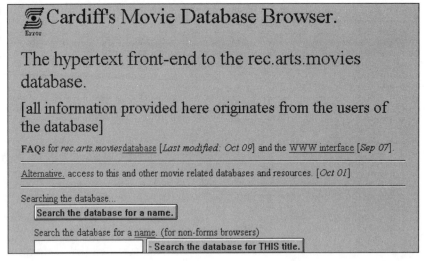

Drama

Type: Gopher
Address: english-server.hss.cmu.edu
Path: Drama
Summary: Play scripts, drama-related materials, reviews, Shakespeare info. Follow path to Shakespeare-Glossary for glossary of Shakespearean terms.

Home Page of Theatre

Type: WWW
Address: http://www.cs.fsu.edu/projects/group4/theatre.html
Summary: Follow the links on this page to find myriad theatre resources. Some highlights: Ray Bradbury's Theatre Episode Guide, ruins of the Roman Theatre, The Fire Sign Theatre and Computers in Theatre. The home page is shown in Figure 10-47.

Figure 10-47: The
Home Page of
Theatre.

THE HOME PAGE OF THEATRE

Welcome to the **HOME PAGE OF THEATRE** in Mosaic, an Internet information browser and World Wide Web client. NCSA Mosaic was developed at the National Center for Supercomputing Applications at the University of Illinois, Urbana-Champaign.

The Home Page of Theatre gives you information on some well known playwrites, provides

Screenwriters' and Playwrights' Home Page

Type: WWW

Address: http://www.teleport.com/~cdeemer/scrwriter.html

Summary: As of this writing, this page is still under construction, but there are already lots of resources for screenwriters and playwrights. There's a guide to screenplay structure, scripts, discussion groups and tips from the pros.

Weird Movie List

Type: FTP

Address: ftp.spies.com

Path: /Library/Media/Film/weird.mov

Summary: Alphabetical list of weird movies, with descriptions. You can also get this list via Gopher. The address is wiretap.spies.com, then choose Wiretap Online Library/ Mass Media/Film and Movies/Weird Movie List.

Travel

Aspen Gopher

Type: Gopher

Address: aspen.com

Summary: Choose Special-Aspen Linkup to get to a Gopher hole devoted to topics of relevance to Aspen, CO. As of this writing, the Aspen Gopher is still under construction. Right now you can get photos, ski maps and other ski information. In the future, you can expect to see stuff about hotels, bed and breakfasts, ski conditions and much more.

Contact: aspen@aspen.com

Clothing Optional

Type: FTP

Address: rtfm.mit.edu

Path: /pub/usenet/rec-answers/nude-faq/beaches

Summary: Lists of clothing-optional beaches, hot springs, parks and resorts worldwide.

Currency Converter

Type: WWW

Address: http://www.ora.com/cgi-bin/ora/currency

Summary: This page is updated weekly. By default, the page shows the currency rates of over 50 countries relative to U.S. currency (e.g., one U.S. dollar is worth 1.3605 dollars in Australia). To get currency rates relative to another country, just click the country you want. Take a look at Figure 10-48 to see how it works.

Figure 10-48: The
Koblas Currency
Converter page.

The Global Network Navigator/Koblas Currency Converter

by David Koblas

Using the **Koblas Currency Converter** is very simple. Just select the desired currency and all other currencies will be coverted relative to the one you selected. The name of the currency will also appear just below this message.

This week's currency rates (one US dollar equals)

Updated weekly—last 28 October 1994

```
    Argentina:    0.99940
    Australia:    1.3548
      Austria:   10.496
      Belgium:   30.830
       Brazil:    0.85000
      Britain:    0.61070
       Canada:    1.3478
        Chile:  400.79
```

GNN TC Internet Resources—Planning

Type: WWW

Address: http://nearnet.gnn.com/gnn/meta/travel/res/planning.html

Summary: Even if the longest trip you ever take is from your computer to your printer, check out this page. It'll take you to all sorts of travel-related resources. You'll find U.S. Army Area Handbooks on Egypt, Indonesia, Israel, Japan, the Philippines, Singapore, Somalia, South Korea and Yugoslavia. And get an inside peek at the documents the State Department gives its people before they travel to a country. Get the latest U.S. State Department travel warnings and consular information sheets. A few more highlights: The Internet Guide to Hostelling; Travel Health - Staying Healthy in Asia, Africa, and Latin America; the CIA World Factbook; Travel Tips for Less Developed Countries; and the Worldwide Telephone Codes list, which is a searchable list of area codes for the entire world.

The Hawaiian Islands

Type: WWW
Address: http://www2.hawaii.edu/visitors/visit.hawaii.html
Summary: This one's maintained by the Hawaii Visitors Center. There's a link to each of the islands.

The Jerusalem Mosaic

Type: WWW
Address: http://shum.cc.huji.ac.il/jeru/jerusalem.html
Summary: Listen to the song of Jerusalem, view Jerusalem from the sky, read about events in the history of Jerusalem.

Figure 10-49: The Jerusalem Mosaic.

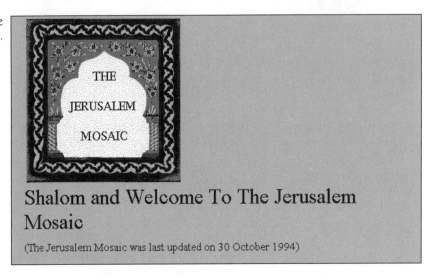

THE JERUSALEM MOSAIC

Shalom and Welcome To The Jerusalem Mosaic

(The Jerusalem Mosaic was last updated on 30 October 1994)

Local Times Around the World

Type: Gopher
Address: austin.unimelb.edu.au
Summary: Choose General Information and Resources/Local Times around the World. Connect to computers in cities around the world to get local time reports.

Subway Maps

Type: Gopher

Address: vishnu.jussieu.fr

Summary: Choose Indicateur des metros (don't worry, there's a file in English too). Download color maps of the Paris and Lyon subways.

Related Newsgroup

rec.travel.marketplace

Weather

National Weather Service Forecasts

Type: Gopher

Address: wx.atmos.uiuc.edu

Summary: Weather reports by geographical region as well as by weather type.

National Weather Service Forecasts II

Type: Gopher

Address: downwind.sprl.umich.edu

Summary: Choose Weather Text, U.S. City Forecasts. Daily weather information for cities all over the country. Pick a state, then a city.

Gateways to More Internet Resources

Carnegie Mellon University English Server

Type: Gopher

Address: english-server.hss.cmu.edu

Summary: A Gopher server developed by the graduate students in the English department of Carnegie Mellon University. Designed to freely distribute documents and information on a wide range of subject matter, this is truly one of the most comprehensive information resources on the Internet.

Cool Site of the Day

Type: WWW
Address: http://www.infi.net/cool.html
Summary: What's a cool site? Here's what Glenn Davis, who maintains this page, has to say: "Every day I look around the World Wide Web for something that I think is cool. I can't tell you what makes a site cool. I just find them, and when I think I have a cool one, I put it in Cool Site of the Day." Don't worry about all the cool sites you've already missed—there's a link to Previous Cool Sites.
Contact: Glenn Davis
gdavis@infi.net

Cool Sites to Visit

Type: WWW
Address: http://kells.vmedia.com:80/alternate/vvc/onlcomp/mosaicqtm/hyperguide/CoolSite4.html
Summary: A collection of cool stuff maintained by Ventana Online. The home page has a list and descriptions of current cool happenings. Go to General Net Resources (from the TOC page) for a terrific collection of information about the Net.

Hytelnet Server

Type: telnet
Address: access.usask.ca
Summary: Log in as hytelnet. Access telnet resources using a hypertext browser. Hytelnet is Peter Scott's implementation of a hypertext database of publicly accessible Internet sites. More than 1,300 sites are currently listed, including libraries, campus-wide information systems, Gopher, WAIS and WWW servers. Provides access to several university and library card catalogs. This is a useful way to search for books and journal articles on a specific topic, but you will not be able to access the full text of these resources via a remote Internet login.

A Hytelnet mailing list is also available by e-mail at listserv@kentvm.kent.edu. Send a one-line mail message: "subscribe hytel-l *your name*" (leave out the quotes), where *your name* is your first and last name (not your e-mail address).

Internet Dog-Eared Pages

Type: Gopher
Address: sunsite.unc.edu
Summary: The most often-used resources on the Internet, compiled in one place.

Inter-Active Yellow Pages

Type: WWW
Address: http://netcenter.com/yellows/index.html
Summary: Commercial products and services on the net. Everything from consumer electronics to travel to "The World's First Totally Useless 900#s." There's also a Windows Hot Tip of the Month.

Internet Resources Meta-Index

Type: WWW
Address: http://www.ncsa.uiuc.edu/SDG/Software/Mosaic/MetaIndex.html
Summary: This page has links to most of the resource directories and indexes on the Net.

JumpStation Front Page

Type: WWW
Address: http://www.stir.ac.uk/jsbin/js
Summary: Query the JumpStation database and get a set of links that correspond to your criteria.

LIBS

Type: telnet

Address: nessie.cc.wwu.edu

Summary: Log in as LIBS. Provides gateway access to many telnet services. Library card catalogs in various countries are accessible, as are several campus-wide information systems. This service is referred to as a gateway because you can access other services through this portal. An example session is shown in Figure 10-50.

Figure 10-50: A sample LIBS session.

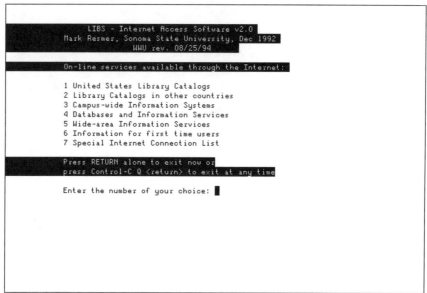

```
        LIBS - Internet Access Software v2.0
     Mark Resmer, Sonoma State University, Dec 1992
                  WWU rev. 08/25/94

        On-line services available through the Internet:

        1 United States Library Catalogs
        2 Library Catalogs in other countries
        3 Campus-wide Information Systems
        4 Databases and Information Services
        5 Wide-area Information Services
        6 Information for first time users
        7 Special Internet Connection List

        Press RETURN alone to exit now or
        press Control-C Q <return> to exit at any time

        Enter the number of your choice: █
```

Marius Watz' WWW Pages

Type: WWW

Address: http://www.uio.no/~mwatz/

Summary: Links that focus on philosophy, the avant-garde, cyberculture and the computer underground. Check out his NEXUS project.

MCLI's Hot Links

Type: WWW

Address: http://hakatai.mcli.dist.maricopa.edu/links/
wwwLinks.html

Summary: Another great collection of Web links.

The Mother-of-all BBS

Type: WWW

Address: http://www.cs.colorado.edu/homes/mcbryan/
public_html/bb/summary.html

Summary: Links to just about everything on the Web. You can
perform a WAIS search on the Bulletin Board.

NetManage WWW Starting Points

Type: WWW

Address: http://www.netmanage.com/netmanage/nm11.html

Summary: Yet another set of links organized by subject.

The Official Roadmap to the Information Superhighway

Type: WWW

Address: http://netcenter.com/roadmap/index.html

The Scout Report

Type: WWW

Address: http://www.internic.net/scout-report/

Summary: A weekly publication produced by InterNIC Information Services. Highlights of new resources and Internet
news updates. Very cool. You can also Gopher to the
Scout Report: internic.net/Information Services/Scout
Report. To subscribe via e-mail, send mail to
majordomo@is.internic.net with the words "subscribe
scout-report" (without the quotes) in the body of the
message. If your mailer automatically appends your
signature, you should include the word "end" (again
without the quotes) on a separate line. This keeps
majordomo from processing unnecessary commands.

The Source

Type: WWW

Address: http://hakatai.mcli.dist.maricopa.edu/smc/ml/
source.html

Summary: A great selection of philosophy, religion and psychology
resources.

W3 Catalog

Type: WWW

Address: http://cui_www.unige.ch/w3catalog

Summary: A searchable catalog of Web resources. As of 10/15/94,
it contained 10,003 entries.

Washington & Lee University's Netlink Server

Type: WWW

Address: http://honor.uc.wlu.edu:1020/

Summary Links to high-level Internet sources, database of links to
public login telnet sites, WWW servers, WAIS servers—
tons of stuff!

The Web's Edge

Type: WWW

Address: http://kzsu.stanford.edu/uwi.html

Summary: "UnderWorld Industries' Cultural Playground." Lots of
alternative stuff. Check out "Stream of Conscience," an
art/poetry web-zine. Figure 10-51 gives you a taste of
what's here.

Figure 10-51: The Web's Edge home page.

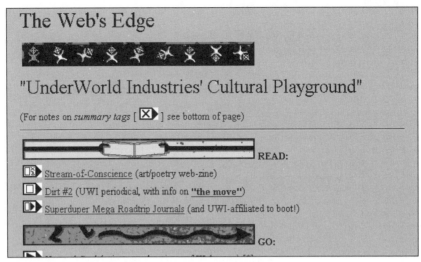

What's Hot and Cool

Type: WWW

Address: http://kzsu.stanford.edu/uwi/reviews.html

Summary: Lots of cool (and hot) alternative-type stuff. Figure 10-52 shows just a few of the links.

Figure 10-52: What's Hot and Cool.

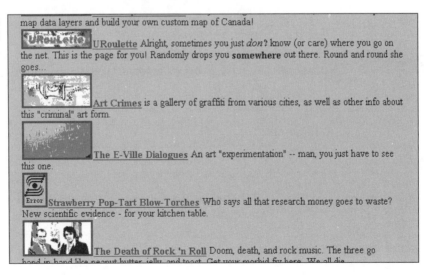

What's New With NCSA Mosaic and the WWW

Type: WWW
Address: http://www.ncsa.uiuc.edu/SDG/Software/Mosaic/ Docs/whats-new.html
Summary: Get the latest Web info here. Descriptions of and links to new home pages.

The World Wide Web Virtual Library

Type: WWW
Address: http://info.cern.ch/hypertext/DataSources/bySubject/ Overview.html
Summary: A very complete subject catalog of Net resources, organized by subject and service type.

Yahoo - A Guide to WWW

Type: WWW
Address: http://akebono.stanford.edu:80/yahoo/
Summary: In one week during October 1994, this topically organized listing grew from 9,558 to 16,096 entries.

The Yanoff List

Type: FTP
Address: ftp.csd.uwm.edu
Path: /pub/inet.services.txt
Summary: A HUGE list of Internet resources, updated regularly. Better than a lot of other resource lists because it gives descriptions of each site. Print it out and start browsing—there's enough to keep you busy at least until the next edition of this book comes out.

Also available by mailing list by sending a subscription request to yanoff@csd4.csd.uwm.edu. The list is also posted regularly to several USENET newsgroups including biz.comp.services and alt.internet.services.

Conclusion

So now you're a pro at practically all things Internet. What's that? You feel like we've just gone around the world in 80 days (or perhaps only 8)? You're still overwhelmed with all the things you can do, people you can meet and places you can visit?

The good news is, you're not on your own. There are plenty of friendly people all over the Net who can offer you help when you need it. And you can always find a wealth of interesting and useful Internet information at the Ventana Online Visitor's Center. (For more on Ventana Online and the Visitor's Center, see Appendix A.) But the real secret to finding your way around the Internet is to forget about where you're going, and just go. Explore. Take a sidetrip. Have fun.

Appendix A
The Companion Disks
& Ventana Online

In this appendix you'll find information about the software included on *The Mac Internet Tour Guide Companion Disks*, and about the valuable services and resources available from Ventana Online (where the latest versions of the companion disk software are always available), including the Visitor's Center and *The Mac Internet Tour Guide Online Companion*.

The Companion Disk Software

The software included on *The Mac Internet Tour Guide Companion Disks* is a compilation of both commercial software and shareware. Ventana Mosaic is our own custom version of Enhanced Mosaic, the predominant World Wide Web reader. The remaining software on the companion disks is distributed with the permission of its authors and is provided here for evaluation purposes. You may try it without obligation, but if you decide to keep a program permanently, please check the Read Me file that is on the disk and make the appropriate shareware payment whenever applicable. Ventana Press and the author provide this software for your use as is and make no guarantee or warranty regarding its performance or compatibility.

To install the software from the companion disks, you'll need about 5mb of free space on your hard drive. We suggest that you make a careful backup of the contents of your hard drive and backups of the companion disks before you begin. Refer to the disk labels and the pages at the back of the book for installation instructions.

Ventana Mosaic

Ventana Mosaic is a special custom version of Enhanced Mosaic. After you install this software, you'll be ready to explore the wonders of the world's largest living book—the World Wide Web, an online hypertext system spanning the Internet. To learn more about Mosaic and the Web, take a look at Chapter 8.

Eudora

Eudora is one of the best Internet e-mail programs available for the Macintosh. It is fully compatible with the POP3 mail server offered by most Internet service providers. To configure Eudora for use with your mail server, see Chapter 4, "Electronic Mail." The complete Eudora documentation set does not fit on the companion disks. You can FTP complete documentation—in Microsoft Word format—from Qualcomm Inc.'s server, or you can order a printed manual and distribution disk from the company for $30.

Fetch

Fetch is a File Transfer Protocol (FTP) program. With Fetch you can quickly and easily download files from or upload files to a remote host on the Internet. Instructions for configuring and using Fetch are provided in Chapter 6, "Transferring Files."

Nuntius

Nuntius is a news reader—a software client that simplifies the process of navigating and reading network news articles. To learn more about network news, and about configuring and using Nuntius, refer to Chapter 5, "Network News & Newsgroups."

StuffIt Expander

StuffIt Expander is a file decompression utility that you'll need for the files and other software resources you download from various sites on the Internet.

TurboGopher

TurboGopher enables you to browse through information resources on the Internet, translating complicated menu structures into familiar folder and file icons. TurboGopher is covered in Chapter 7, "Using Gopher."

InterSLIP & MacTCP

InterSLIP, a freeware product owned by and provided courtesy of InterCon Systems Corporation, is a Control Panel that enables you to establish a connection to the Internet with a modem and an ordinary telephone line.

MacTCP is licensed Apple software that is required to establish an Internet connection. It is a Control Panel that allows your Mac to communicate with other computers using the TCP/IP protocols on the Internet.

For information about configuring MacTCP and InterSLIP, and about establishing your own Internet connection, refer to the special offer page near the end of this book, or contact your Internet service provider or network administrator.

Ventana Online & the Visitor's Center

Ventana Online was created to offer information, software and support for computer users and customers of Ventana Communications, as well as Online Companion Archives for our press and media products. The information is regularly updated, with new publications and software packages added as they become available, so check with us often.

Most of the files mentioned in this book, as well as megabytes of related information, are maintained at Ventana Online's FTP and World Wide Web sites. What you hold in your hands is really only the core of *The Mac Internet Tour Guide*. The full package includes all the carefully organized data and programs available to you on the Ventana Online server. The server's anonymous FTP address is ftp.vmedia.com; the address for the World Wide Web site is http://www.vmedia.com/.

The Ventana Online Visitor's Center is a place where *Tour Guide* readers and others can stop and rest on their ramblings through the Net. And better still, it's where you'll find the latest versions of all the great freeware and shareware programs discussed in *The Mac Internet Tour Guide*, as well as the latest updates, news, tips, tricks and other hot information. Visitor's Center services include

■ Ventana's Nifty Site of the Week, where we showcase many of the great Internet resources available, and give archive maintainers well deserved recognition. A new site is featured each week.

- Our Online Companion Archives, where we provide online support for many of our print and software products.

- The Ventana Online Software Archive, where you can find an annotated reference to much of your favorite Internet freeware and shareware, including the latest versions of the programs discussed and demonstrated throughout *The Mac Internet Tour Guide*. Current versions of interesting Macintosh programs for use on the Internet are available via anonymous FTP. Special Read Me files and other goodies are available there.

- The Ventana Desktop Publishing Archive, where you can find information about freeware and shareware for popular desktop publishing programs plus links to information about desktop publishing on the Internet.

Access the Ventana Online Visitor's Center and *The Mac Internet Tour Guide Online Companion* using Mosaic (or another Web reader) at http://www.vmedia.com/mitg.html, or by FTP at ftp.vmedia.com/ pub/companions/itg/Mac/. The Ventana Online Visitor's Center is open to anyone, not just *Tour Guide* readers, so spread the word.

Glossary

access method—The rules that manage how all the computers and other devices on a network can send information through the same physical medium in an orderly fashion.

access privileges—The privileges to open and make changes to folders and their contents; they are given to or withheld from users. By setting access privileges, you can control access to confidential information stored in folders on a server.

Access Privileges window—When using the AppleShare file server, a window that displays the access privileges, owner, group and other information about a folder or volume. You use the Get Privileges command in the File menu of the Finder or the Access Privileges desk accessory in the Apple menu to display the window and to review, set or change access privileges for a folder or volume.

activate—To make a nonactive window active by clicking anywhere inside it.

active window—The frontmost window on the desktop; the window where the next action will take place. An active window's title bar is highlighted.

addressing—A scheme, determined by network protocols, for identifying the sending device and destination device for any given item of information traveling on a network.

administrator—The person who sets up a network resource, registers users and their passwords, and maintains the resource.

alert—A warning or report of an error in the form of an alert box, a sound from the computer's speaker, or both. See also **alert box**.

alert box—A box that appears on the screen to give a warning or report an error message. Its appearance is usually accompanied by a sound warning, usually the selected system beep.

alias—(n.) An alternate name used to invoke or identify a command, a network host, a list of users or some other applicable entity. (v.) To provide an entity with an alternate name, or to make an alias of a file or folder.

American Standard Code for Information Interchange—See **ASCII**.

AppleTalk network system—The system of network software and hardware used in various implementations of Apple's communications network.

AppleTalk protocol—Apple Computer's network standard that defines how devices communicate with each other across a network.

Archie—A network service used for locating files that are publicly accessible by anonymous FTP.

ARPAnet—A wide area network that linked government, academic and industrial installations around the world. Primarily connecting research sites, the ARPAnet was developed in the 1960s by the Advanced Research Projects Agency of the U.S. Department of Defense.

ASCII—Acronym for American Standard Code for Information Interchange (pronounced "ASK-ee"). A standard that assigns a unique binary number to each text character and control character. ASCII code is used for representing text inside a computer and for transmitting text between computers or between a computer and a peripheral device.

asynchronous—Not synchronized by a mutual timing signal or clock. Compare **synchronous**.

asynchronous transmission—A method of data transmission in which the receiving and sending devices don't share a common timer, and no timing data is transmitted. Each information character is individually synchronized, usually by the use of start and stop bits. The time interval between characters isn't necessarily fixed. Compare **synchronous transmission**.

bandwidth—The range of transmission frequencies that a network can use. The greater the bandwidth, the greater the amount of information that can travel on the network at one time.

baseband—A transmission method in which a network uses its entire transmission frequency range to send a single communication or signal. Compare **broadband**.

baud—(1) A unit of data transmission speed: the number of discrete signal-state changes (signal events) per second. Often, but not always, equivalent to **bits per second**. Compare **bit rate**. (2) The maximum speed at which data can be sent down a channel, such as a telephone line; often confused with the actual speed at which the data is transmitted between two computers, measured in bits per second.

BBS—See **bulletin board system**.

bit—A contraction of *binary digit*. The smallest unit of information that a computer can hold. The value of a bit (1 or 0) represents a simple two-way choice, such as yes or no, on or off, positive or negative, something or nothing.

bit rate—The speed at which bits are transmitted, usually expressed as **bits per second**, or bps. Compare **baud**.

bits per second—See **bit rate**.

bridge—(1) A device that lets you connect two or more networking systems together. (2) A combination of hardware and software that connects two or more networks. Bridges are used to increase the number of devices and the distances covered in a network.

broadband—A transmission method in which the network's range of transmission frequencies is divided into separate channels and each channel is used to send a different signal. Broadband transmission is often used to send signals of different kinds simultaneously, such as voice and data. Compare **baseband**.

bulletin board system (BBS)—A computerized version of the bulletin boards frequently found in grocery stores—places to leave messages and to advertise things you want to buy or sell. One thing you get from a computerized bulletin board that you can't get from a cork board is free software.

bus topology—A layout scheme in which devices on a network are connected along the length of a main cable, or bus, rather than in a daisy chain or a loop.

byte—The number of bits used to represent a character. For personal computers, a byte is usually eight bits.

cable—An insulated bundle of wires with connectors on the ends. Examples are serial cables, disk drive cables and LocalTalk cables.

carrier—The background signal on a communication channel that is modified to carry information. Under RS-232-C rules, the carrier signal is equivalent to a continuous MARK (1) signal; a transition to 0 then represents a start bit.

CCITT—Abbreviation for Consultative Committee on International Telegraphy and Telephony; an international committee that sets standards and makes recommendations for international communication.

choose—To pick a command by dragging through a menu. You often choose a command after you've selected something for the program to act on; for example, selecting a disk and choosing the Open command from the File menu.

Chooser—A desk accessory that lets you configure your computer system to print on any printer for which there's a printing resource on the current startup disk. If you're part of an AppleTalk network system, you use the Chooser to connect and disconnect from the network and choose among devices connected to the network. You can also specify a username that the system uses from time to time—when you're printing on a LaserWriter, for example.

CIX—Abbreviation for Commercial Internet Exchange; an agreement among Internet service providers that allows them to account for commercial network traffic.

Clear To Send—An RS-232-C signal from a DCE to a DTE that is normally kept false until the DCE makes it true, indicating that all circuits are ready to transfer data. See also **Data Communication Equipment**, **Data Terminal Equipment**.

click—(v.) To position the pointer on something and then press and quickly release the mouse button. (n.) The act of clicking.

client—A computer that has access to services on a network. A computer that provides services is called a **server** (which see). A user at a client may request file access, remote login, file transfer, printing or other available services from servers.

communications protocol—See **protocols**.

configuration—(1) A general-purpose computer term that can refer to the way you have your computer set up. (2) The total combination of hardware components—central processing unit, video display device, keyboard and peripheral devices—that make up a computer system. (3) The software settings that allow various hardware components of a computer system to communicate with one another.

configure—To change software or hardware actions by changing settings. Configurations can be set or reset in software or by manipulating hardware jumpers, switches or other elements.

connect time—The amount of time you spend connected to an information service.

daisy chain—(n.) A colloquial term for a group of devices connected to a host device, where the first device in the "chain" is connected to the host, the second device is connected to the first, the third device is connected to the second, and so on. (v.) To link together sequentially.

daisy-chain topology—A network topology where each device on the network is directly connected to the next with a modular extension cable and a connecting device.

data—Information, especially information used or operated on by a program. The smallest unit of information a computer can understand is a bit.

data bits—In the stream of bits being sent from your computer to a peripheral device or another computer, the bits that contain meaningful information; distinguished from bits used to indicate that a character is about to start, has stopped, or is correct.

Data Carrier Detect (DCD)—An RS-232-C signal from a DCE (such as a modem) to a DTE (such as a Macintosh) indicating that a communication connection has been established. See also **Data Communication Equipment**, **Data Terminal Equipment**.

Data Communication Equipment (DCE)—As defined by the RS-232-C standard, any device that transmits or receives information. Usually this device is a modem.

Data Set Ready (DSR)—An RS-232-C signal from a DCE to a DTE indicating that the DCE has established a connection. See also **Data Communication Equipment, Data Terminal Equipment**.

Data Terminal Equipment (DTE)—As defined by the RS-232-C standard, any device that generates or absorbs information, thus acting as an endpoint of a communication connection. A computer might serve as a DTE.

Data Terminal Ready (DTR)—(1) One of the handshake lines in a data transmission interface. See also **hardware handshake**. (2) An RS-232-C signal from a DTE to a DCE indicating a readiness to transmit or receive data. See also **Data Communication Equipment, Data Terminal Equipment**.

default—A value, action or setting that a computer system assumes, unless the user gives an explicit instruction to the contrary. Default values prevent a program from stalling or crashing if no value is supplied by the user.

Defense Data Network (DDN)—A single, wide area, packet-switching network that integrated the ARPAnet research network and the MILnet defense network.

device—(1) A hardware component of a computer system, such as a monitor, disk drive or printer. Also called a *peripheral device,* because such equipment is often physically separate from, but attached to, the computer. (2) A part of the computer, or a piece of external equipment, that can transfer information. (3) Any piece of equipment that can be attached to a network—a computer, a printer, a file server, a print server or any other peripheral device.

dialog box—(1) A box that contains a message requesting more information from you. Sometimes the message warns you that you're asking your computer to do something it can't do or that you're about to destroy some of your information. In these cases, the message is often accompanied by a beep. (2) A box that a Macintosh application displays to request information or to report that it is waiting for a process to complete.

download—To transfer files or information from one computer to another.

electronic mail—A network service that enables users to send and receive messages via computer.

Ethernet—A high-speed local area network that consists of a cable technology and a series of communication protocols. The hardware (cable) provides the physical link to connect systems together. The TCP/IP protocol allows different computers to exchange information over a network. The Ethernet specification was developed by Digital Equipment Corporation, Intel Corporation and Xerox Corporation. Ethernet is a registered trademark of Xerox Corporation.

Ethernet backbone—A network topology with separate AppleTalk networks interconnected to Ethernet gateways that are, in turn, connected to a single, continuous Ethernet cable.

Ethernet cable system—A system of high-performance coaxial cables widely used in the communications industry. Ethernet cables can be part of an AppleTalk network system.

EtherTalk—A high-speed AppleTalk network system that uses the cables of an Ethernet network. Ethernet is a widely used communications network. The Apple software and interface card that allow AppleTalk networking protocols to run on high-speed Ethernet media at 10 megabits per second—more than 40 times faster than the standard rate supported by Macintosh computers of 230.4 kilobits per second.

even parity—The use of an extra bit set to 0 or 1 as necessary to make the total number of 1 bits an even number; used as a means of error checking in data transmission. Compare **MARK parity**, **odd parity**, **space parity**.

FAQ—Abbreviation for Frequently Asked Question; a list of frequently asked questions (and their answers). Most mailing lists and all network news newsgroups provide FAQ postings on a regular basis.

file—(1) Any named, ordered collection of information stored on a disk. Application programs and operating systems on disks are examples of files. You make a file when you create text or graphics, give the material a name, and save it to disk; in this sense, *file* is synonymous with *document*. A Macintosh file consists of a *data fork* and a *resource fork*.
(2) For UNIX operating systems, an array of bytes; no other structure is implied by UNIX systems as they even treat devices like files.

file server—(1) A network device, usually consisting of a computer and one or more large capacity disks, on which network users can store files and applications in order to share them. (2) A specially equipped computer that allows network users to store and share information. (3) A combination of controller software and a mass-storage device that allows computer users to share common files and applications through a network.

file transfer protocol—A protocol that exchanges files with a host computer.

flame—A noxious and usually personal attack against the author of a network news article. A *flame war* is a series of related flame messages exchanged back and forth between two *flamers,* usually resulting in messages that barely relate to the original topic which spawned them in the first place.

FTP—(n.) (1) Abbreviation for File Transfer Protocol; a protocol that determines how files are transferred from one computer to another. (2) A software program that transfers files using FTP. (v.) The act of transferring files using FTP.

full duplex—A four-wire communication circuit or protocol that allows two-way data transmission between two points at the same time. Compare **half duplex**.

full-duplex communication—A method of data transmission where two devices transmit data simultaneously. This method allows the receiving device to echo back each character of your message as it is received.

gateway—A device that connects networks that use different protocols. In effect, it translates between the protocols so that devices on the connected networks can exchange data.

Gopher—A menu-based means (and set of governing protocols) of exploring information resources.

half duplex—A two-wire communication circuit or protocol designed for data transmission in either direction but not both directions simultaneously. Compare **full duplex**.

half-duplex communication—A way of communicating between your computer and another computer or a peripheral device in which you can only send data or receive it at one time—not both. The other computer cannot echo back each character of your message as it is received.

handshaking—The exchange of status information between a **DCE** and a **DTE** used to control the transfer of data between them. The status information can be the state of a signal connecting the DCE and the DTE, or it can be in the form of a character transmitted with the rest of the data. See also **Data Carrier Detect**, **Data Set Ready**, **Data Terminal Ready**, **XOFF**, **XON**.

hardware handshake—A protocol that tells the computer to start or stop sending data by setting the DTR (Data Terminal Ready) line logic state. Also known as the Data Transfer Ready protocol. Compare **XON/XOFF**.

host computer—(1) A multi-user computer, such as a minicomputer or mainframe, that serves as a central processing unit for a number of terminals. (2) The computer that receives information from and sends data to terminals over telecommunication lines. The computer that is in control in a data communication network. The host computer may be a mainframe computer, minicomputer or microcomputer.

IAB—Abbreviation for Internet Architecture Board; the "council of elders" that makes decisions about Internet standards.

IETF—Abbreviation for Internet Engineering Task Force; a subgroup of the Internet Architecture Board that concerns itself with solving technical problems on the Internet.

internet—A network made up of two or more interconnected local area or wide area networks.

Internet—A worldwide, interconnected group of networks. Internally, the internet is composed of heterogeneous networks (such as ARPAnet and CSnet) that use different message formats and protocols. Through the use of gateways that convert formats and protocols between networks, the internet appears externally as a single network, with hosts on interconnected networks appearing as interconnected hosts.

internet address—(1) An address for a computer on a network. The internet address consists of a network number and a host number that is unique for that network. (2) The AppleTalk address and network number of a socket.

ISOC—Abbreviation for the Internet Society; an organization formed to support a world-wide information network, and the governing body of the Internet Architecture Board.

kilobit (kbit)—A unit of measurement, 1024 bits, commonly used in specifying the capacity of memory integrated circuits. Not to be confused with **kilobyte** (which see).

kilobyte (k)—A unit of measurement consisting of 1024 (2^{10}) bytes. Thus, 64k memory equals 65,536 bytes. The abbreviation *k* can also stand for the number 1024, in which case *kbyte* or *kb* is used for kilobyte. See also **megabyte** (which see).

Knowbot—A knowledge robot; a software program that provides information retrieval.

LAN—See **local area network**.

local area network (LAN)—A group of computers connected for the purpose of sharing resources. The computers on a local area network are typically joined by a single transmission cable and are located within a small area such as a single building or section of a building. Compare **wide area network**.

local system—The computer from which a user originates a network command. Compare **remote system**.

local system administration—Management of a single computer. This includes such functions as starting up and shutting down the system, adding and removing user accounts, and backing up and restoring data. Compare **network administration**.

LocalTalk cable system—A system of cables, cable extenders and connector boxes that connect computers and network devices as part of the AppleTalk network system.

LocalTalk connector—A piece of equipment, consisting of a connection box, a short cable and a machine-specific connector, that enables an Apple computer to be part of an AppleTalk network system. Also called a LocalTalk connector box.

log in—To identify yourself to a system or network and start to use it. Usually logging in requires a password, depending on the system. Same as log on; opposite of **log off** (which see).

login name—In UNIX systems, the name of a user's account. Used for identification purposes.

login prompt—The prompt (usually login: on UNIX systems) by which a system tells you it is ready to accept your login name.

log off—To indicate to a system or network that you have completed your work and are terminating interaction.

MARK parity—A method of error checking in data transmission in which the most significant bit of every byte is set to 1. The receiving device checks for errors by looking for this value on each character. Compare **even parity**, **odd parity**, **space parity**.

megabit (mbit)—A unit of measurement equal to 1,048,576 (2^{16}) bits, or 1024 kilobits, commonly used in specifying the capacity of memory ICs. Not to be confused with **megabyte** (which see).

megabyte (mb)—A unit of measurement equal to 1024 kilobytes, or 1,048,576 bytes. See also **kilobyte**.

modem—Short for modulator/demodulator; a peripheral device that links your computer to other computers and information services using the telephone lines.

modem command—An instruction to a computer system, usually typed from the keyboard, that directs a modem attached to the computer to perform some immediate action.

multi-user—(adj.) Characterizes a mode or ability of an operating system to support several people using the same computer at once.

multi-user system—An operating system, such as UNIX, that allows many users to access application software simultaneously.

name—The name presented to users of a network to identify a given network service.

naming protocol—A protocol used by AppleTalk to associate a name with the physical address of a network service.

network—A collection of interconnected, individually controlled computers, together with the hardware and software used to connect them. A network allows users to share data and peripheral devices such as printers and storage media, to exchange electronic mail, and so on.

network administration—Management of the software and hardware that connects computers in a network, including such functions as assigning addresses to hosts, maintaining network data files, and setting up internetwork routing. Compare **local system administration**.

network administrator—The person who is responsible for setting up and maintaining the network.

network connection—A combination of hardware and software that lets you set up a particular implementation of the AppleTalk network system, such as LocalTalk or EtherTalk.

network device—A computer, printer, modem, terminal or any other physical entity connected to a network.

Network File System (NFS)—A protocol suite developed and licensed by Sun Microsystems that allows different makes of computers running different operating systems to easily share files and disk storage.

network manager—The person responsible for maintaining and troubleshooting the network.

network number—A unique number to each network in an internetwork that has been assigned by a seed router.

network system—A family of network components that work together because they observe compatible methods of communication.

NFS—See **Network File System**.

NIC—Abbreviation for Network Information Center; an organization responsible for supplying information for any of the component networks that make up the Internet.

NOC—Abbreviation for Network Operations Center; an organization responsible for the day-to-day operation of the component networks that make up the Internet.

node—(1) A device that's attached to a network and communicates by means of the network. (2) Any network device that has an address on the network. (Some network devices, such as modems, may be connected to a network but not be a node themselves.)

node number—A number that distinguishes one node from all others on the network.

NREN—Abbreviation for National Research and Education Network; an effort to combine the networks operated by the U.S. government into a single high-speed network.

odd parity—The use of an extra bit in data transmission set to 0 or 1 as necessary to make the total number of 1 bits an odd number; used as a means of error checking. Compare **even parity**, **MARK parity**, **space parity**.

off-line—(adj.) Not currently connected to or under the control of the computer. Used to refer to equipment such as printers and disk drives, information storage media such as disks, and the information they contain. Compare **online**.

online—(adj.) Currently connected to and under the control of the computer. Used to refer to equipment such as printers and disk drives, information storage media such as disks, and the information they contain. Compare **off-line**.

OSI model—The Open Systems Interconnection (OSI) reference model for describing network **protocols** (which see), devised by the International Standards Organization (ISO); divides protocols into seven layers to standardize and simplify protocol definitions.

packet—A unit of information that has been formatted for transmission on a network.

port—(n.) (1) A socket on the back panel of a computer where you plug in a cable for connection to a network or a peripheral device. (2) A connection between the central processor unit and main memory or a device (such as a terminal) for transferring data. (3) A unique number that identifies a particular Internet service. (v.) To move software from one hardware architecture to another.

PPP—Abbreviation of Point-to-Point Protocol; a protocol that enables a computer to communicate with other computers using TCP/IP over standard telephone lines and high-speed modems.

protocols—The rules that govern interaction on a network. Protocols determine where, when and how information is transmitted.

random-access memory (RAM)—The part of the computer's memory that stores information temporarily while you're working on it. A computer with 512k RAM has 512 kilobytes of memory available to the user. Information in RAM can be referred to in an arbitrary or random order, hence the term random-access. (As an analogy, a book is a random-access storage device in that it can be opened and read at any point.) RAM can contain both application programs and your own information. Information in RAM is temporary, gone forever if you switch the power off without saving it on a disk or other storage medium. Compare **read-only memory**.

read-only memory (ROM)—Memory whose contents can be read but not changed; used for storing firmware. Information is placed into read-only memory once, during manufacture. It remains there permanently, even when the computer's power is turned off. Compare **random-access memory**.

remote—(adj.) At a distance. Unable to be connected directly using local wiring, but requiring communications devices. Compare **local**.

remote computer—A computer other than your own but in communication with yours through telephone lines, network wiring or other communication links. A remote computer can be at any distance from your computer—from right beside it to thousands of miles away.

remote site—A computer or network that is accessed through a long distance communications medium, such as telephone lines, network wiring, ISDN or a satellite.

remote system—On a network, any computer other than the local system.

RFC—Abbreviation for Request for Comments; a collection of papers that define the Internet standards and proposed standards.

server—A computer that provides a service across a network. The service may be file access, login access, file transfer, printing and so on. A computer from which a user initiates the service is called a **client** (which see).

service—A specialized function that a network provides to users, such as file sharing and electronic mail.

service provider—An organization that provides connections to the Internet.

signature—A text file, usually five lines or less, containing your identification and contact information that is added to your network news articles and e-mail messages.

SLIP—Abbreviation for Serial Line Internet Protocol; a protocol that enables a computer to communicate with other computers using TCP/IP over standard telephone lines and high-speed modems.

socket—On a network, a communication mechanism originally implemented on the BSD version of the UNIX operating system. Sockets are used as endpoints for sending and receiving data between computers.

space parity—A method of error checking in data transmission in which the most significant bit of every byte is set to 0. The receiving device checks for errors by looking for this value on each character. Compare **even parity, MARK parity, odd parity**.

standard—A set of specifications for designing hardware or software that is recognized by multiple vendors, an official standards organization, or both.

synchronous—Able to perform two or more processes at the same time, such as sending and receiving data, by means of a mutual timing signal or clock. Compare **asynchronous**.

synchronous transmission—A transmission process that uses a clocking signal to ensure an integral number of unit (time) intervals between any two characters. Compare **asynchronous transmission**.

TCP/IP—Abbreviation for Transmission Control Protocol/Internet Protocol; a suite of networking protocols developed at the University of California for the U.S. Department of Defense.

telnet—A terminal emulation protocol that lets you log in remotely to other computers on the Internet, using a command-line interface.

terminal—A keyboard and display screen through which users can access a **host computer** (which see).

terminal emulation—Software that enables a personal computer to communicate with a **host computer** by transmitting in the form used by the host's terminals.

topology—The physical layout of a network.

traffic—Transmissions traveling across a network.

tty—A terminal; abbreviated from teletypewriter, which was the first terminal device used on UNIX operating systems.

USENET—A network of about 3 million users (mostly UNIX users) who communicate using the UNIX-to-UNIX Copy Protocol (UUCP).

WAIS—Abbreviation for Wide-Area Information Server; an Internet service for looking up specific information in Internet databases.

WAN—See **wide area network**.

wide area network—Computers and/or networks connected to each other using long distance communication methods, such as telephone lines and satellites. Compare **local area network**.

World Wide Web (WWW)—A hypertext-based Internet service used for browsing Internet resources.

XOFF—A special character used for controlling the transfer of data between a **DTE** and a **DCE**. When one piece of equipment receives an XOFF character from the other, it stops transmitting characters until it receives an **XON**. See also **handshaking, XON**.

XON—A special character used for controlling the transfer of data between a **DTE** and a **DCE**. See also **handshaking, XOFF**.

XON/XOFF—A communications protocol that tells the computer to start or stop sending data by sending the appropriate character: either an **XON** or an **XOFF**. Compare **hardware handshake**.

Bibliography

Adoba, Bernard. *The Online User's Encyclopedia*. New York: Addison-Wesley, 1994.

Arick, Martin R. *The TCP/IP Companion*. Wellesley, Massachusetts: QED, 1993.

Bayers, Albert F. III, Peter Rutten, and Kelly Maloni. *Net Guide*. New York: Random House, 1994.

Benedikt, Michael, ed. *Cyberspace: First Steps*. Cambridge, Massachusetts: MIT Press, 1991.

Brand, Stewart. *The Media Lab: Inventing the Future at MIT*. New York: Viking, 1987.

Branwyn, Gareth. *Mosaic Quick Tour for Mac*. Chapel Hill, North Carolina: Ventana Press, 1994.

Comer, Douglas E. *Internetworking with TCP/IP, Principles, Protocols, and Architecture, Volume I*. 2nd ed. Englewood Cliffs, New Jersey: Prentice Hall, 1991.

Gibson, William. *Neuromancer*. New York: Ace Books, 1986.

_____. *Virtual Light*. New York: Bantam Books, 1993.

Gore, Al. "Infrastructure for the Global Village," *Scientific American*, vol. 265, no. 3, pp. 150–153. New York: Scientific American, September 1991.

Grief, Irene, ed. *Computer-Supported Cooperative Work: A Book of Readings*. San Mateo, California: Morgan Kauffman Publishers, 1988.

Hahn, Harley, and Rick Stout. *The Internet Compete Reference*. Berkeley, California: Osborne McGraw-Hill, 1994.

Hiltz, Roxanne. *Online Communities: A Case Study of the Office of the Future*. Norwood, New Jersey: Ablex Press, 1984.

Kapor, Mitchell. "Civil Liberties in Cyberspace," *Scientific American*, vol. 265, no. 3, pp. 158–164. New York: Scientific American, September 1991.

Krol, Ed. *The Whole Internet User's Guide & Catalog*. 2nd ed. Sebastopol, California: O'Reilly & Associates, 1994.

Lambert, S., and W. Howe. *Internet Basics*. New York: Random House, 1994.

LaQuey, Tracy, and Jeanne C. Ryer. *The Internet Companion: A Beginner's Guide to Global Networking*. Reading, Masachusetts: Addison-Wesley, 1993.

Quarterman, John S. *The Matrix: Computer Networks and Conferencing Systems Worldwide*. Burlington, Massachusetts: Digital Press, 1990.

Rheingold, Howard. *The Virtual Community: Homesteading on the Electronic Frontier*. New York: Addison-Wesley, 1993.

Rucker, Rudy, R.U. Sirius, and Queen Mu. *Mondo 2000: A User's Guide to the New Edge*. New York: HarperCollins, 1992.

Index

A

Abbreviations   119
Access privileges, TCP/Connect II
    167–168
Addressing system   33–35
Alice in Wonderland   25
America Online, e-mail   55–56
Anonymous FTP   41, 144
AppleLink, e-mail   56–57
Archie   242–243
    for Macintosh   243–244
    searching with TurboGopher   245–247
ARPAnet   8
Art resources   256–260
Articles   108
Asterisk (*)
    wildcard   89
At sign (@)
    partial domain names   94
AT&T Mail, e-mail   56

B

Bandwidth   11
Bang
    See exclamation point
Bang-path addresses   53
Bboards   115
Binary compatibility   104
BinHex files, decoding
    TCP/Connect II   174
    TurboGopher   185
Blind courtesy copies
    Eudora   69–70
    TCP/Connect II   83
    that aren't   109
Boards   115
Book resources   260–263
Bounced e-mail messages   46
Bozo filters   125, 139
Browsing information   6
    TurboGopher   186–187

BTW (by the way)   119
Bulletin boards   108, 115
Business resources   263–266

C

Case sensitivity
    Internet addresses   37
    Mosaic   204
    TCP/Connect II   89
CMacTeX typesetting software   61
Commercialization of the Internet   10
Compact Pro file compressor   242
CompuServe, e-mail   54
Computing resources   266–268
Connection types   18–22
Consensual anarchy   7, 30
Context sensitivity, WAIS   239
Courtesy
    See etiquette
Courtesy copies
    Eudora   69–70
    TCP/Connect II   83
Crackers   251
CTerm terminal emulator   235
Culture resources   268–270

D

Dedicated connection   19
Dial-in connection   18
Disinfectant software   151–152
Domain names   33–36
    partial   94
Downloading files
    Fetch   160–163
    Mosaic   216–218
    TCP/Connect II   171–175
    TurboGopher   188–191, 199

E

Editors
    See text editors
Education resources   270–272
Electronic bulletin boards   108
Electronic Communications Privacy Act
    (ECPA)   49–50
Electronic Frontier Foundation (EFF)
    250–252
Electronic magazines
    See 'zines
Electronic mail
    See e-mail
Electronic mailing lists
    canceling subscriptions   99
    subscribing to   45, 97–99
E-mail   5
    America Online   55–56
    AppleLink   56–57
    archiving, TCP/Connect II   83
    AT&T Mail   56
    attaching files
        Eudora   100
        TCP/Connect II   101
    bounced messages   46
    checking for mail automatically   61
    CompuServe   54
    courtesy copies   69–70
    creating mailboxes
        Eudora   73
        TCP/Connect II   86
    creating messages
        Eudora   68–70
        TCP/Connect II   82–83
    cross-network reference   58
    deleting messages, Eudora   74–75
    EmilyPost software   48
    encryption   59
    etiquette   46–48
    Eudora software   37

file transfers 59
filters, TCP/Connect II 87–91
finding addresses 91–96
fonts 61–62
gateways 52
highlighting messages,
   TCP/Connect II 90
line length 61
lines per message 61
locating addresses 196
   Finger 236–239
   Knowbots 234–235
   Netfind 235–236
Macintosh-related addresses 95–96,
227
managing
   Eudora 72–75
   TCP/Connect II 86
MCI Mail 54–55
MIME software 59
moving mail between mailboxes
   Eudora 73–74
   TCP/Connect II 82
PEM software 59
Ph servers 61
privacy 49–50
receiving files
   Eudora 101
   TCP/Connect II 101–103
replying to messages
   Eudora 70–71
   TCP/Connect II 84–85
retrieving and reading
   Eudora 66–68
   TCP/Connect II 80–82
saving files 62
sending messages
   Eudora 72
   TCP/Connect II 82–83
signature lines 65

uses 44–45
UUCP 52–53
EmilyPost software 48
Empty Trash command 75
Encryption software 14
Environment resources 272–275
Ethnocentricity 41
Etiquette 40–41
   e-mail 46–48
   newsgroups 114–117
   uploading files 165
Eudora 37
   attaching files to e-mail 100
   configuring 59–65
   courtesy copies 69–70
   creating mailboxes 73
   creating messages 68–70
   deleting e-mail 74–75
   Empty Trash command 75
   free copy 362
   managing e-mail 72–75
   moving messages between
      mailboxes 73–74
   password rejection 66
   receiving files 101
   replying to messages 70–71
   retrieving and reading e-mail 66–68
   sending messages 72
   switch settings 63–64
   Trash mailbox 74–75
Exclamation point (!)
   in bang-path addresses 53
   Mosaic new entries 210

F

FAQ (Frequently Asked Questions)
116, 250
Fetch 39
   configuring 154–160

description   152–154
downloading files   160–163
expanding compressed files   158
free copy   362
passwords   155, 157, 164
uploading files   163–164
File extensions   163
File transfer   5
File types   148–150
Files
  downloading
    Fetch   160–163
    Mosaic   216–218
    TCP/Connect II   171–175
    TurboGopher   188–191, 199
  expanding compressed   158
  receiving
    binary compatibility   104
    Eudora   101
    size limitations   104
    TCP/Connect II   101–103
  sending with e-mail   45
  transferring, TCP/Connect II   171–176
  uploading
    Fetch   163–164
    TCP/Connect II   176
Film resources   345–347
Filters, e-mail
  bozo   125, 139
  TCP/Connect II   87–91
Finance resources   275–277
Finger   36, 92–93, 236–239
Flame bait   118
Flame wars   108, 118
Flames   108, 118
Flaming   118
  See also EmilyPost software
Follow-up articles   108
Food & drink resources   277–280
Forums   108

Fractal generator   20
Freeware resources   146
FTP (File Transfer Protocol)   143–144
  anonymity   41
  Fetch software   39
FTP servers
  configuring   169–171
  locating   155
FTP sites, accessing with Mosaic   220
FTPd   190
Fun & games resources   280–281
FYI (for your information)   119

G
Gateways to resources   351–358
Gopher   179–180
  accessing with Mosaic   221–222
  server addresses   198–199
  See also TurboGopher
Government resources   316–322
Graphics, Mosaic   220
Greater than sign (>)
  quoting text   71
Growth rate of Internet   10

H
Hackers   251
Health resources   282–287
History of the Internet   8–10
History resources   287–288
Home page, Mosaic   204
Hotlink   201
HTML (HyperText Markup
  Language)   222–223
Humor resources   288–291
Hypermedia   202
Hypertext   201

I

IMHO (in my humble opinion)   119
Info-Mac Gopher server
   browsing with TurboGopher   192–193
Internet Architecture Board (IAB)   7,
   252–253
Internet Cruise software   171
Internet Engineering Task Force (IETF)
   7, 253
Internet Relay Chat (IRC)   109
Internet Research Task Force (IRTF)   253
Internet resources   291–300
Internet Society   7, 252–253
Internet/NREN Business Journal   65
InterSLIP   20, 24
   free copy   363
IP addresses   33

J

Jobs resources   300–301

K

Knowbots   234–235

L

Languages resources   301–302
LAP (Link Access Protocol)   24
Law resources   303–305
Link Access Protocol (LAP)   24
Links, Mosaic   206
List servers, querying   45
Listserv mail servers   97
Literature resources   260–263
LOCIS (Library of Congress Information
   System)   23
Logging off   41

M

Macintosh
   archives   151
   e-mail addresses   95–96, 227
   FTP sites   175
MacPGP software   14
MacPPP software   20, 24
MacSLIP software   24
MacTCP
   free copy   363
MacTCP software   6, 24–25
Mail servers   45
Mailboxes
   creating
      Eudora   73
      TCP/Connect II   86
   moving mail between
      Eudora   73–74
      TCP/Connect II   82
Mandelbrot generator   20
MandelTV software   20
MCI Mail   7
   e-mail   54–55
Medicine resources   282–287
Message threads   108, 130
Messages, e-mail   45
MIME (Multipurpose Internet Mail
   Extensions)   59
Mirror sites   41
Modem connections, Mosaic   220
Moderated newsgroups   112
MOOGopher   141
Mosaic   203
   accessing FTP sites   220
   accessing Gopher sites   221–222
   browsing the Web   203–218
   downloading files   216–218
   free copy   362
   graphics   220

modem connections   220
moving across pages   219
Multimedia   202
  resources   306–307
Music resources   307–313

N

Netfind   235–236
Network news   5
Network News Transfer Protocol
  (NNTP)   109
Network Operations Center   8
New age resources   313
News readers
  Nuntius   120–125
  TCP/Connect II   125–128
News resources   313–314
News servers   109
Newsgroups   5, 109
  art related   260
  book related   263
  business related   266
  computer related   268
  culture related   270
  customizing   126–127
  descriptions of popular   112–113
  environment related   275
  etiquette   114–117
  filtering   139
  finance related   277
  following message threads   38
  food & drink related   280
  government related   322
  health & medicine related   287
  history related   288
  humor related   291
  Internet related   300
  jobs related   300–301

language related   302
law related   305
Macintosh related   113–114
moderated   112
music related   313
Nuntius news reader   38
politics related   322
posting articles
  Nuntius   132–134
  TCP/Connect II   140–142
reading articles
  Nuntius   129–132
  TCP/Connect II   134
science fiction related   336
science related   334
social issues related   322
sports related   343
subscribing to
  Nuntius   121–122
  TCP/Connect II   135–139
travel related   351
weird topics   344–345
'zine related   263
NNTP (Network News Transfer Protocol)
  network news   109
Note Pad II software   231
NSF (National Science Foundation)   9
NSFNET   9
Nuntius   38
  configuring   120–125
  free copy   362
  posting newsgroup articles   132–134
  reading newsgroups   129–132
  subscribing to newsgroups   121–122

O

OBO (or best offer)   119
Occult resources   314–315

P

Pages, WWW 202
    building your own 222–223
Passwords
    Fetch 155, 157, 164
    recommended syntax 40
    rejected by Eudora 66
    rejected by TCP/Connect II 80
    TCP/Connect II FTP module 168
Pathnames 162
Peer-to-peer networking 8
Performance Systems International (PSI)
    White Pages directory 94
Ph servers 61, 79
Philosophy resources 315
Politics resources 316–322
POP (Post Office Protocol)
    with TCP/Connect II 79
POP3 (Post Office Protocol version 3)
    required to run Eudora 59
Popcorn software 159
Posts 108
PPP (Point-to-Point Protocol) 18, 20, 147
Privacy, e-mail 49–50
Privacy-enhanced Electronic Mail
    (PEM) 59
Privatization of the Internet 10–11
Pronunciation rules 35
PSIWP
    See Performance Systems International
    (PSI)
Public domain resources 146

Q

Question mark (?)
    wildcard 89
Quoting conventions 71

R

Reference resources 322
Religion resources 323–325
Resource requirements 22–25
RFC (Request for Comments) 248–249
Romance resources 326
ROTFL (rolling on the floor
    laughing) 119
RTFM (read the funny manual) 119

S

Science fiction resources 334–336
Science resources 326–334
Searching for information
    Archie 242–243
    BBEdit 85
    Finger 236–239
    Gopher protocol 179–180
    Macintosh Archie 243–244
    Netfind 235–236
    TurboGopher 40
    WAIS 239–242
Security issues 39
    resources 336
SGML (Standard Generalized Markup
    Language) 222
Shareware resources 147
Sharing resources 41
Showbiz resources 336–337
Signature lines
    Eudora 65
    Nuntius 125
    TCP/Connect II 127–128
SLIP (Serial Line Internet Protocol) 18, 20
Smiley 116, 118
Smithsonian Institution photo archive 46
SMTP (Simple Mail Transfer Protocol)
    with TCP/Connect II 79

Social issues resources   316–322
Software resources   337
Sports resources   338–343
Star Trek resources   343–345
Store-and-forward service   45
StuffIt Expander decompression
   utility   148
   free copy   362
StuffIt Lite compression utility   186
Subscribing to
   electronic mailing lists   45, 97–99
   newsgroups
      Nuntius   121–122
      TCP/Connect II   135–139

T

TANSTAAFL (there ain't no such thing as
   a free lunch)   119
TCP/Connect II   75–103
   FTP module
      configuring   165–171
      decoding BinHex files   174
      downloading files   171–175
      uploading files   176
   mail module
      archiving mail   83
      attaching files to e-mail   101
      configuring   75–79
      courtesy copies   83
      creating mailboxes   86
      e-mail filters   87–91
      highlighting messages   90
      managing e-mail   86
      moving messages between
         mailboxes   82
      password rejection   80
      receiving files   101–103

   replying to messages   84–85
   retrieving and reading e-mail   80–82
   sending e-mail messages   82–83
   news module
      configuring   125–127
      filtering newsgroups   139
      posting newsgroup articles   140–142
      reading newsgroups   134
      subscribing to newsgroups   135–139
   Telnet module
      configuring   230–232
      opening a session   232–234
TCP/IP (Transmission Control Protocol/
   Internet Protocol)   6, 31–32
Technical support   182
Technology resources   345
Telnet
   configuring
      NCSA   226–228
      TCP/Connect II   230–232
   opening a session
      NCSA   228–230
      TCP/Connect II   232–234
Terminal emulation
   CTerm   235
   TCP/Connect II Telnet module   230
   ZTerm   169
TeX typesetting software   61
Text editors
   BBEdit   85
   selecting for Nuntius   124
   selecting for TurboGopher   182–186
Text files, displaying with Finger   237
Theater resources   345–347
Top-level domain   35–36
Trash mailbox   74–75
Travel advisories   33
Travel resources   348–351

TurboGopher   40
   Archie searches   245–247
   Bookmarks   193–198
   browsing Info-Mac Gopher
   server   192–193
   configuring   182–186
   decoding BinHex files   185
   downloading files   188–191, 199
   free copy   362
   tips   199–200
   See also Gopher

U

Unacceptable uses of the Internet   38–39
Underscore (_)
   in MCI Mail addresses   55
Uniform Resource Locator (URL)   206
UNIX   7
Uploading files
   etiquette   165
   Fetch   163–164
   TCP/Connect II   176
USENET User List service   93
User types
   business   16–17
   government   16
   individual   18
   university   14–15
Users, locating
   Finger   92–93
   PSI White Pages directory   94
   USENET User List   93
   Whois directory   94
UUCP (UNIX-to-UNIX Copy
   Protocol)   22
   e-mail   52–53
   network news   109

V

Ventana Online   363–364
Ventana Online Web server   218
Viruses   150–152
Visitor's Center   363–364

W

WAIS (Wide Area Information
   Server)   239–242
Weather resources   351
WELL (Whole Earth 'Lectronic Link)   180
Whois directory   94
Wildcards   89
WWW (World Wide Web)
   browsing with Mosaic   203–207
   building your own pages   222–223
   description   201–202

Z

'Zines   34
   resources   260–263
ZTerm terminal emulator   169

# Colophon

The Mac Internet Tour Guide was produced on a Power Macintosh 8100 using PageMaker 5.0. Body text is set in Adobe Palatino. Subheads and running heads are set in DTC Kabel. Sidebars are set in Adobe Futura Condensed. The cover art was produced on a Macintosh Quadra 800 using Adobe Illustrator.

Page proofs were output to a LaserJet 4 Plus and final film output was produced on a Linotronic 330.

Notes

Notes

Maximize Your Mac

Voodoo Mac, Second Edition

$24.95
464 pages, illustrated

Whether you're a power user looking for new shortcuts or a beginner trying to make sense of it all, *Voodoo Mac* has something for everyone! Computer veteran Kay Nelson has compiled hundreds of invaluable tips, tricks, hints and shortcuts that simplify your Macintosh tasks and save time—including disk and drive magic, font and printing tips, alias alchemy and more!

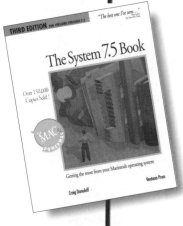

The System 7.5 Book, Third Edition

$24.95
736 pages, illustrated

The all-time best-selling *System 7 Book*, now revised, updated and re-titled! *The System 7.5 Book* is the industry's recognized standard and the last word on the Macintosh and Power Mac operating systems. Includes a complete overview of AppleHelp, AOCE, e-mail, fax, PC Exchange, MacTCP, QuickTime and more!

Mac, Word & Excel Desktop Companion, Second Edition

$24.95
362 pages, illustrated

Why clutter your desk with three guides? This money saver gets you up and running with Apple's System 7.5 software and the latest versions of Microsoft Word and Excel for the Mac. A complete overview; examples of each program's commands, tools and features; and step-by-step tutorials guide you easily along the learning curve for maximum Macintosh productivity!

The Official America Online for Macintosh Membership Kit & Tour Guide, Second Edition

$27.95
568 pages, illustrated

This book takes Mac users on a lively romp through the friendly AOL cyberscape. Best-selling author Tom Lichty, a.k.a. MajorTom, shows you how to make friends, find your way around, and save time and money online. Complete with software to get you started. BONUS: 20 free hours of online time for new members.

America Online's Internet, Macintosh Edition

$24.95
336 pages, illustrated

A hands-on introduction to AOL's intuitive Internet interface. It's familiar, it's convenient, and it's a local call for most people in the U.S. Includes details on navigating with Gopher; using e-mail; reading newsgroups; troubleshooting and technical notes on the Internet; and a no-risk, manufacturer's money-back guarantee. New users get 10 hours of free online time. Companion disk includes the most recent AOL software, ready for installation on any Macintosh.

Mosaic Quick Tour for Mac

$12.00
208 pages, illustrated

The *Mosaic Quick Tour* introduces the how-to's of hypertext travel in a simple, picturesque guide. Mosaic, called the "killer app" of the Internet, lets you view linked text, audio and video resources thousands of miles apart. Use Mosaic to do all of your information hunting and gathering—including Gopher searches, newsgroup reading and file transfers via FTP.

Design & Conquer

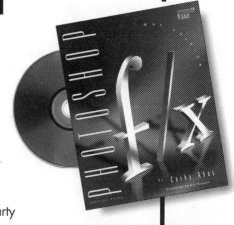

Looking Good With QuarkXPress

$34.95
544 pages, illustrated

Looking Good With QuarkXPress showcases the graphic devices, layouts and design tools built into the latest version of QuarkXPress. Basic principles of graphic design come to life on every page with examples of newsletters, brochures, mailers and more—all in a straightforward guide that is accessible to users at all levels. The companion CD-ROM features templates, fonts, clip art, backgrounds and XTensions.

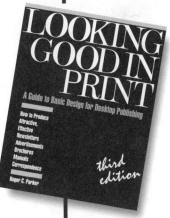

Looking Good in Print, Third Edition

$24.95
464 pages, illustrated

For use with any software or hardware, this desktop design bible has become the standard among novice and experienced desktop publishers alike. With more than 300,000 copies in print, *Looking Good in Print, Third Edition* is even better, with new sections on photography and scanning. Learn the fundamentals of professional-quality design along with tips on resources and reference materials.

Newsletters From the Desktop, Second Edition

$24.95
392 pages, illustrated

Now the millions of desktop publishers who produce newsletters can learn how to improve the designs of their publications. Filled with helpful design tips and illustrations, as well as hands-on tips for building a great-looking publication. Includes an all-new color gallery of professionally designed newsletters, offering publishers at all levels a wealth of ideas and inspiration.

To order any Ventana Press title, complete this order form and mail or fax it to us, with payment, for quick shipment.

TITLE	ISBN	Quantity	Price		Total
Voodoo Mac, 2nd Edition	1-56604-177-5	_____ x	$24.95	=	$ _____
The System 7.5 Book, 3rd Edition	1-56604-129-5	_____ x	$24.95	=	$ _____
Mac, Word & Excel Desktop Companion, 2nd Edition	1-56604-130-9	_____ x	$24.95	=	$ _____
The Official America Online for Macintosh Membership Kit & Tour Guide, 2nd Edition	1-56604-127-9	_____ x	$27.95	=	$ _____
America Online's Internet, Mac Edition	1-56604-175-9	_____ x	$24.95	=	$ _____
Mosaic Quick Tour for Mac	1-56604-195-3	_____ x	$12.00	=	$ _____
Photoshop f/x	1-56604-179-1	_____ x	$39.95	=	$ _____
Advertising From the Desktop	1-56604-064-7	_____ x	$24.95	=	$ _____
The Presentation Design Book, 2nd Edition	1-56604-014-0	_____ x	$24.95	=	$ _____
Looking Good With QuarkXPress	1-56604-148-1	_____ x	$34.95	=	$ _____
Looking Good in Print, 3rd Edition	1-56604-047-7	_____ x	$24.95	=	$ _____
Newsletters From the Desktop, 2nd Edition	1-56604-133-3	_____ x	$24.95	=	$ _____

Subtotal = $ _____

Shipping = $ _____

TOTAL = $ _____

SHIPPING:

For all standard orders, please ADD $4.50/first book, $1.35/each additional.
For "two-day air," ADD $8.25/first book, $2.25/each additional.
For orders to Canada, ADD $6.50/book.
For orders sent C.O.D., ADD $4.50 to your shipping rate.
North Carolina residents must ADD 6% sales tax.
International orders require additional shipping charges.

Name _____ Company _____

Address (No PO Box) _____

City _____ State _____ Zip _____

Daytime Telephone _____

____ Payment enclosed ____ VISA ____ MC Acc't # _____ Exp. Date _____

Signature _____

Mail or fax toll free to: Ventana Press, PO Box 2468, Chapel Hill, NC 27515 ☎ 800/743-5369 Fax 919/942-1140

Check your local bookstore or software retailer for these and other best-selling titles, or call toll free: 800/743-5369

Ventana Software License

PLEASE READ THIS LICENSE CAREFULLY BEFORE USING THE SOFTWARE. BY USING THE SOFTWARE, YOU ARE AGREEING TO BE BOUND BY THE TERMS OF THE LICENSE. IF YOU DO NOT AGREE TO THE TERMS OF THIS LICENSE, PROMPTLY RETURN THE UNUSED SOFTWARE TO THE PLACE WHERE YOU OBTAINED IT AND YOUR MONEY WILL BE REFUNDED.

1. License. The application, demonstration, system and other software accompanying this License, whether on disk, in read only memory, or on any other media (the "Software") the related documentation and fonts are licensed to you by Ventana. You own the disk on which the Software and fonts are recorded but Ventana and/or Ventana's Licensors retain title to the Software, related documentation and fonts. This License allows you to use the Software and fonts on a single Apple computer and make one copy of the Software and fonts in machine-readable form for backup purposes only. You must reproduce on such copy the Ventana copyright notice and any other proprietary legends that were on the original copy of the Software and fonts. You may also transfer all your license rights in the Software and fonts, the backup copy of the Software and fonts, the related documentation and a copy of this License to another party, provided the other party reads and agrees to accept the terms and conditions of this License.

2. Restrictions. The Software contains copyrighted material, trade secrets and other proprietary material. In order to protect them, and except as permitted by applicable legislation, you may not decompile, reverse engineer, disassemble or otherwise reduce the Software to a human-perceivable form. You may not modify, network, rent, lease, loan, distribute or create derivative works based upon the Software in whole or in part. You may not electronically transmit the Software from one computer to another or over a network.

3. Termination. This License is effective until terminated. You may terminate this License at any time by destroying the Software, related documentation and fonts and all copies thereof. This License will terminate immediately without notice from Ventana if you fail to comply with any provision of this License. Upon termination you must destroy the Software, related documentation and fonts and all copies thereof.

4. Export Law Assurances. You agree and certify that neither the Software not any other technical data received from Ventana, nor the direct product thereof, will be exported outside the United States except as authorized and as permitted by the laws and regulations of the United States. If the Software has been rightfully obtained by you outside of the United States, you agree that you will not re-export the Software nor any other technical data received from Ventana, nor the direct product thereof, except as permitted by the laws and regulations of the United States and the laws and regulations of the jurisdiction in which you obtained the software.

5. Government End Users. If you are acquiring the Software and fonts on behalf of any unit or agency of the United States Government, the following provisions apply. The Government agrees:
    (i) if the Software and fonts are supplied to the Department of Defense (DoD), the Software and fonts are classified as "Commercial Computer Software" and the Government is acquiring only "restricted rights" in the Software, its documentation and fonts as that term is defined in Clause 252.227-7013(c)(1) of the DFARS; and
    (ii) if the Software and fonts are supplied to any unit or agency of the United States Government other than DoD, the Government's rights in the Software, its documentation and fonts will be as defined in Clause 52.227-19(c)(2) of the FAR or, in the case of NASA, in Clause 18-52.227-86(d) of the NASA Supplement to the FAR.

6. Limited Warranty on Media. Ventana warrants the diskettes and/or compact disc on which the Software and fonts are recorded to be free from defects in materials and workmanship under normal use for a period of ninety (90) days from the date of purchase as evidenced by a copy of the receipt. Ventana's entire liability and your exclusive remedy will be replacement of the diskettes and/or compact disc not meeting Ventana's limited warranty and which is returned to Ventana or an Ventana authorized representative with a copy of the receipt. Ventana will have no responsibility to replace a disk/disc damaged by accident, abuse or misapplication. ANY IMPLIED WARRANTIES ON THE DISKETTES AND/OR COMPACT DISC, INCLUDING THE IMPLIED WARRANTIES OF MERCHANTABILITY AND FITNESS FOR A PARTICULAR PURPOSE, ARE LIMITED IN DURATION TO NINETY (90) DAYS FROM THE DATE OF DELIVERY. THIS WARRANTY GIVES YOU SPECIFIC LEGAL RIGHTS, AND YOU MAY ALSO HAVE OTHER RIGHTS WHICH VARY BY JURISDICTION.

7. Disclaimer of Warranty. You expressly acknowledge and agree that use of the Software and fonts is at your sole risk. The Software, related documentation and fonts are provided "AS IS" and without warranty of any kind and Ventana and Ventana's Licensor(s) (for the purposes of provisions 7 and 8, Ventana and Ventana's Licensor(s) shall be collectively referred to as "Ventana") EXPRESSLY DISCLAIM ALL WARRANTIES, EXPRESS OR IMPLIED, INCLUDING, BUT NOT LIMITED TO, THE IMPLIED WARRANTIES OF MERCHANTABILITY AND FITNESS FOR A PARTICULAR PURPOSES. VENTANA DOES NOT WARRANT THAT THE FUNCTIONS CONTAINED IN THE SOFTWARE WILL MEET YOUR REQUIREMENTS, OR THAT THE OPERATION OF THE SOFTWARE WILL BE UNINTERRUPTED OR ERROR-FREE, OR THAT DEFECTS IN THE SOFTWARE AND FONTS WILL BE CORRECTED. FURTHER-MORE, VENTANA DOES NOT WARRANT OR MAKE ANY REPRESENTATIONS REGARDING THE USE OR THE RESULTS OF THE USE OF THE SOFTWARE AND FONTS OR RELATED DOCUMENTATION IN TERMS OF THEIR CORRECTNESS, ACCURACY, RELIABILITY, OR OTHERWISE. NO ORAL OR WRITTEN INFORMATION OR ADVICE GIVEN BY VENTANA OR A VENTANA AUTHORIZED REPRESENTATIVE SHALL CREATE A WARRANTY OR IN ANY WAY INCREASE THE SCOPE OF THIS WARRANTY. SHOULD THE SOFTWARE PROVE DEFECTIVE, YOU (AND NOT VENTANA OR A VENTANA AUTHORIZED REPRESENTATIVE) ASSUME THE ENTIRE COST OF ALL NECESSARY SERVICING, REPAIR OR CORREC-TION. SOME JURISDICTIONS DO NOT ALLOW THE EXCLUSION OF IMPLIED WARRANTIES, SO THE ABOVE EXCLUSION MAY NOT APPLY TO YOU.

8. Limitation of Liability. UNDER NO CIRCUMSTANCES INCLUDING NEGLIGENCE, SHALL VENTANA BE LIABLE FOR ANY INCIDENTAL, SPECIAL OR CONSEQUENTIAL DAMAGES THAT RESULT FROM THE USE OR INABILITY TO USE THE SOFTWARE OR RELATED DOCUMENTATION, EVEN IF VENTANA OR A VENTANA AUTHORIZED REPRESENTATIVE HAS BEEN ADVISED OF THE POSSIBILITY OF SUCH DAMAGES. SOME JURISDICTIONS DO NOT ALLOW THE LIMITATION OR EXCLUSION OF LIABILITY FOR INCIDENTAL OR CONSEQUENTIAL DAMAGES SO THE ABOVE LIMITATION OR EXCLUSION MAY NOT APPLY TO YOU.
In no event shall Ventana's total liability to you for all damages, losses, and causes of action (whether in contract, tort (including negligence) or otherwise) exceed the amount paid by you for the Software and fonts.

9. Controlling Law and Severability. This Licensee shall be governed by and construed in accordance with the laws of the United States and the State of California, as applied to agreements entered into and to be performed entirely within California between California residents. If for any reason a court of competent jurisdiction finds any provision of this License, or portion thereof, to be unenforceable, that provision of the License shall be enforced to the maximum extent permissible so as to effect the intent of the parties, and the remainder of this License shall continue in full force and effect.

10. Complete Agreement. This License constitutes the entire agreeement between the parties with respect to the use of the Software, the related documentation and fonts, and supersedes all prior or contemporaneous understandings or agreements, written or oral, regarding such subject matter. No amendment to or modification of this License will be binding unless in writing and signed by a duly authorized representative of Ventana.

Ventana Communications Group, Inc.
P.O. Box 2468
Chapel Hill, NC 27515
Phone: 919/942-0220
FAX: 919/942-1140

End-User Software Sublicense Agreement

PLEASE READ THIS CAREFULLY BEFORE OPENING THE DISK OR CD-ROM ENVELOPE. BY OPENING THE ENVELOPE YOU AGREE TO BE BOUND BY ALL OF THE TERMS IN THIS AGREEMENT. IF YOU DO NOT AGREE TO ALL OF THESE TERMS DO NOT OPEN THE ENVELOPE OR USE THE SOFTWARE, BUT PROMPTLY RETURN THE UNOPENED ENVELOPE TO VENTANA.

1. <u>License</u> The enclosed computer software, Ventana Mosaic™ ("Software") is not being sold or purchased, but is being licensed to you by Ventana Communications Group, Inc. ("Ventana"), under a nonexclusive, nontransferable and paid-up license for use only under the following terms, and Ventana, and Spyglass, Inc. ("Spyglass"), licensor of Ventana Mosaic, reserve any right not expressly granted to you herein. Under the terms of this license you own the media on which the Software is recorded, but Spyglass retains all rights of ownership to the Software and all copies of the Software. This license shall be governed by the laws of the state of North Carolina.

2. Under this license you may:

   a.) Make one (1) copy of the Software solely for backup or archival purposes.

   b.) Make use of the Software on one computer at a time, by one user at a time. If such computer is accessible by multiple users or other computers, you must obtain additional licenses for each additional user.

   c.) Transfer your rights under this license for the Software, provided that you give Ventana prior notice of such transfer and that any transferee shall read and accept all of the terms and conditions of this license.

3. <u>Proprietary Rights</u>. This Software is protected by copyright pursuant to federal and state law as well as international law. The Software also contains trade secrets proprietary to Spyglass. Licensee acknowledges the foregoing and agrees to reproduce Ventana's and Spyglass's copyright notices and any other proprietary notices when the Software is copied.

4. <u>Restrictions</u>. Subject to the provisions of federal law, you expressly agree you will not:

   a.) Make or distribute copies of the Software in any form, directly or indirectly, without prior written agreement with Ventana.

   b.) Reverse engineer, disassemble, decompile or otherwise reduce the Software to a human perceptible form or otherwise attempt to re-create the source code.

   c.) Modify, adapt, sublicense, sell, lend, rent or lease the Software.

   d.) Create any derivative work, or incorporate the Software in any other work.

   e.) Remove or in any other way obscure any copyright notices or other proprietary rights of Ventana or Spyglass.

   f.) Use the Software on more than one computer.

   g.) Export the Software without full compliance with the rules and regulations of the Bureau of Export Administration.

   h.) Use more than one copy of the Software even if more than one copy of the Software is included as part of a multiple-component package.

If any provision of the license shall be inapplicable by law to any U.S. Government end-user, each such end-user acknowledges that use, duplication or disclosure by the Government is subject to restrictions as set forth in subparagraph (c)(1)(ii) of The Rights in Technical Data and Computer Software clause at DFARS 252.227-7013.

5. <u>Severability and Termination</u>. If any part of this license is found unenforceable by a court, it shall be limited only to the extent necessary to make it enforceable, without otherwise affecting the license. This license shall remain in effect until terminated. The license will be terminated immediately and without notice by your failure to comply with any provisions of this License Agreement. Upon termination, you shall be entitled to retain the media but must destroy the Software and all copies thereof. You may terminate this license at your own discretion by destroying the Software and all copies or returning the same to Ventana.

6. <u>Warranty, Disclaimer and Limitation of Liability</u>. Ventana warrants that the Software will perform in accordance with the technical specifications set forth in the documentation. A copy of the documentation can be obtained from Ventana prior to accepting this license for the Software by contacting Ventana at the address and phone number set forth above. Ventana further warrants that the disk on which the Software has been encoded is free from original workmanship defect at the time of such encoding. Ventana's sole obligation in the event of a claim under the foregoing warranties will be to provide a replacement copy of the Software upon receipt of the Software postage prepaid and upon confirmation of such defect.

VENTANA DISCLAIMS ANY WARRANTY OF MERCHANTABILITY OR FITNESS FOR PARTICULAR PURPOSE. The Software is licensed in "as is" condition, and except as set forth herein, Ventana makes no warranty of any kind, express or implied. Some states restrict the right to exclude certain warranties, therefore your rights that you may have may vary from state to state.

In no event will Ventana be held liable for monetary damages for any amount in excess of the amount paid for the license grant pursuant to this Agreement. Ventana shall have no liability beyond the obligations set forth above, and shall in no event be liable for additional monetary damages whether incidental, consequential or otherwise, arising out of the use of the Software, irrespective of whether Ventana shall have been informed of the possibility of such damages. Because some states do not allow the exclusion or limitation of liability for consequential or incidental damages, such limitation may not apply to you.

Mosaic is a trademark of the University of Illinois.

FREE Registration!

Getting Started With the Companion Disks

If you're like I am, you bought this book, immediately turned to the back of the book and extracted the disks. Now you are eager to install the disks and start surfin' the Internet. Let me encourage you to read the book that accompanies these disks. It contains a wealth of helpful tips and cool information. But the programmers at Ventana have worked hard to make it as easy as possible get started, even if you don't first read the book. The sections that follow describe how to install the software contained on *The Mac Internet Tour Guide Companion Disks*, how to establish an account with IBM Global Network, as well as how to use the Ventana Launcher to start your Internet software. Follow the directions in the next two pages and you'll be ready to go surfin'!

Installing the Companion Disks

To install the software from the companion disks, follow these steps:

1. Place the first disk in the drive.

2. When the ITG Installer appears on the Mac Desktop, double-click the program's icon.

3. Follow the prompts on the screen, removing and replacing disks as instructed. After the software is installed, the installer displays the Getting Started window.

Signing Up With IBM Global Network

Before you can connect to the Internet, you need to set up an account with an Internet service provider and you need to configure the Internet software that you have just installed to work properly with the service provider.

You can use the *Mac Internet Tour Guide* software with nearly any Internet service provider, but included with this book is a special free sign-up offer from IBM Global Network and its IBM Internet Connection service (see accompanying special offer description). To take advantage of this offer and to establish an account with IBM Global Network, follow these steps:

1. Click the IGN button in the Getting Started window. The IBM Global Network Sign Up window appears.

2. In the Sign Up window, type your name, address, phone number and fax number (if any).

3. Type three user IDs (5 to 7 letters in length, with no spaces or punctuation) into the 1st Preference, 2nd Preference and 3rd Preference text boxes. If all three of your preferences have been used by another IBM Global Network subscriber, IBM will derive a unique user ID from your first preference. The user ID that IBM finally chooses will become a portion of your electronic mail (e-mail) address.

4. Click the Modem button to display the modem window.

5. Select a Baud Rate (the speed of your modem), the comm port to which your modem is connected, as well as a modem default (the type of modem you have—when in doubt, choose Hayes).

6. Make sure your modem is turned on and connected to both your computer and the phone line. Click the Sign Up button. The program dials the IBM Internet Connection service and proceeds to establish an account with the IBM Global Network.

7. When your account has been established, the program disconnects from the IBM Internet Connection service and displays an information window, which shows you your new user ID, a password assigned by IBM, your new e-mail address, and the IBM Global Network access phone number that is nearest to your address.

   The Getting Started program writes this information to the configuration files that your Internet programs will use, but you should still record this information in a safe place. You'll need to know your user ID any time you give someone your new e-mail address. Just add **@ibm.net** to your user ID. For example, if your user ID is **johns**, your e-mail address is **johns@ibm.net**.

   You also might want to write down the following pieces of information from the information window: hostname, domain name, mail server and news server.

   The 800 customer service number for Advantis, the U.S. carrier for IBM Global Network, also appears in this information window. Write down this number in case you ever have a problem connecting to the Internet.

8. Click the Finished button to close the program.

Signing Up With Another Service Provider

If you decide to use a service provider other than IBM Global Network, follow these steps:

1. Click the Other button in the Getting Started window. The Ventana Configure window appears.

2. Use the telephone to call a representative of the service provider with whom you want to establish an account. Fill in the Ventana Configure window based with information supplied by the service provider.

3. Request assistance from the service provider about writing an appropriate gateway script for using InterSLIP to establish a SLIP connection with the service provider.

Launching the Internet Applications

One of the programs installed on your hard disk is the Ventana Launcher. This program is a convenient launching pad for all the Internet software that accompanies *The Mac Internet Tour Guide*. To run your Internet software, follow these steps:

1. Use InterSLIP to dial and connect to your Internet service provider.

2. Double-click the Ventana Launcher icon to display the Ventana Launcher window. This window contains buttons that launch the following Internet applications: Ventana Mosaic, Eudora, Nuntius, TurboGopher, Fetch and Telnet. There is also a button that displays a window from which you can access configuration information for these programs.

3. From the Options menu, select File Locations to display the File Locations window. Specify the locations of each of the Internet applications. **Note:** Refer to Chapter 9 for information on obtaining NCSA Telnet.

4. Click a button for the program you want to start. Refer to the various chapters of this book for a discussion of how to use each of these programs. After you exit an application, the screen returns to the Ventana Launcher window.

5. To quit, click the Close button.